D1125936

a novel by SAM PERRONI

Kind Eyes

A Life Lost. A Life Found. Lincoln's Last Murder Trial.

Editor: Julie Kastello
Milwaukee, Wisconsin

Copy Editor: Kristine Krueger
Plano, Texas

Page Design: Cheryl A. Michalek
Milwaukee, Wisconsin

Illustrator: Michael Lindas
Little Rock, Arkansas

Jacket Artwork: EXIT Marketing
Little Rock, Arkansas

Author Photograph: Jackie Nelson
Narragansett, Rhode Island

ISBN 978-0-615-30512-7

*This book is dedicated to the memory
of my mother, Virginia Faye, who could
have been anything if given the opportunity.*

CHAPTER 1

Sherry fiddled with the power door lock as the new limousine made its way down South Morris Avenue to Park Hill Cemetery. Bloomington's oldest cemetery was familiar to all who grew up in this nurturing Illinois town. Surrounded by oceans of corn standing like a million soldiers and pastures of amber wheat bejeweled with hackberry, Bloomington was home to the Kickapoo Indians before the first European settlers arrived at the turn of the 19th century.

The hearse carrying Eliza "Ellie" Harrison Stoddard slowly pulled into the cemetery's front entrance ahead of a line of cars. When the procession stopped, Ellie's family followed the simple coffin to her final resting place. Following a fitting sermon about an exceptional woman, the family greeted a respectable group of friends.

Ellie's second husband had served as the town's assistant fire chief before he died 14 years earlier. Ellie's oldest daughter, Marge, and favorite granddaughter, Sherry, were downcast over Ellie's passing but content with knowing she had lived a difficult life to the fullest.

As the black Cadillac pulled away from the cemetery, Sherry was in the backseat between her mother and her mother's sister,

Fannie. Silence was normally unacceptable when the three women were together, but this moment was different.

As the neighborhood slowly passed them by, Marge filled the uncharacteristic silence. "You know, I never noticed how comfortable this street is. I've lived here all my life and nothing has changed. I don't like change, Sherry, do you?"

"I haven't given it much thought, Mom," Sherry answered, perplexed that her mother was discussing inconsequential matters when they had just buried her grandmother.

"As you get older you will," added Aunt Fannie.

"Dave's birthday is Wednesday…" said Sherry, mentioning her son in an effort to change the subject.

"Your Nana would take me and your Uncle Tom with her on this street when she was selling Avon," continued Marge. "I was only seven years old. Tom was three. I hope I was good. Besides her Aid to Dependent Children, it was her only income. Can you imagine taking two kids with you door-to-door selling beauty care products? I don't know how she did it."

"You never told me about that," Sherry said. "Didn't your father help her?"

"Not a dime. We only heard from him when he wanted something," said Marge with disgust.

"I'm sorry," said Sherry, gently touching her mother's hand.

"Don't be. I became a stronger person watching Mom struggle. I even became a lawyer because of it. Well, enough of that. Did you say something about Dave?"

"His birthday," said Sherry.

"Birthday...oh, yes…he'll be five…" Marge said distractedly, her mind still on her mom. "Would you help me go through Nana's things, Sherry? I need to look for some papers. Her lawyer needs them to handle her estate."

"Estate? She only had her car and home," said Aunt Fannie,

checking her makeup.

"But she didn't have a will, so everything will have to go through probate," Marge explained, searching in her purse for the probate lawyer's card.

"Why does everything have to be so complicated, Mom?" asked Sherry, taking the card from her mother's hand.

"So the lawyers can make a living," quipped Aunt Fannie.

"Amen," Marge added.

Under a tepid afternoon sun, Marge and Sherry entered Ellie's flawless two-story frame home to search for her papers. Ellie had lived in the same house for 53 years, but the house was so well-maintained it didn't show its age. Countless photographs—the memories of a lifetime—adorned the papered walls and decorated the dated furnishings. And everything had its place.

In the dimly lit attic, the two women became immersed in Ellie's dusty mementos and personal belongings scattered among the junk. While Marge reminisced over her old toys and clothes, Sherry slowly sifted through a distressed cedar trunk that had been pushed against the wall. Most of the possessions were old clothes and books, but a wooden box bearing the name of her great-great-grandmother, Virginia Faye Harrison, caught Sherry's attention.

Sherry began investigating the contents. A yellow silk scarf covered some costume jewelry. A simple gold pocket watch and chain slipped off a small, tattered Bible. A brittle issue of *Harper's Weekly* dated April 29, 1865, covered a handwritten legal paper titled "Order." And beneath it was a neat stack of papers fastened at the top with a faded red ribbon and washed-out blue cover containing the words "Trial of P.Q. Harrison for the murder of Greek Crafton on the 16th of July, 1859."

"What's this?" asked Sherry, picking up the papers and lifting the cover.

"What's what? Oh! It's a trial transcript. A record of a criminal trial," said Marge as she sat down on the floor with her daughter. "I haven't seen that for more than twenty years."

"Who's P.Q. Harrison?" Sherry asked, turning the well-preserved pages.

"He was Virginia's brother. Virginia was thirteen years old when it happened," Marge replied as she looked over her daughter's shoulder at the transcript.

"When what happened?" asked Sherry.

"It was the summer of eighteen fifty-nine..." Marge began.

⚜

The courthouse caretaker had begun preparing for the Harrison murder trial a week earlier. Paint was touched up. The worn pine courtroom floor was dusted and mopped, and the padded leather chairs used by the lawyers and the judge were rubbed with oil to provide maximum comfort and appearance.

Wednesday, Aug. 31 was poised to be another hot, sultry day in Springfield, Illinois. The sun had been unmercifully intense for several days in a row. The katydids were louder than usual, and the residents were doing their best to work early and stay out of the sun in the afternoons. From the talk in town, a large turnout was expected for a murder trial that had divided a community and devastated two respected families. The judge had told the sheriff to summon 101 able-bodied men over the age of 18 as prospective jurors. The panel would be mostly farmers sprinkled with a close-knit group of local businessmen.

Although serious enough, criminal jury trials—especially murder cases—were a source of entertainment for the community. There was a sense of theater in the proceedings, and the oratory skills of the lawyers were always the subject of much debate. People had their favorites and were even known to place an occasional wager on a trial's outcome.

The Harrison case was certainly no exception. It had generated interest as far north as Chicago and as far south as Charleston. The Springfield newspapers had featured the case on its front pages, and reporters planned to be in attendance from the surrounding villages and towns. There was even talk of newspapermen coming from the *Chicago Tribune* and *East St. Louis Daily Journal*.

Peachy Harrison had been up since daybreak. Abraham Lincoln and Stephen T. Logan, his co-counsel, had come to his jail cell the night before to review their final strategy and plans with him. Logan, at 61 years old, was a former circuit judge and one of Illinois' premier courtroom lawyers. After learning that Lincoln had agreed to represent Harrison, Logan sent word to Lincoln that he would assist him without charge if Lincoln desired his help. Lincoln was delighted to have his old law partner at his side.

Logan was an able trial strategist and researcher. He also had a reputation for being an exacting taskmaster whose pleadings comported with strict standards of wording and punctuation. With Lincoln's jury persuasiveness, it would be a formidable team indeed.

Logan also had a selfish motive for volunteering his services. He felt Lincoln's days as a trial lawyer were numbered due to his interest in presidential politics. Because of his unwavering love of the courtroom and genuine admiration for Lincoln, Logan wanted to defend a final murder case with Lincoln before he left the practice of law.

It was 8:30 a.m. when Sheriff Andrew came to Peachy's solitary cell. "It's time, Peachy. Court starts in thirty minutes. How you gettin' along?" asked the sheriff in earnest as he watched Peachy stare at the dusty floor from a seated position on his bunk.

"I'm putting all my faith in Mr. Lincoln and Mr. Logan, but to be honest with you, Sheriff, I'm scared," said Peachy as he slipped on his recently shined boots.

"Every man I see walk out of here is scared, Peachy. I didn't expect you to be any different," said the sheriff. "A man doesn't really know what he is made of until he faces real fear."

"Yeah, I guess that's true. But I'm still scared. Look—Ma wouldn't let me go to court with dirty boots," said Peachy, managing a smile while standing for his escort.

The sheriff opened the cell door, and he and his deputy began walking Peachy the short distance to the stately brick courthouse. As they approached the veranda, which showcased two impressive Doric pillars, a substantial crowd had gathered to greet them. Some of the crowd called out in support and others just stared at them curiously.

When the three men entered the courthouse, people were lining the hallway to the courtroom door. As he entered the courtroom, Peachy was stunned to find it overflowing with jurors and spectators—even the balcony was filled to capacity. Most people were talking to their neighbors. Some were silently absorbing every detail of the moment.

But at Peachy's entrance, the talking turned to murmurs and all eyes were fixed on the killer. As the sheriff placed Peachy in the prisoner's dock near defense counsel's table—where he would stand for the entire trial—Peachy saw his family sitting in the front row of the unforgiving wooden benches. Despite their collective tension, they smiled at him as if to say, *We're with you.*

On the opposite side of the aisle from his family, John Crafton and his family were also seated in the front row. With his meaty arms crossed, Crafton was intently focused on Peachy.

Feeling Crafton's anger, Peachy quickly turned away and began to examine the unfamiliar courtroom. He had never been in court before. The judge's impressive walnut bench, centered in the front of the courtroom, rose tastefully above the wooden plank floor. The bench was adorned with a skillfully carved outline of an American eagle. Two flags of the United States stood proudly like bookends on either side of the bench, adding sharp color to the hard white walls that formed their backdrop. A beautiful crimson leather chair with brass buttons was staged behind the bench and turned slightly toward a door on the right.

To the left of the bench was a large Franklin stove used for heat in the winter, with yards of stovepipe running wildly across the ceiling looking for an exit. Near the stove, Peachy saw the jury box. Twelve ominous Windsor chairs, consisting of two rows of six about 10 feet from the prosecution's table, faced him directly.

To the left of the prisoner's dock and slightly in front of the bench was the witness box. It sat higher than the lawyers' tables and jury box and was equipped with a single straight-backed wooden chair. A simple table and chair sat in front of the bench. Peachy would learn, as the trial began, that this was the court reporter's table.

The courtroom as a whole was an intimidating and commanding sight, but Peachy knew he would feel better when Lincoln and Logan arrived. He wanted to believe the scene was the product of a poorly digested meal and he would wake up from the nightmare soon enough. *How could this have happened?* he thought as his mind returned to the Saturday he hoped to one day forget.

Saturday, July 16 was a vibrant day in Pleasant Plains, Illinois, a small dusty village 17 miles from Springfield. The sun was bright and warm, and the high thin clouds looked like errant brushstrokes across the pale blue sky. The townsfolk were busy shopping and talking about the First Methodist Church supper and dance that was to take place that evening.

Greek and John Crafton were up early to double-check the list of farm supplies they needed to buy at the general store. In the well-equipped blacksmith shop at the entrance to their family farm, Greek mentioned the church supper and dance to his father, who reacted with characteristic enthusiasm. John joked about his dancing prowess and Greek teased that his mother would surely make John look good. The banter revealed their deep affection for one another, an affection both were uncomfortable expressing aloud. It was 7:20 a.m. when both men climbed into the family wagon for the 30-minute ride to town.

Peachy had been up since sunrise. His mother had fixed her traditional Saturday family breakfast of biscuits, gravy and pork sausage. As Peachy went outside to hitch up the horse to the family buggy, he was approached by his baby sister.

"Can I ride to town with you?" Virginia asked. Peachy felt his sister was only trying to be protective and he really wanted to say no.

The day before, Virginia had overheard a brief conversation in the general store between one of Greek's friends and the owner. Virginia reported that Greek and his father were planning to be at the store the next morning to pick up supplies. Virginia knew that her father had asked Peachy to go to the store the next day as well. Realizing the possibility of a chance encounter, Virginia told Peachy about the conversation so he could avoid Greek. Peachy said nothing to his sister. He was tired of being afraid. He was tired of feeling helpless and weak, and he thought, *I'm not hiding anymore.*

After a few seconds, struggling with his pride, Peachy put his hand on Virginia's cheek. "I guess I couldn't stop you with a horsewhip."

"Not with your aim," said Virginia with a laugh. A radiant smile broke over her face as she took her seat in the buggy.

"I'll be right back, Virginia. Don't leave without me," Peachy called out.

Peachy entered the small farmhouse and found his mother in the warmly decorated eating area. Mary Rose was arranging some flowers she had picked in her garden.

"Need anything in town?" asked Peachy.

"Not today, son," Mary Rose said, forcing a smile as she moved to adjust his collar. She had an unsettled feeling that wouldn't leave her. Maybe it was the way Peachy's eyes didn't quite meet hers, or perhaps it was simply a mother's instinct. But she knew something was wrong, and she embraced her youngest son quickly before he could walk away.

"OK. I'll see you later, I guess," said Peachy. Climbing into the buggy, he could feel the knife scabbard under his shirt. He placed his hand on it for reassurance. It was 7:30 a.m. and they had a 15-minute ride to town.

Virginia's faced beamed as the brother and sister arrived in Pleasant Plains. She had forgotten that some new fabric was scheduled to arrive at Patty's Seamstress Shop across from Short & Hart's General Store. The eye-catching fabric was in the shop's front window. It was yellow—Virginia's favorite color. As the buggy came to a smooth stop, Virginia hopped out and headed straight for Patty's. Halfway across the street, she glanced watchfully at Peachy and the front of the general store. "I'll be right there," called Virginia as he climbed the steps to the store.

Peachy casually entered the modest general store to see Ben Hart, one of the owners, leaning against the back of the counter reading a newspaper. Short & Hart's had been a fixture in the quiet village for years.

"Hey, Ben," Peachy greeted him. "How you doin' today?"

"So far, so good, Peachy. Where's your dad?" inquired Ben, extending his hand.

"Farmin'," Peachy replied. "He pampers that corn like it was his children, Ben. What are you reading?"

"Abraham Lincoln's speech to the Republican Party of Springfield. Take a look at this and tell me what you make of it, Peachy," said Ben, easing the paper across the counter.

Ben handed Peachy the folded newspaper and Peachy began to read an article in which Lincoln continued to denounce the spread of slavery to new states and territories. Lincoln believed that slavery should be contained in the southern states, where he felt it would eventually die out.

While Ben and Peachy read the paper, Greek and John pulled up to the front of the general store. Greek jumped out of the well-maintained wagon and hitched the mule. His father paused at the store entrance to look at some new farm tools.

Greek walked into the store and immediately saw Peachy. His eyes flared. As he headed straight for Peachy, he threw his hat to the floor. Deeply absorbed in the newspaper, neither Peachy nor Ben noticed Greek until he had wrapped Peachy's arms from behind. Peachy managed to grab the iron railing attached to the counter.

"I don't want to fight you," said Peachy through gritted teeth. Greek worked to loosen Peachy's grip from the railing as the struggle continued. At the same time, Ben came around the counter and grabbed Greek from behind.

"Let him go!" shouted Ben. As Ben held Greek, John Crafton, who heard the commotion, ran to the three men and grabbed Ben from behind, pulling him from Greek.

"Leave him alone!" yelled John, pushing Ben away. "Greek can and should whip him."

The men struggled as Greek made an attempt to move Peachy to the front of the store. As he did, his hand slipped from Peachy's right arm. Then Greek drew his fist back to hit Peachy in the face.

Reaching into his shirt, Peachy's open hand hit the knife handle. He pulled the knife from the scabbard and plunged it into Greek's side—twice.

The second stab took Greek's breath away, and he stumbled back. John, realizing his son had been stabbed, reached for Peachy. "What have you done? He was not armed!" John shouted.

Peachy, who was now in a rage, instinctively sliced at John with the knife and cut John's arm. When John saw his wound, he began throwing objects at Peachy—a set of scales, a glass and a stool. "You'll pay for this!" John screamed.

A small crowd, including Greek's friend Jon Bone, had gathered at the store entrance.

"Have I no friends here?" asked Peachy as John continued to yell at him. No one moved. Greek, who had slumped over some feed sacks, slowly rose and turned toward the front door. As he passed through the door, he staggered into the arms of the town doctor, J.L. Million. Dr. Million immediately saw blood on Greek's hands and shirt.

"What happened?" demanded the doctor, surveying the crowd.

"He stabbed me," gasped Greek, short of breath.

"Somebody help me," said Dr. Million as he and a few of the farmhands carried Greek to his office, where he did his best to dress Greek's wounds.

As Greek was being carried to Dr. Million's office, Peachy dropped the bloody knife and ran to his buggy. Virginia, who had heard someone say that Peachy had stabbed Greek, rushed hysterically to her brother. She stopped as her brother reached the buggy and put her hand on her brother's arm.

"Peachy! What happened, Peachy?" asked Virginia as she turned her brother around. Peachy just stared at her.

"Let's go home. Ma will help us," said Virginia as the two got in the buggy for their silent trip home.

Peachy's thoughts were abruptly interrupted. It was 8:45 a.m., and the prosecuting attorneys entered the courtroom. Some of the spectators present greeted them with a respectful handshake. Others just watched.

John M. Palmer, a tall man, brown-haired and strong-faced, was the chief deputy prosecuting attorney. He sat down at the prosecution table with his assistant, Joseph R. Jamison, and James B. White, the career prosecuting attorney for Sangamon County, Illinois.

Jamison was a young lawyer in his early 20s. He went to work for the prosecuting attorney after receiving his law license a year earlier. Jamison's father was a prominent Chicago lawyer who had pulled strings to get Joseph a job in the prosecutor's office, so his son could get some trial experience. Jamison, a short man with a thin black mustache, pranced when he walked—a manifestation of his inherited arrogance.

White, who was both handsome and charming, was the elected prosecutor. He was there solely to send a message to the jurors that the case was important. He also wanted to make sure the newspapers printed his name as one of the lawyers because he was running for re-election.

Those present were suitably impressed with the prosecution trio.

John Crafton watched closely as the prosecutors seated themselves. He recalled the day he met with White's chief deputy.

John and his three boys arrived in Springfield early on Wednesday, July 20. Springfield, the state capital of Illinois, was also the county seat for Sangamon County. The prosecuting attorney's office was directly across from the county courthouse. The office was official-looking with an appropriately lettered window facing the street, and the flag of the United States posted on either side of the entrance.

Palmer had been the chief deputy prosecuting attorney for five years and was regarded as a skilled and relentless courtroom lawyer. He was young, handsome and affable. He also had a reputation for being a worthy opponent who could build a case against an accused like a seasoned carpenter builds a house—one piece of evidence at a time.

Palmer's opponents, while they didn't always like him, universally respected him. Whenever they faced Palmer in court, they knew he was going to be prepared and that they were in for a battle. He had a way about him that could lead a jury to the prosecutor's promised land *nolens volens*—willing or not. Juries trusted him and most often shared in his confidence of the defendant's guilt. And, Palmer abhorred losing. This combination made him a dangerous prosecutor indeed.

Palmer was also interested in politics and was in the middle of his own campaign for Congress. He had previously met John Crafton at the Clary's Grove Fourth of July picnic while Palmer was stumping for office.

John and his sons entered the prosecutor's office and approached the young male clerk.

"We're here to see Mr. Palmer. I'm John Crafton." The boys remained quiet.

"I'll see if Mr. Palmer can speak with you. He has court today," said the clerk.

"Tell him it's important," said John sternly.

The clerk walked down a short hall from the reception area and entered an office, closing the door behind him. While the clerk was away, the Craftons' attention was diverted to the pale green walls of the office, which were adorned with a law license, letters from supporters and newspaper articles about Palmer's involvement with the elected prosecutor and other recognizable figures, including Abraham Lincoln.

Palmer's political views differed from those of Lincoln, especially on the issue of slavery. While personally against slavery, Palmer believed each new state should decide the issue separately without interference from the federal government. He, however, had a great deal of respect for Lincoln, whom he regarded as an astute politician and formidable opponent in the courtroom.

In a few minutes, Palmer's clerk returned. "Mr. Palmer will see you now. Please follow me."

John and his sons walked down the hall and entered Palmer's sparsely appointed but neatly kept office.

"Good to see you, Mr. Crafton. I don't believe I've had the pleasure of meeting your sons," said Palmer, extending his hand with a slight bow. After a respectful exchange of greetings with the Crafton boys, Palmer turned his attention to John.

"I know why you're here," Palmer began as he pulled his desk chair to the middle of the room. "Have a seat. Sheriff Andrew has informed me of the distressing circumstances surrounding the death of your son Greek. You and your family have my heartfelt sympathy."

John looked at Palmer sternly. "Peachy murdered Greek and he was unarmed. I saw everything. He should be hanged for what he did," John said, his voice cracking.

John's boys sat motionless with their eyes fixed on Palmer. Palmer paused. "I understand your feelings. I've asked the sheriff to investigate a few things for me. Of course, he will take statements from you and the other witnesses. When he gives me a report, I'll consult with Mr. White and make my recommendation."

John stood up, with his sons following his lead, and extended his strong hand to Palmer. "All me and my family want is justice, Mr. Palmer. I know you'll do the right thing."

The Craftons left the office, and Palmer told his clerk to immediately contact him if he received any information from Sheriff Andrew. Palmer knew this case would generate a great deal of interest from the community and the newspapers. He also wondered aloud to his clerk who the Harrison family might hire as a defense attorney if he did file murder charges. That could affect the size of the crowd at the courthouse, the number of reporters in attendance and ultimately, the trial's outcome.

John Crafton's attention returned once again to the prosecution team. The prosecutors didn't look at Peachy when they took their seats. Peachy's importance was becoming secondary to the litigators' notoriety. Everyone present was about to see the most celebrated courtroom battle in Sangamon County history.

At 8:50 a.m., Lincoln, Logan and Logan's assistant, Shelby Cullom, entered the courtroom. The room buzzed. Several of the spectators in attendance grabbed Lincoln's hand or whispered to a friend as he walked by.

Lincoln, clean shaven and with a full head of hair that looked like it had been combed with his fingers, was dressed in a slightly wrinkled white linen suit, white shirt and black bow tie. He greeted some of the audience in his typical soft-spoken, cordial manner. The defense attorneys eventually passed the bar—the wooden railing that separates the well of the courtroom from the spectators—and walked to their assigned table. Lincoln carefully placed his legal papers on the defense table that had been partially cut away to accommodate his long legs.

He then walked directly toward Peachy, putting his large, powerful hand gently on the back of Peachy's hand as Peachy gripped the railing of the prisoner's dock.

"Try not to look guilty, Peachy," Lincoln whispered.

"What do you mean, Mr. Lincoln?" asked Peachy in a low voice.

"Everyone in this courtroom—most definitely the jury—will be watching you as this trial proceeds. They may never hear from you since you have a right not to testify. With that in mind, they may base part of their judgment on whether you look and act like a murderer, Peachy. So always stand straight with your head up, and don't react to the evidence or the prosecutor. Keep your eyes fixed on the witness or the jury. In other words, keep your best poker face," Lincoln instructed.

Peachy grinned for the first time since entering the courtroom and nodded his head in agreement. "I understand, sir."

"Oh, and keep a positive mind-set no matter what happens in this courtroom," said Lincoln before returning to his chair.

Virginia could not hear the exchange between Lincoln and her brother, but it comforted her to see them together and to remember the day she and her mother met Lincoln for the first time.

❦

The day after Peachy's arrest, the Harrison family left for Springfield. Mary Rose had a first cousin, Diane, who lived off the main road to the city. Mary Rose was very close to her cousin and wanted her to hear the news of Peachy's arrest from family instead of through town gossip. As the Harrisons turned off the main road to Diane's, Mary Rose noticed a weathered sign announcing a debate that had taken place between Abraham Lincoln and Stephen A. Douglas at the Vrooman Mansion in

Bloomington.

Diane, who had lived alone since her husband died in a logging accident 15 years earlier, met them in the front yard. Everyone in the Harrison family loved Diane. She was a happy, affectionate person who always made you smile. She was also an exceptional cook who specialized in making sweets. Diane was particularly fond of Virginia, whose spirit and curiosity she relished.

After exchanging greetings and hugs, everyone sat down for breakfast. Diane sensed that something was wrong and asked Mary Rose outright what was troubling her. Mary Rose gave Diane the details as she knew them and told her they were going to Springfield to see Peachy. Everyone listened intently. Diane was jolted by the news and the gravity of the situation and asked if she could go to Springfield with them. The Harrisons were grateful for her company.

As they were preparing to leave, Mary Rose pulled Diane aside. "Before Abraham Lincoln lost the Senate campaign to Douglas, he was a courtroom lawyer, wasn't he?" Mary Rose asked.

"I think so, Mary Rose," Diane replied. "I'm not sure why, but I think he wants to be President."

"Does he still try cases, and does he take on murder cases?" Mary Rose inquired, her eyes growing large.

"I'm sure he would if he was paid enough," said Diane. "As far as I've heard, he's good. Can you afford him, Mary Rose? I also heard he represents the railroad, and you know how much money they have."

"I'm going to try to hire him. Maybe he would let us pay him at harvesttime. I've got to try," said Mary Rose with tears in her eyes.

"I agree, Mary Rose. It can't hurt to try," said Diane, nodding her head in agreement. When the women hugged, Mary Rose felt a calmness she had not experienced in many days.

After arriving at the county jail, the family was led to Peachy's cell. He was pleased to see them but visibly anxious about what was going to happen next. To the utter amazement of everyone but Diane, Mary Rose announced she was going to try to hire Abraham Lincoln to represent Peachy.

After a moment of uncomfortable silence, Peachy's father, Peyton, expressed his thoughts. "Ma, how can we afford Mr. Lincoln?"

"I don't know," Mary Rose answered.

"How will you talk to him, Ma?" asked Peachy.

"After we leave here, I'm going to his office. I saw it when we passed the statehouse," said Mary Rose.

Virginia listened carefully and then asked the first question that burst from her confused young mind. "What if he's not there?"

"I'll track him down. I'm not leaving Springfield till I see him," Mary Rose answered defiantly.

"I don't think it's gonna work," Peachy lamented.

"We've got to stay faithful and never give up," his mother insisted. Peachy lifted his head and glanced at her. Her confident smile was all he needed. It inspired him as it always had.

The family visited for more than an hour. Diane had successfully distracted them with funny childhood stories about the adventures she and Mary Rose shared growing up together. When the visit was over, they each hugged Peachy, but no one could find the right words to say good-bye.

"Keep your chin up, son. We ain't done yet," said Peyton, breaking the uncomfortable silence.

Once they left the jail, Peyton took Mary Rose to the Lincoln-Herndon Law Offices. Because they knew Lincoln was not expecting them, they agreed that Mary Rose would ask for the meeting while the rest of the family waited in the wagon.

As her mother stepped out of the wagon, Virginia had second thoughts about letting her go alone. "Can I go with you?" Virginia asked. She knew her father would be hard-pressed to sit still while his wife asked someone of Lincoln's stature to represent their son when they couldn't pay for his services. Mary Rose sensed her daughter's dilemma and thoughtfully consented to her company.

Climbing two flights of stairs to the third floor of a building that also housed a foundry, the United States Marshal, the federal prosecutor and federal court, Mary Rose and Virginia entered the small reception area of Lincoln's office to find a pleasant-looking man there to greet them.

"Hello. Come in. I'm William Herndon. Can I help you folks?"

"We would like to see Mr. Lincoln, if that would be convenient," said Mary Rose in a forced calm voice.

"I'm sorry. Mr. Lincoln has gone home to take his dinner," said Herndon. Disappointed, Mary Rose began to say she would return later, but Herndon quickly interrupted. "I don't know Mr. Lincoln's schedule. He's very busy these days, as you can imagine."

"I understand. Thanks for your courtesy," said Mary Rose as she left the cluttered office with Virginia close behind.

As they were leaving the building, Mary Rose noticed a young foundry worker sweeping up in front of the building. She asked him if he knew where Lincoln lived. Pointing down the street, the boy told them to go one block and turn left. "Keep going straight. It's the big house on the corner of Eighth and Jackson with the white picket fence. You can't miss it."

The rest of the family waited while Mary Rose and Virginia walked down the neatly kept neighborhood street to the Lincoln home. When they arrived at the Lincoln home, they knew it instantly. Mary Rose thought to herself, *It's exactly the type of house Mr. Lincoln should be living in.* The home was large but simple. The yard was neat but not immaculate. There were toys on the grass bordering the brick sidewalk leading to the front door, and the flowers were well-tended—obviously by a meticulous hand.

Stopping at the fence, Mary Rose took a deep breath, grabbed Virginia's moist hand and climbed the wooden stairs to the front door. Her strength seemed to leave her as she raised her arm to knock on the stately oak door.

Tap. Tap. Tap.

For an instant, she was afraid that she hadn't knocked hard enough. But in a few seconds, a small, neatly dressed woman appeared. "May I help you?" she asked without smiling.

"Why, yes," said Mary Rose with a warm smile. "Would it be possible for us to see Mr. Lincoln?"

"He's taking his dinner, but if you would like to wait, I will ask him if his schedule would permit a meeting. I'm his wife, Mary Todd Lincoln," she added, extending her hand with a slight smile.

"Thank you, Mrs. Lincoln. I'm Mary Rose Harrison and this is my daughter, Virginia. We'll sit here on the steps."

Mrs. Lincoln closed the door. A short time later, Mary Rose and Virginia heard the door reopen. This time, a towering man stood in the doorway. Mary Rose's heart raced as she wondered if she would be able to speak. Virginia was frozen as she stared at the tallest man she had ever seen.

The figure studied both women for a few seconds, his gaze actually helping them compose themselves. The women were taken by him immediately. There was something about his look and manner that made them feel at ease and secure.

"Mrs. Harrison, I'm Abraham Lincoln," he said as he extended his large hand toward Mary Rose. As he bent over, Mary Rose thought to herself that his handshake was surprisingly tender for such a big and imposing man.

Lincoln then turned. "And this must be Virginia," he said. Instead of bending over to greet her, Lincoln stooped down so he would be at her eye level. "I'm very proud to meet you, Virginia. I know your parents must take a great deal of pride in you." Virginia's face blushed as she combed her fingers through her long, light brown hair.

Lincoln invited the women to come in and sit in the parlor. As Lincoln sat down in a chair, they were seated on a custom-made haircloth sofa designed to accommodate his long frame.

Just then, one of his boys ran past the parlor and up the stairs wearing a strange assortment of Indian garb and carrying a wooden hatchet. When it came to his sons, Lincoln was an indulgent father. The boys' pranks, even when they bordered on mutiny, and their sportive ways appeared to be a source of perpetual joy to a man, who at times, preferred solitude to company.

Of course, like most enterprising young boys, they were inclined to take flight occasionally. The Lincolns' neighbors witnessed many high-spirited chases. One story, in particular, became the neighborhood favorite.

Mary was giving their dirt-loving 3-year-old, Willie, a much-needed bath. When she turned to get a bath toy, the little pistol bolted out the back door stark-naked and ran up the street to a neighbor's fence. The boy crawled under the fence into a cow pasture, where he dashed across the green grass dotted with dried cow patties.

Lincoln was enjoying the pleasant day on the front porch reading his newspaper when, out of the corner of his eye, he caught the pink-and-white escapee running at full speed across the field. He stood up, laughing out loud, while Mary Todd, in a frenzy, encouraged him to pursue the boy. He caught the tyke in the middle of the pasture and gathered him up in his arms while smothering him with kisses. Pitching the boy across his shoulders, Lincoln carried

Willie back to his peeved mother and fresh bathwater.

Lincoln grinned at Virginia as he adjusted his black suspenders while inching forward in his chair. Focused, and with his long legs extending well beyond his arms, he put his chin on the knuckles of his left hand and his elbow on his left knee.

"Mrs. Harrison, how can I help you?"

"It's my son. He's been charged with murder," Mary Rose related.

"Peachy Harrison is your son?" asked Lincoln as he leaned back in his chair.

"Yes, how did you know his name?" replied Mary Rose, startled.

"In my calling, word of murder charges travels fast," said Lincoln.

"We came to ask if you would represent him. We don't have much money, but we are not paupers. We can pay, say, a dollar a month for as long as it takes. Peachy's a good boy. He's never been in trouble with the law before. I can't bear the thought of losing him, and we know it's important to have a good lawyer," said Mary Rose, seizing the moment.

Lincoln listened intently to the distraught mother. When Mary Rose finished, Virginia caught his eye. They spoke not a word. But in that brief moment, Virginia felt the full effect of his inherent kindness and understanding.

Then, Lincoln talked to them. "I cannot comprehend the burden you and your family must feel. Uncertainty can be one of the cruelest times in life. This is especially true when it involves a matter of this importance."

Mary Rose nodded in appreciation.

"My political advisors may believe that I do not have the time for your son's case, but I will represent your son if that is his wish. And there will be no fee."

"But we can't let you do that, Mr. Lincoln. We're proud people and we want to pay you," said Mary Rose with all the determination she could muster.

"I know, Mrs. Harrison, but I don't want to charge you a fee. It's payment enough that you and your family have such confidence in me. So let's compromise. My fee will be thirty dollars payable at the rate of six dollars per year."

"We'll pay after harvest, and I promise we won't be late," said Mary Rose.

"I have the utmost confidence in the truthfulness of that statement, Mrs. Harrison," said Lincoln, smiling.

Lincoln's customary fee in murder cases was $300, but he couldn't tell Mary Rose. It would have troubled her unnecessarily. "I'll meet with your son this evening after I leave the office to see if he's in agreement. If so, I will pitch into his case like a dog at a root," said Lincoln, standing up.

Unable to contain their excitement, both women hugged Lincoln and thanked him profusely.

"One more thing, Mary Rose. I shall not make any promises," Lincoln cautioned. "After twenty-three years, I've learned one thing for certain about the trial of a criminal case. You can never tell what will happen. All I can do is promise you that you may be disappointed in the judge or the jury, but you will not be disappointed in me."

"I understand, Mr. Lincoln," Mary Rose acknowledged. As they were leaving, Lincoln gave them a cordial wave and a smile.

"By the way, you may call me Abe, if you like," he called out.

As Virginia's daydream ended, she thought to herself that the exceptional man she met that day would always be "Mr. Lincoln" to her.

CHAPTER 2

The seasoned courtroom crowd became respectfully subdued as court was about to go into session. The sheriff's deputy stood at the door beside the judge's bench, checking his pocket watch. At precisely 9 a.m., the door opened and the sheriff entered with a short, robed man following close behind.

As the judge ascended the three stairs to his walnut bench, the courtroom crier, T.W.S. Kidd, opened court in a loud and commanding voice. "All rise!" announced the crier, and everyone packing the warm courtroom rose as one. "Oyez! Oyez! Oyez! The Circuit Court for Sangamon County, Illinois, is now in session pursuant to adjournment, the Honorable Edward Young Rice Jr. presiding. All ye who have business before this court draw near and ye shall be heard. God save the state of Illinois, the union and this honorable court."

The judge positioned himself in his leather chair. He was a wiry middle-aged man with gray beginning to overtake his full head of brown hair. Dark spectacles highlighted his bushy eyebrows, which were growing out of control, and his head appeared large for his small body. His black robe covered his starched white shirt and complemented his neatly placed black bow tie.

"Good morning, everyone," he said pleasantly. "Please be seated. Court is now in session in the case of the People versus Harrison."

The audience, which had risen thunderously to attention when the judge entered the courtroom, sat down quietly. The court reporter took his place in front of the judge, and the deputy moved quietly to the end of the jury box.

"This is a murder case, and Peachy Quinn Harrison is the accused," said the judge, addressing the audience in an official tone of voice. "Are the People ready for trial?"

"Yes, your Honor," Palmer replied.

"And the prisoner?"

Lincoln drew himself up and addressed the court with confidence. "Peachy Harrison is ready for trial, your Honor."

Nodding in approval, the judge turned and addressed his attention to the men called in for jury duty–referred to in the law as talesmen. "The sheriff has told you why you were summoned to the courthouse. Twelve of you will sit in judgment of the accused. The lawyers for both sides will be examining your qualifications, but before I permit them to do so, I want to know if any of you are related by blood or marriage to the prisoner."

A bearded young man in the back of the room stood up. "Judge, Peachy is my first cousin. His ma is my aunt."

"What is your name?" the judge asked.

"It's Kenneth Stone."

"Well, Mr. Stone, it wouldn't be right for you to sit on your cousin's jury, so I am going to excuse you from service in this case."

Making his way to the back of the courtroom, Mr. Stone volunteered, "I think that's fair, judge. I wouldn't pay much mind to the prosecution anyhow."

Everyone—except the prosecutors—broke out in laughter.

"Anyone else?" the judge continued.

Hearing no response, Judge Rice called upon the prosecution to conduct its voir dire of the panel. Palmer spent the next hour and a half questioning the prospective jurors. He covered several areas: possible friendships with the Harrison family, the names of the witnesses that might be called, the crime of murder and whether the talesmen had ever been in a fight where someone had been shot or stabbed. He asked the jurors whether they could find Harrison guilty of murder if the prosecution proved its case beyond a reasonable doubt. Everyone knew what that meant. The stakes were as high as they get in a court of law. All of the jurors nodded in the affirmative.

Finally, Palmer asked about the death penalty. This area of Palmer's voir dire was the most sensitive subject in murder cases. With the penalty for murder fixed at death by hanging, Palmer needed to know if the jurors would decide the case on sympathy or, perhaps, disregard the death penalty on religious or moral grounds.

Palmer became incomparably serious.

Palmer: My last question is always the most difficult for me. The penalty in this case is death. Do any of you have strong feelings, one way or the other, about the death penalty?

The courtroom became uncommonly still. The resulting silence consumed what felt like an eternity before a juror spoke.

Juror: If you prove 'em guilty, then that's the punishment, an eye for an eye.

Judge Rice: Your name, sir?

Juror: Mark Gollaghers.

Palmer: Mr. Gollaghers...so sympathy for the defendant would not be a factor in your decision?

Gollaghers: Not if I do my duty.

Palmer: You mean your duty under the law?

Gollaghers: What other duty is there?

Palmer: Anyone else?

Juror: I don't know if I could do it.

Judge Rice: Your name, please.

Juror: William January.

Palmer: Mr. January. You don't know if you could convict the defendant, no matter what the evidence is?

January: I don't know. I think I could be fair.

Palmer: But if I prove the defendant guilty, could you convict him with the knowledge he would hang?

January: I...I don't know. I would try.

Palmer: Your Honor, could counsel be permitted to approach the bench?

Judge Rice: Permission granted. You may approach.

Lincoln and Palmer walked to the side of the judge's bench away from the jury. Palmer began to whisper.

Palmer: Judge, the People would ask that Mr. January be excused. It's apparent that he quite likely cannot follow the law.

Judge Rice: Mr. Lincoln, what is your position?

Lincoln: Your Honor, Mr. January said he could be fair. That is all that is required.

Judge Rice: Since we have plenty of jurors, I am going to excuse Mr. January. I'm concerned that he may not follow my instructions due to his obvious hesitation over the death penalty.

Palmer: Thank you, Judge.

Lincoln: Note our exceptions, Judge.

Judge Rice: So noted.

Palmer returned to the podium facing the jury panel and Lincoln went to his chair. Lincoln leaned over and whispered to Logan as Palmer prepared to continue his examination. Lincoln had wanted Mr. January on the jury.

Judge Rice: Mr. January, you may be excused. If you prefer, you may remain in the courtroom to observe.

January: Yes, Judge.

Judge Rice: Mr. Palmer, you may proceed.

Palmer: Does anyone else feel like Mr. January? Since I

see no hands raised, I'm finished with my examination. Thank you for your patience.

Judge Rice: Thank you, Mr. Palmer.

Based on their answers to Palmer's questions, the judge excused a few more of the prospective jurors and then called on the defense for their examination.

Logan was first. He stood in front of the podium and conducted, without notes, a detailed and probing inquiry into a host of subjects. He had conducted similar inquiries in hundreds of cases. Lincoln remarked to Logan before trial that obtaining a fair-minded jury was imperative in any criminal case, but more so in a case like Peachy's. The case was a close one in Lincoln's mind, and he wanted the defense to identify as many prospective jurors as they could who might, if they sat on the jury, go into the case favoring the prosecution. Logan agreed and accomplished his part of the examination with characteristic precision.

It was a quarter past twelve o'clock as Lincoln stood, suit jacket unbuttoned, to address the jurors. He knew the men being examined were getting hot and hungry.

"You'll be pleased to know that I will be the last lawyer to examine you," said Lincoln. The jurors received the comment with enthusiasm.

"So, if you will give me your full attention for just a while longer, I swear I will be finished before one o'clock, and I will answer a burning question many of you have had on your mind since I walked into the courtroom."

Lincoln then paused and cocked his head as if to say something profound. "I'm 6 feet 4 inches tall, and I can pick a cherry tree clean as a whistle without using a stepladder." The audience laughed. Even the judge broke into a smile.

Now, the men wanted to listen to him—at least most of them did—and they, for the moment, became more relaxed in the highly charged atmosphere.

Initially, Lincoln examined the men about the State's burden of proof: whether they could hold the prosecution to that burden in the Harrison case and whether they recognized and understood that self-defense was a legal justification for homicide—the death of a person at the hands of another. He even got some of the men to share their experiences about defending themselves—though none of them had ever killed another man.

Lincoln approached his examination methodically. He wanted the men to begin to feel what Peachy must have felt and to recognize that a criminal trial was nothing more than life reenacted in the courtroom. Lincoln's natural ability to put himself in the place of another man and to understand that person's feelings and emotions was, without the jurors realizing it, having a psychological effect on them. As seasoned trial lawyers would say, "He was getting into the jury box" with the talesmen.

At 10 minutes until 1 p.m., Lincoln concluded his remarks by extracting a promise from the prospective jurors. If they sat on the jury, they would agree not to make up their minds until they heard all of the evidence.

"My uncle used to tell me, 'Abe, no matter how thin you pour a flapjack, it always has two sides.' Can I count on you to remember that piece of wisdom as we go through this trial together?" he asked.

"Yes," said some of the jurors while most just nodded in the affirmative.

Lincoln left the podium and sat down. The judge ordered the sheriff to pull the names of 12 men. After each name was called, the juror was directed to a designated place in the jury box.

When the jury box was filled, Judge Rice administered the oath and then looked at juror No. 1, who was sitting in the front row about 6 feet from the judge's bench. "Mr. Anderson, you will be our foreman," he directed.

Anderson nodded, and Lincoln whispered again into Logan's ear. "I'm not sure about him. His uncle was hanged in Fort Smith, Arkansas, for stealing horses ten years ago, and I heard he said his uncle deserved it."

"Maybe he did," Logan retorted. "Perhaps that means he lives by the rules. As you know, one of the rules in this case is self-defense."

Lincoln studied the jury as the judge finished scribbling the jurors' names on his jury chart. In time, Lincoln would come to know their faces and they his client's, in the unusually distant familiarity that happens in every criminal jury trial. But now the 12 engaged men sat as stiff as their oak chairs, avoiding all eye contact with anyone but the judge.

Lincoln and Logan shook hands in satisfaction as the judge excused the jurors. He admonished them to not discuss the case until they retired to deliberate and requested they return at 8:30 the following morning.

As the jurors—10 farmers, an engineer and a carpenter—filed out of the courtroom, Virginia inched to the edge of her seat. When the spectators began to follow the jurors into the bright sunlight, Virginia headed straight for Lincoln. He was stuffing his legal papers into a worn leather folding case, and she tugged on his suit coat to get his attention.

"Virginia, it's good to see you today," said Lincoln as he turned to greet her. "Do you have something you want to say to me?"

"Yes, sir," Virginia responded anxiously.

Lincoln sat down as if he had nothing else to do. "Here, my dear. Sit with me and tell me what's on your mind."

By this time, the courtroom had cleared with the exception of Lincoln and the Harrison family. Peachy had been taken back to jail.

"Mr. Lincoln, what does this mean? Do we have a good jury? Are we winning?" Virginia asked rapid-fire.

"Those are bright and fair questions," Lincoln replied. "They are also very difficult questions to answer. It requires me to size up men's hearts, Virginia, and that is a trait I don't profess to have. I'll tell you that all 12 jurors must agree on a verdict, and I feel we have a few men on the jury who will receive our defense favorably.

"We also have some who, I believe, may favor the prosecution's side. That means Mr. Logan and I must work very hard to persuade the remainder of the jurors that our side is just. Then, we must hope that a majority of the jurors will persuade the others that there is reasonable doubt in this case," Lincoln explained.

"I think I understand," said Virginia. "We must be patient. Well, if anyone can convince them, Mr. Lincoln, I know you can."

After a few more moments of discussion, Lincoln, Virginia and the Harrisons left the courtroom. As they parted, the Harrisons saw Lincoln heading toward the jail. Lincoln wanted to visit with his client about the events of the day before he went home to prepare for the following day's opening statements and testimony.

⁓

Thursday's *Springfield Register* carried a front-page article about the trial.

TRIAL OF PEACHY QUINN HARRISON
INDICTED FOR THE MURDER OF GREEK CRAFTON

Circuit Court of Sangamon County – Hon. E.F. Rice, Judge

FIRST DAY

WEDNESDAY, AUGUST 31, 1859

Court met at nine o'clock, as usual. The Courthouse was filled with a large crowd, in expectation of the coming trial. The number present and the earnest expression in the countenance of all evidenced the deep and general interest taken by the public in this remarkable trial.

After dispatching some other business, the case of the People of the State of Illinois v. Peachy Quinn Harrison was taken up. The District Attorney, Mr. James B. White, assisted by John M. Palmer, of Macoupin, and Joseph R. Jamison, of Chicago, appeared for the State. The Hon. Abraham Lincoln, Hon. Stephen T. Logan and S.M. Cullom, Esquire, appeared on behalf of the defendant.

The day's session was entirely consumed in the examination of jurors. After the examination of one hundred and one citizens, a jury of twelve good and lawful men was impaneled as follows:

Benjamin Brown, Farmer
James A. Brundage, Farmer
William Patterson, Farmer
Jefferson Pierce, Farmer
Zenas Brambwell, Engineer
Moses Pilcher, Carpenter
William Hinchey, Farmer
George Anderson, Farmer
Josephus Gatton, Farmer
M.H. Pickrell, Farmer
Charles Nuckollus, Farmer
Isaac Peyton, Farmer

It now being a quarter past one o'clock, court was adjourned, after charging the jury and placing them in the care of two officers until half past eight o'clock tomorrow morning. Mr. Isaac H. Gray, proprietor of the American House, will lodge the jurors for the duration of the trial.

On Thursday, the second day of trial began with a similar level of anticipation and excitement. The lawyers arrived early. The courtroom was packed and 11 jurors were promptly seated in the jury box by the deputy. The sheriff had informed the judge that juror Patterson had taken ill. After informing counsel of the problem, it was agreed that several alternate jurors would be examined in the court's chambers and a substitute selected. Juror Charles A. White, a farmer, was chosen and assumed his seat in the jury box. Newspaper reporters, along with a court-room sketch artist, were seated behind the Craftons. The only noticeable addition to the crowd was the presence of witnesses for both sides—about a dozen in all.

Judge Rice, in his crisply pressed robe, entered the courtroom after the customary opening by the crier and took his seat.

"Good morning, everyone," the judge said.

Like a congregation greeting its pastor, most of those present responded, "Good morning, Judge."

Judge Rice then addressed the lawyers. "Is everyone ready to proceed?"

"Yes, your Honor," said Palmer and Lincoln simultaneously.

Lincoln stood to address the judge. "May it please the court, the defense requests the Rule."

The Rule required the witnesses on both sides to remain out-side the courtroom until they were called to testify. This courtroom procedure was designed to prevent the possibility that a witness may be influenced by hearing the testimony of others. Palmer asked that the sheriff be made an exception. Lincoln agreed since the sheriff had duties to perform while the trial progressed.

Judge Rice obliged. "Your request is granted."

The sheriff, with Palmer's help, began politely shepherding the witnesses into the hallway.

John Crafton looked puzzled. "Why do I have to leave?" he asked, obviously perturbed.

"Lower your voice, John, please. The judge has agreed to Lincoln's request to sequester the witnesses," Palmer explained.

"Sequester? What's that?" Crafton asked in a hushed voice as he moved to the rear of the courtroom.

"That means the witnesses are not permitted to hear each other's testimony. You have to stay outside the courtroom until you testify," Palmer answered.

"But I want to hear what that no-account Republican lawyer has to say about me and my family," said Crafton with his finger in Palmer's face.

"I understand, John. But I need you as a witness and if you don't leave, you can't testify. No exceptions other than the sheriff," Palmer said sternly.

"I guess I got no choice," Crafton said as he walked into the crowded hallway.

"That's right, you can stay in the courtroom after you testify," said Palmer, patting Crafton on the shoulder before he returned to his table.

Now it was time for the lawyers to address the jury with their opening statements. Because the State had the burden of proof, Palmer would go first.

The judge slipped on his spectacles. "Mr. Palmer, you may now plead your case to the jury."

"Thank you, your Honor," Palmer said as he walked to the center of the courtroom well facing the jury. He buttoned his black suit jacket. His dark hair was perfectly groomed and his tie neatly placed, but his polish would prove to be no match for his case preparation.

"May it please this honorable court," Palmer began. "Gentlemen of the jury, the defendant, Peachy Quinn Harrison, has been charged with the crime of murder by a duly impaneled grand jury for Sangamon County. The indictment against him states: 'The grand jury for the July term of the Sangamon County Circuit Court, State of Illinois, in the year of our Lord one thousand eight hundred fifty-nine, hereby upon their letters present, charge one Peachy Quinn Harrison with the crime of murder, to wit, the aforesaid Peachy Quinn Harrison, on the sixteenth day of July, eighteen hundred fifty-nine, not having fear of God before his eyes, but instead having been moved and seduced by instigation of the devil, did then and there feloniously, willfully and with malice aforethought inflict a mortal knife wound upon one Jonathan "Greek" Crafton, which caused the death of the aforesaid Jonathan "Greek" Crafton against the peace and dignity of the People of the State of Illinois,' " Palmer said, reading the handwritten pleading.

"The indictment is signed by the foreman of the grand jury and myself," Palmer said as he eased closer to the jury box. "Now, malice aforethought means that a person kills another deliberately and intentionally," he explained. "We will prove that the defendant stabbed Greek Crafton—who was unarmed—causing his death, because he held great animosity for Greek. Our evidence will include a death threat by the defendant, the purchase of a bowie knife a short time after the threat, the fact that the defendant had a motive to kill Greek and the fact that the defendant fled—to avoid the reach of the law—when a warrant was issued for his arrest."

Turning toward Peachy, Palmer pointed at him with his arm fully extended. Pausing for dramatic effect, he raised his voice as he said, "The plain truth is that the defendant is a murderer!" The jurors looked at Peachy and then back at Palmer. "And the People are confident that when you hear the evidence, you will agree that a true and just verdict would be one of guilty as charged."

A flash of panic raced through Peachy's body like a charge of electricity, but he remembered Lincoln's advice and resisted the natural tendency to react.

"Thank you for your service," Palmer said as he crossed to the prosecutor's table and sat down.

"Mr. Lincoln, who will be speaking for the prisoner?" asked Judge Rice as he looked at counsel for the defense.

"I will, your Honor," Lincoln replied confidently. Lincoln rose and walked by the prisoner's dock where Peachy was glued to Lincoln's every move. As Lincoln passed, he laid his hand on Peachy's shoulder, patting him gently. Lincoln walked to the jury box and paused briefly. He looked every juror in the eye.

After a thoughtful moment, he said passionately, "Peachy Harrison is innocent. He's not a murderer." Lincoln came from behind the podium.

"Under the law of this great state, a man may kill another if he had a well-founded danger of great bodily harm at the hand of another. There will be no quarrel in this case about how Greek Crafton died. My client stabbed him. I know Peachy would give his place in Heaven to have that fateful day back. But he stabbed Greek in self-defense.

"Greek Crafton was a big, strong man. Peachy, as you can see, is a small man with limited strength. For some reason, Greek developed a keen dislike for Peachy and used his size to intimidate Peachy. Greek made it clear that he wanted to fight Peachy and do him harm. Greek even told others he was going to whip Peachy."

Lincoln stepped closer to the jury box. "As Peachy's fear grew, he decided to arm himself. On the day of the fatal encounter, Greek, without provocation, attacked my client, and Peachy defended himself," Lincoln said gesturing with his fist.

"We share in the Craftons' bereavement, but Greek, as you

will hear, brought this upon himself. We sincerely believe that when the evidence is in, you will conclude that a fair verdict in this case would be one of not guilty. On behalf of my client and his family, we thank you for your kind attention," Lincoln concluded and then left the podium to sit down.

Both sides were now clearly presented. The lines were drawn and the fight for persuasion was on.

"Call your first witness, Mr. Palmer," Judge Rice ordered.

Palmer nodded to the sheriff. Palmer had decided to start with the town doctor. Palmer rose, buttoning his suit coat, and quickly moved to the podium to begin his direct examination.

Palmer: Your Honor, the People call Dr. J.L. Million to the stand.

Judge Rice: Dr. Million, please step forward and take the oath.

Dr. Million was a short, chubby man. His thin hair exposed a shiny bald spot at the back of his head, and his worn suit looked as if he had slept in it.

Court Reporter: Dr. Million, please place your right hand on the Bible. Do you swear that your testimony before this court and jury will be the truth, the whole truth, and nothing but the truth, so help you God?

Dr. Million: I do.

Judge Rice: Please be seated, Doctor.

Palmer: State your full name for the jury, please.

Dr. Million: Joshua Lewis Million.

Palmer: And you are a physician, are you not?

Dr. Million: I am.

Palmer: How long have you been a physician?

Dr. Million: Twenty-one years.

Palmer: Where did you study medicine?

Dr. Million: Philadelphia, Pennsylvania.

Palmer: Where do you reside, Doctor?

Dr. Million: At Pleasant Plains in this county.

Palmer: Do you have an office?

Dr. Million: I have an office in my home in Pleasant Plains, and I share an office in Springfield with Dr. Herbert. I come here on Tuesdays and Friday mornings.

Palmer: Over the years, have you treated people with knife wounds?

Dr. Million: Many.

Palmer: On Saturday, the sixteenth of July of this year in Sangamon County, did you treat one Greek Crafton?

Dr. Million: Yes, sir, I did.

Palmer: Did you know the parties here? The defendant, Peachy Harrison, and Greek Crafton in his lifetime?

Dr. Million: Yes, sir.

Palmer: Where did they reside?

Dr. Million: In the vicinity of Pleasant Plains.

Palmer: It's true, is it not, that Greek Crafton is dead?

Dr. Million: Yes.

Palmer: Now, Doctor, what do you know of the cause of his death?

Dr. Million: He died from a knife wound inflicted in his left side, I believe between the eleventh and twelfth ribs on the left side. That wound, in my opinion, penetrated into the cavity of the abdomen. I could not ascertain positively what organs were injured, but I supposed from the course the knife took that the spleen and stomach were penetrated.

Palmer: Where did you see him initially?

Dr. Million: Well, sir, I saw him…I suppose…a minute or two after this affray occurred. He was at the front door of the general store where the difficulty took place. This store was in Pleasant Plains and belonged to Mr. Short and Mr. Hart. When I first saw Greek, he was in rather a staggering condition. He called to me and he reclined on me in rather a failing position…and I caught him. He was taken to my house, my office, by myself and one or two other gentlemen who were at the store. I suppose my office is something like a hundred yards from the store—not far.

Palmer: Was an examination made of his condition?

Dr. Million: His intestines, a portion of them, were protruding and I returned them to their place and dressed the wound, taking three or four stitches, and applied some plasters over it.

Palmer: Did you…were you able to conduct a further examination of his person at that time?

Dr. Million: Yes, I think about the seventh or eighth rib on his right side, it looked like a knife had glanced against the rib making a cut about three inches in length. That took about eight or nine stitches, I believe. Both wounds had been laid open by a sharp pointed knife.

Palmer: What was their direction?

Dr. Million: It being between two ribs, it was difficult to say—only from his symptoms—which way the course was. I imagine that the knife took a horizontal direction. It would be horizontal if he was standing erect. It cut across.

Palmer: Could you tell the organ touched by the knife by any inference or by any other means?

Dr. Million: About an hour and a half after the injury, he vomited a large quantity of blood and that could not, I suppose, have gotten into the stomach without the stomach being cut. It might also have cut the duodenum.

Palmer: Duodenum? What's that?

Dr. Million: It's where the esophagus meets the stomach.

Palmer: Can you show us…show the jury…the area on the sketch you're holding in your hands?

Dr. Million: Certainly.

Dr. Million pointed to the organs for the judge and jury. Those in attendance strained their necks to see—all except Sarah Crafton, Greek's mother, who covered her eyes with a trembling hand.

Palmer: How long did Greek live?

Dr. Million: The wounds were inflicted about eight o'clock Saturday morning—not noticing that time particularly— and he died at home about nine o'clock Monday night.

Palmer: In your opinion, what caused Greek's death?

Dr. Million: I think his death was caused by the deep knife wound. He got an infection and bled to death.

Palmer: I have no further questions. Your witness, Mr. Lincoln.

As Dr. Million's testimony ended, tears filled Sarah's eyes. At that same moment outside the courtroom, John Crafton, frustrated that he couldn't hear the other witnesses' testimony, once again replayed in his mind the day his oldest son died.

⚮

Family and friends had traveled to the Crafton farm to show their support and to comfort Greek while he nursed his grievous wounds. Greek was a strong young man with a promising future as a farmer or blacksmith. It was unthinkable that Greek would die this way. There was no doubt in John's mind that Greek would make a full recovery. He had to live. John had plans for his oldest son.

As Greek's condition failed to improve, his brothers became increasingly angry. They were pressing their father to allow them to pay Peachy a visit, but John told them the law should deal with Peachy.

On Monday afternoon, July 18, the Rev. Peter Cartwright, the well-known and inspiring minister of the Craftons' church, traveled the washed-out, dusty road to the Crafton farm. He explained that he had come to aid the family and give comfort to Greek, whom he understood was in grave condition. The family welcomed Rev. Cartwright into their modest home and obliged him when he asked to have some time alone with Greek.

As the afternoon sun slipped into dusk, Greek's condition deteriorated. He was becoming unresponsive, and his color turned ashen. The family was losing hope, and Greek's friends became subdued. Everyone joined hands and prayed, but at 9:04 p.m., Greek died.

The next day, Greek was laid to rest on the Crafton farm. Greek's mother took to her bed in despair. John and his sons spent the morning crafting a family cemetery behind the log farmhouse on a small rise. They planted an oak tree next to the cemetery to symbolize Greek's life—young and strong—and John told his boys they were going to fashion an ornate iron fence to enclose the sacred piece of ground.

After the final shovel of dirt was gently tamped on Greek's grave, John told his sons they were going to Springfield the next day to see the prosecutor. He was determined to seek retribution.

⚘

Observing no movement by the defense, Judge Rice asked the obvious, "Mr. Lincoln, any cross-examination of Dr. Million?"

Lincoln eased his long frame from under the counsel table saying, "No, your Honor."

> *Judge Rice:* Thank you, Dr. Million. You may leave now or you may stay. It is your choice. Call your next witness, Mr. Palmer.

> *Palmer:* The People call Henry Frederick to the stand, your Honor.

The sheriff led Frederick past the spectators to the court reporter's table. He was 26 years old, 6 feet tall, of slender build but with broad shoulders. He had blue eyes, short auburn hair and sandy whiskers and walked with a peculiar long, loping step to the well of the courtroom.

> *Court Reporter:* Mr. Frederick, please place your right hand on the Bible. Do you swear that your testimony before this court and jury will be the truth, the whole truth, and nothing but the truth, so help you God?

> *Frederick:* I do, sir. Yes, sir.

Frederick nervously seated himself in the witness chair and glanced at Peachy, who stood impassively in the prisoner's box.

Palmer: Mr. Frederick, where do you reside?

Frederick: Reside, sir?

Palmer: Live…where do you live?

Frederick: Oh, sorry. Pleasant Plains in this county.

Frederick smiled apologetically.

Palmer: Are you acquainted with the defendant, Peachy Harrison?

Frederick: Yes, sir.

Palmer: Did you know Greek Crafton when he was alive?

Frederick: Yes.

Palmer: Are you and Peachy Harrison friends?

Frederick: Yes.

Palmer: How close of a friendship do you have?

Frederick: We been friends since we were small boys.

Palmer: Did you want to come here today?

Frederick: No…no, sir.

Palmer: Your Honor, I would like to ask the court to declare Mr. Frederick a hostile witness so I may lead him and impeach him, if necessary.

Judge Rice: What's your position on this, Mr. Lincoln?

Lincoln's feet became temporarily entangled in the table legs as he rose to a stooped position.

Lincoln: Mr. Logan will address this matter, may it please the court.

Judge Rice: Very well. Mr. Logan?

Logan rose, his gray suit jacket already stained with perspiration.

Logan: This is highly irregular and we object. Mr. Frederick has shown no propensity to testify falsely.

Judge Rice: It is apparent to the court that Mr. Frederick is a reluctant witness, so I will grant Mr. Palmer's request.

Logan: Save our exceptions, your Honor.

Judge Rice: Yes. You may proceed, Mr. Palmer.

Palmer: Thank you, your Honor. Mr. Frederick, you and the defendant went to the Clary's Grove Fourth of July picnic together, did you not?

Frederick: Yes.

Palmer: On the way, you came in contact with Greek and John Crafton, correct?

Frederick: Yes.

Palmer: Did an altercation take place?

Frederick: Altercation?

Palmer: Was there an argument?

Frederick: I guess so. They had words.

Palmer: Tell me about the words, please.

Frederick: I don't recollect exactly.

Palmer: Well, let me see if I can help you recollect. On the Fourth, the residents of Pleasant Plains and neighboring villages were making their way to the annual Clary's Grove picnic, and you picked up the defendant at his home in your buggy, correct?

Frederick: Yes.

Palmer: As you got close to the picnic, you met Greek and John Crafton, isn't that true?

Frederick: Yes.

Palmer: You were not aware that there was growing animosity between the defendant and Greek, were you?

Frederick: Does animosity mean not friends?

Palmer: Yes.

Frederick: I knew they were not getting along, but I didn't know how bad.

Palmer: What was said, Mr. Frederick?

Frederick: Like I said, I don't recollect exactly, but…

Palmer: Didn't the defendant ask Greek about his brother Peter?

Frederick: He said something like, "Where's Peter?"

Palmer: What did Greek say?

Peachy had grasped the prisoner's dock railing with both hands. He caught himself squeezing the railing until his hands began to quiver and a bead of sweat formed on his forehead. The events of the Fourth of July were racing through his mind.

⸙

As visitors and residents—young and old—made their way to the picnic, Henry arrived at the Harrison farm place in his weather-beaten buggy. Peachy and Henry liked each other's company. In many ways, they were like brothers. Sparring with words or teasing and joking their way through a boring afternoon, they had fun with each other.

As they approached the entrance of Clary's Grove, they met Greek and John Crafton at the crossroads. Henry, unaware of the tension that had been mounting between Greek and Peachy, stopped the buggy to visit. After some small talk, Peachy asked Greek about his brother.

"Where's Peter, Greek?"

"Peter's in town with a buggy gettin' some ladies to go to the picnic. I…I understand that you've told Peter not to talk about the company you've been keeping," Greek said, clearly agitated.

"All I said to Peter was that he didn't need to mention Rebecca…" Peachy quickly replied.

"At some convenient time, we'll settle this," Greek interrupted.

"It don't make no difference to me whether we settle it or not," Peachy shot back.

"Then, we can settle it now…I guess," said Greek as he jumped out of the Crafton buggy and pulled off his shirt.

"I don't want to fight you," said Peachy, looking at Henry for support.

"This isn't the time or place for fightin'," Henry said calmly.

"If you ever cast any reflections on my character, I'll whip you," Greek said with his fists raised toward Peachy.

"You damn son of a bitch!" yelled Peachy. "If you try to hurt me, you will regret it."

Greek lunged toward Peachy, who was still in Henry's buggy, but Henry pushed Greek back with his foot. As Henry grabbed the lines, Greek picked up a clod of dirt and threw it at Peachy, striking Henry on the shoulder while he made another attempt to get in the buggy.

Henry snapped the lines. As they were pulling away, Peachy shouted at Greek. "If you ever lay hands on me, I'll kill you."

❧

Peachy's thoughts were abruptly interrupted by Palmer's raised voice.

Palmer: Isn't it a fact, Mr. Frederick, that Greek challenged Mr. Harrison about a statement he, the defendant, made to his brother Peter?

Frederick: Yes. Yes, he did. He called him on it.

Palmer: And the defendant called Greek a son of a bitch, didn't he?

Frederick: Yes.

Palmer: Greek came after him for that, didn't he?

Frederick: Yeah. Greek tried to grab Peachy out of the buggy twice. I pushed him back and cracked the lines to get us out of there.

Palmer: And as you were leaving, the defendant yelled at Greek, "If you ever lay hands on me, I'll kill you," didn't he?

Frederick didn't answer, but instead he looked at Peachy with dismay.

Palmer: Didn't he, Mr. Frederick?

Frederick: But he was mad. He didn't mean it.

Palmer: He didn't? A man's dead. No further questions, your Honor.

Several members of the audience shifted in their seats. Some spectators whispered audibly as Palmer returned to his table.

Judge Rice: Thank you, Mr. Palmer. Cross-examination?

Lincoln rose, looking straight ahead at the judge. As he moved to the podium, he gave Peachy a reassuring nod.

Lincoln: Henry, what do you do for a living?

Frederick: I'm a carpenter.

Lincoln: It would be my guess, I reckon, that you would rather be building a barn than sitting in that chair with Mr. Palmer circling you?

Frederick: Sure would. All of this makes me more nervous than a drunk in church.

Chuckles broke the tense silence that had engulfed the courtroom when Lincoln began his examination.

Lincoln: I understand. Just a few more questions, Henry. Greek wanted to fight Peachy that day, didn't he?

Frederick: Yes, sir. He did.

Lincoln: And Peachy told him he did not want to fight, didn't he?

Frederick: That's right.

Lincoln: But Greek charged Peachy anyway, didn't he?

Frederick: Yes.

Lincoln: He had fire in his eyes.

Frederick: Yes…yes.

Lincoln: Greek even threw a dirt clod at Peachy as you rode away...

Frederick: …And it hit me square in the shoulder.

Lincoln: Thank you, Henry. I have no further questions, your Honor.

Judge Rice: You may leave, Mr. Frederick. Or you may stay. The choice is yours. Gentlemen of the jury, we are going to take our dinner recess. Don't talk about the case. Everyone remain seated while the jury leaves the courtroom. Court will be in recess for one hour and thirty minutes.

As the jurors filed out of the courtroom, Lincoln tried to make eye contact with some of them. He wanted to establish a connection with the jurors and get a sense of how Frederick's testimony may have affected them. Only one juror looked his way.

In a muffled voice, Logan expressed his frustration to Lincoln. "Damnation! That didn't help. Henry's reluctance made him look like he was trying to protect Peachy."

"I know. I told him not to worry about what he heard, but he just didn't want to hurt his friend," Lincoln said, shaking his head side to side.

"I need some air and a washroom break," Logan responded as he removed his perspiration-soaked jacket.

Frederick's testimony had shaken the defense and rocked the Harrisons.

CROCO

CHAPTER 3

The sun burned high in the cloudless afternoon sky, its heat transforming the courtroom into an oven. The spectators' return merely stirred the stale air and added to the heat. Everyone silently hoped the judge would order a breeze.

At precisely 2 p.m., the spectators, who were talking loudly, were silenced by the sheriff announcing the jury's return to the jury box. Court was reconvened and Judge Rice shifted his court files to make a place to write.

Judge Rice: Call your next witness, Mr. Palmer.

Palmer: The People call Sheriff H.F. Andrew to the stand, your Honor.

Judge Rice: Sheriff, please come forward to be sworn.

As the sheriff walked to the court reporter's table, he recalled his difficult assignment investigating and testifying against a family friend before the grand jury.

On July 25, he had traveled to Springfield to meet with Palmer about his investigation into Greek's death. He explained to Palmer what he had been told by the witnesses and gave Palmer the weapon that Peachy had dropped in the store. Palmer was very interested in the evidence and was troubled by Peachy's purchase of the knife, his threat at Clary's Grove and the fact that Greek was unarmed. Palmer acknowledged that Peachy would probably claim self-defense but concluded after due deliberation that Peachy should be charged with murder.

Palmer explained that he was going to talk to the prosecuting attorney and if the prosecutor agreed, he would ask the grand jury to return an indictment. If the grand jury returned an indictment, the sheriff's office would be obliged to arrest Peachy and hold him for trial. As sheriff, he dutifully acknowledged his responsibility to the chief deputy prosecutor.

The following day, Palmer met with James B. White in White's office at the courthouse.

"Do you have anything to report on the Harrison case?" White asked.

"Yes, sir. The Crafton family is up in arms. They want Harrison's hide," Palmer answered as he reached for the report.

"I'm sure they do, John," White said. "Do you think we should go to the grand jury and ask for a murder indictment?"

"I think there's enough evidence to get an indictment. Now, he's going to claim self-defense," warned Palmer.

"What else can he do? Practically the whole town of Pleasant Plains saw him do it," said White.

"I'll see Judge Trimble today," Palmer said as he began to draft his indictment.

At Palmer's request, Judge Bailey Trimble called in the grand jury panel for a special session to be convened on July 28. The panel consisted of 23 men who were all citizens of the county. After instructing the men on their duties, the judge appointed a Springfield banker, Silas Dunn, to serve as the grand jury foreman.

That afternoon, the grand jury gathered in a special room adjacent to the prosecutor's office. White was presenting the evidence for the People with Palmer assisting. By law, the defendant was not allowed to present evidence or have a representative in the room when the grand jury was in session.

Palmer: Gentlemen, today we are presenting the case of the People versus Peachy Quinn Harrison. We are asking for a murder indictment. Greek Crafton of Pleasant Plains was stabbed in the general store there on the sixteenth of July of this year. We would like to call Sheriff H.F. Andrew to summarize the case.

White: Please tell the grand jury who you are.

Sheriff Andrew: I'm the duly elected sheriff of Sangamon County.

White: At Mr. Palmer's request, did you investigate a stabbing that occurred on July sixteenth at Pleasant Plains?

Sheriff Andrew: Yes, I did.

White: Who did you interview?

Sheriff Andrew: Dr. Million, Ben Hart, Henry Frederick, John Crafton and Jon Bone.

White: What did they tell you?

Sheriff Andrew: Dr. Million told me that he treated Greek

Grafton and John Crafton for knife wounds. Greek had been stabbed twice. One wound was caused by a knife slicing Greek's left side. Dr. Million was able to stop the bleeding by sewing him up. The second wound was a deep stab between Greek's ribs on his left side. All Doc could do for Greek on that was to stitch it and put a plaster on it.

White: Did Dr. Million keep Greek at his office?

Sheriff Andrew: No. He let the family take him home.

White: Did Greek die of his wounds?

Sheriff Andrew: Yes.

White: What else did you learn?

Sheriff Andrew: Turns out that Greek was stabbed on Saturday morning by Peachy Harrison while the two men fought in Short and Hart's store.

White: Was it a knife fight?

Sheriff Andrew: Not really. As far as I can tell, Greek did not know Peachy had a knife on him, and Greek was unarmed.

White: Was there bad blood between the two?

Sheriff Andrew: It looks like there was. Henry Frederick told me about a shouting match that took place at Clary's Grove on the Fourth of July. Peachy called Greek a son of a bitch and threatened to kill Greek if he ever laid hands on him.

White: Were there any eyewitnesses to the stabbing?

Sheriff Andrew: Yes, one.

White: Who was that?

Sheriff Andrew: Ben Hart. He's part owner of the general store in Pleasant Plains.

White: What did he say?

Sheriff Andrew: He told me Greek jumped Peachy when Peachy wasn't looking, and then Peachy stabbed Greek with a knife Peachy bought at his store.

White: You've told us Greek wasn't armed, but did Greek threaten to kill Peachy?

Sheriff Andrew: Nobody said that.

White: What else?

Sheriff Andrew: Mr. Hart gave me a bloody knife that Peachy dropped on the floor when he ran out.

White: I don't have any more questions for the sheriff. Are there any questions from the grand jurors?

Grand Juror: Greek…is he John Crafton the blacksmith's boy?

Sheriff Andrew: Yes, he is.

Grand Juror: That's a good family.

Second Grand Juror: That's what I heard.

White: Anything else?

Dunn: Mr. White, what is the law on self-defense?

White: A man can kill another man if his life is threatened.

Dunn: Did Greek threaten to kill Peachy?

White: No witness—that I know of—has said that.

Dunn: Thank you, gentlemen. If there are no other questions, I think it's time to vote.

White: Mr. Palmer and I will leave now.

Dunn: You may be excused, Sheriff, and thank you.

After the prosecutors left the room, Dunn told the grand jury he didn't see where Peachy had the right to kill Greek and he thought they should vote for the murder indictment. He recommended that they sleep on it and return in the morning. The grand jury agreed.

The following day, the grand jury for Sangamon County handed down a true bill charging Peachy Harrison with the murder of Greek Crafton with malice aforethought. The vote was unanimous.

Later that day, word was sent to Sheriff Andrew that a warrant for Peachy's arrest had been issued by the circuit court. But passions were high in Peachy's case and were not reserved for family members.

The *Illinois Journal* promptly had an opinion on the Harrison indictment.

SUNDAY, JULY 31, 1859

EDITORIAL

INDICTMENT OF HARRISON

We are informed that members of the Grand Jury have found a bill against young Peachy Quinn Harrison *for the murder* of Greek Crafton. By what mode of precedence they made up their minds to such an indictment is a mystery. If there ever was a case of killing in self-defense, we think the facts show one. The public would not have a word to say even had the jury seen fit to call it manslaughter; but among those who seem entirely disinterested and impartial in the matter, who have known Greek and Peachy as boys together, and have the same friendship for both, there is much surprise and astonishment manifested. If the Grand Jury in this case would see its way clear to indict Harrison, we do not see how it can fail to indict our local tax collector for larceny on the much stronger testimony against him. But we guess "that's a bay horse of a different color."

Harrison's trial is set for Wednesday, August 31.

And the *Springfield Register* took grave exception to the *Illinois Journal's* editorial.

MONDAY, AUGUST 1, 1859

EDITORIAL

THE HARRISON INDICTMENT

The Grand Jury, on Saturday, found a bill of murder against Peachy Quinn Harrison for the killing of Greek Crafton. Whether rightly or not, it is not for the public press now to express an opinion, in justice to either party. That we regret to see that the *Journal* makes such finding a subject of censure; coupling it with matters connected with the political efforts of that paper.

The *Journal's* paragraph is one which cannot but be depreciated by every thinking man. It is unjust to the party it assumes to defend, who, if really not indictable for murder, cannot be benefitted by mingling his cause with the partisan commentary of the newspaper press; and so his friends feel it.

The killing of Crafton is a subject of judicial examination. Investigation by the Grand Jury is a part of the necessary routine. If their finding is to be subject of newspaper commentary pending the trial, and in a manner to excite prejudice by joining such comment with matters having partisan connection, the decision of court and jury must necessarily be the subject of similar preparatory controversy. We express no opinion in regard to the finding of the Grand Jury, but, as a law-abiding citizen, we protest against the conduct of the public journal which assumes to prejudge judicial investigation; and more especially, when that journal attempts to bring partisan feeling to bear in matters before the courts affecting not only the integrity of the officers of the law, and them under examination for its alleged infraction, but affecting the life of a human being.

The finding of the Grand Jury may or may not be wrong. Grand Juries are but human but their action is not final. They only present a case, which, in their opinion, requires the action of court and petit jury. To prejudge their actions, and especially in the manner adopted by the *Journal*, is not only to do injustice to the public but to the parties involved.

If the actions of our courts are to be moulded by outside public opinion, expressed through the political press, we may as well conclude to decide judicial questions by popular election—to set aside constitution and law, and leave such self exponents of law and gospel as the editors of the *Journal* to decide, not only as to the making of the laws, but the manner of their execution by the courts.

We repeat that the *Journal* does injustice to Mr. Harrison. Its attorneyship can be of no benefit to him, and if its expressions affect anything, it can only be to his detriment by providing the impression that such extraordinary means as the use of a partisan press, in a judicial investigation, is sought to further his interests, through party friends, in the absence of confidence in his innocence of the charge upon which he is arraigned.

We have full confidence that the court and jury will do its duty, and that justice will be done, upon thorough examination of the subject. In common with all the good citizens, we deplore the causes which have led to the trial, and it is only cause of additional regret that anyone should be so foolish as to attempt to produce results in a manner adopted by the *Journal* in its issue yesterday.

The *Register* prompted a pointed rebuttal from the *Illinois Journal.*

TUESDAY, AUGUST 2, 1859

EDITORIAL

THE REGISTER AND THE GRAND JURY

Our paragraph in reference to the severe action of the Grand Jury in the Harrison case affords occasion for a very effecting comment on the part of the *Register.* That sheet is wonderfully afraid that we are trying to give the case a political turn, which was as remote as possible from our intention. Upon what the *Register* predicates its fears, is not so apparent, unless it ascends that the acts of a Grand Jury are, forsooth, above all scrutiny or "censure," which we would inform the editor, is not our understanding of the matter. We do not believe, as the *Register* seems to, that Grand Juries are omnipotent inquisitions, but we hold that they are just as responsible to public opinion for what they do as individuals. But it sounds rather laughable in the *Register* to talk about our lugging politics into the courts when it is notorious that the very Grand Jury, which that sheet apologizes for, is a pat political machine, made up entirely of the very strongest democratic partisans, for a particular purpose. If the *Register* is sincere in its deprecation of partisanism in judicial proceedings, let it begin by venting a small vial full of indignation at the composition of its present Grand Jury, before it presumes to arraign others on the charge.

But aside from all this, and from the evident effort of the *Register* to call attention, politically, to the case of young Peachy Quinn Harrison, we trust that court and the traverse jury will act fairly and do their whole duty in the premises.

And a surrebuttal from the *Register* followed.

WEDNESDAY, AUGUST 3, 1859

EDITORIAL

PUBLIC JUDGMENT

The *Journal* makes a lame excuse for its paragraph pre-judging the Harrison case, now pending in the circuit court, and charges us with what we condemned in its first paragraph. The justice of this we are willing to leave to public judgment. We repeat what we said on Tuesday: nobody can be benefitted by such attorneyship as that volunteered by the *Journal*. It is unjust to either side, and can result in no public good. We do not consider courts or juries immaculate, but there is a proper and improper time to discuss the correctness of their action. In the present instance, we think the *Journal* has chosen the latter, to say nothing of the manner of its discussion. That's all.

⁓

The sheriff shifted his dusty hat from one hand to the other as he approached the witness chair.

> *Court Reporter:* Please place your right hand on the Bible, Sheriff. Do you swear that your testimony before this court and jury will be the truth, the whole truth, and nothing but the truth, so help you God?

> *Sheriff Andrew:* Yes.

> *Palmer:* State your name, please.

The sheriff cleared his throat and grinned nervously before he answered.

Sheriff Andrew: Harold F. Andrew.

Palmer: You are the duly elected sheriff of Sangamon County, Illinois, are you not?

Sheriff Andrew: I am.

Palmer: Did you investigate Greek Crafton's death?

Sheriff Andrew: At your request, yes, sir.

Palmer: And you appeared before the grand jury with what you found out, correct?

Sheriff Andrew: Last month.

Palmer: The grand jury returned a murder indictment.

Sheriff Andrew: Yes, sir.

Palmer: And a warrant for the defendant's arrest was issued, correct?

Sheriff Andrew: Right.

Palmer: Did you attempt to serve the arrest warrant?

Sheriff Andrew: Me and my deputy went to the Harrison farm on Saturday, thirty July…yes, sir.

Palmer: Was the defendant there?

Sheriff Andrew: No, sir.

Palmer: Where was he?

Sheriff Andrew: I don't know.

Palmer: Did the family know?

Sheriff Andrew: If they did, they didn't tell me.

Palmer: Did you go back?

Sheriff Andrew: Not that day. Word was sent to me that he was going to surrender on Monday.

Palmer: What date?

Sheriff Andrew: First of August.

Palmer: Did he?

Sheriff Andrew: Did he what?

Palmer: Did he surrender?

Sheriff Andrew: No.

Palmer: Did you go back to the Harrison farm?

Sheriff Andrew: Yes, on Tuesday.

Palmer: Was he there when you went back?

Sheriff Andrew: Yes.

Palmer: Did you arrest him?

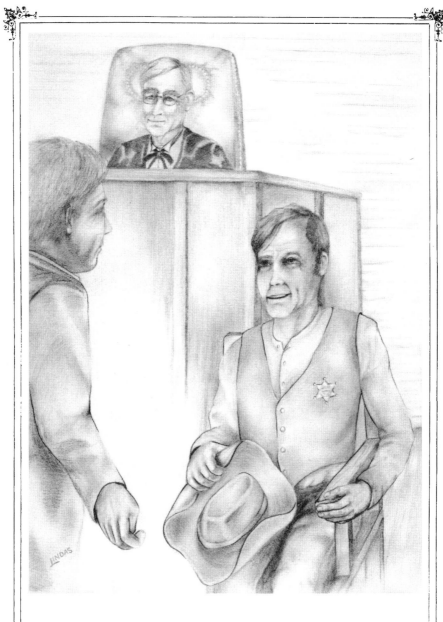

John Palmer questions Sheriff Andrew

Sheriff Andrew: Yes, sir.

Palmer: Did you ask him where he had been?

Sheriff Andrew: Yes, sir.

Palmer: What did he say?

Sheriff Andrew: Fishing.

Palmer: Pass the witness, your Honor.

Judge Rice: Cross-examination? Mr. Logan?

Logan moved to the podium. His poufy hair seemed to thrive on the heat.

Logan: Yes, your Honor. Sheriff, doing double duty today?

Sheriff Andrew: No rest for the weary.

Logan: So true. When you went before the grand jury, you only presented evidence obtained from a few witnesses, correct?

Sheriff Andrew: Five.

Logan: When you went to arrest our client on the thirtieth of July, you got the warrant the day before, right?

Sheriff Andrew: Yes, sir.

Logan: You don't know if our client knew there was a warrant, do you?

Sheriff Andrew: Well, everyone in the county knew.

Logan: But you didn't ask our client if he knew about the warrant, did you?

Sheriff Andrew: No, sir.

Logan: Thank you, Sheriff. No further questions.

Judge Rice: Gentlemen of the jury, we are going to recess for fifteen minutes. I need a glass of water. Please don't discuss the case. Everyone remain seated until the jury leaves the courtroom.

The judge's knee-length robe was trapping heat like a hayloft. And the defense lawyers took advantage of the reprieve to prepare for cross-examination of the damaging witnesses to come.

ᨁᦄᦄ

Judge Rice: Call your next witness, Mr. Palmer.

Palmer: The People call Jon C. Bone to the stand, your Honor.

Jon Bone, a small, leathery-skinned man wearing a plaid shirt and baggy light- colored pants, and holding a dusty bowler hat, walked in shyly and approached the witness chair.

Court Reporter: Put your right hand on the Bible, please.

Bone: I'm left-handed.

Judge Rice: Put your right hand on the Bible anyway. That's just the way we do it.

Court Reporter: Do you swear to tell the truth, the whole truth, and nothing but the truth, so help you God?

Bone: Yes, sir. I do.

Palmer: Where do you reside, sir?

Bone: Near Pleasant Plains in Sangamon County.

Palmer: Did you know the deceased…Greek Crafton?

Bone: I did.

Palmer: Do you know the defendant?

Bone: I know him.

Palmer: Now, around the seventh of July this year, were you in Short and Hart's General Store?

Bone: I was looking for a pickax.

Palmer: What time of day was it?

Bone: Afternoon…could have been around dinnertime.

Palmer: Was anyone else in the store with you?

Bone: I…I was alone when I heard them.

Palmer: Heard them?

Bone: I heard Peachy and Mr. Hart talking.

Palmer: What were they talking about?

As Bone was testifying, Peachy remembered the conversation he had with Hart vividly.

"Have any knives for sale, Ben?"

"Hey, Peachy. Sure do!" Hart said, reaching under the counter. "Take a look at this one. It's a bowie knife with a German silver handle."

"How much is it, Ben?"

"Three dollars."

"I'll take it," Peachy said as he reached in his pocket. "Does it come with a scabbard?"

Peachy's thoughts were again interrupted.

Bone: Peachy wanted to buy a bowie knife with a scabbard.

Palmer: What kind of scabbard was it?

Bone: It was black leather. Different persons carry them in different places. This was hung across the breast in some way. He put it on.

Juror: Who put it on?

Judge Rice: I'm going to allow the juror's question, Mr. Palmer, so the witness may answer.

Bone: Why, Peachy Harrison. I think his remark was, "Does it fit under the shirt?"

Palmer: Did it?

Bone: Yes.

Palmer: How long was the blade?

Bone: Between five and six inches long in the blade—a regular bowie knife—sharp in the edge.

Palmer: Was anything further said between the defendant and Mr. Hart?

Bone: I heard Mr. Hart thank Peachy and ask about his family.

Palmer: What did the defendant say?

Bone: He didn't say nothin'. He just walked out.

Palmer: Thank you. No further questions. Pass the witness.

Judge Rice: Mr. Logan or Mr. Lincoln?

Though smothering in the sweltering courtroom, Logan buttoned his jacket as he moved to the podium.

Logan: Yes, Judge. Mr. Bone, did our client say what he intended to do with the knife?

Bone: Not that I heard.

Logan: Do you believe a man has the right to defend himself?

Palmer half rose. "Objection. What he believes is irrelevant."
Logan barely waited for the prosecutor to finish.

Logan: I withdraw my last question, Judge.

Judge Rice: Very well. Anything further?

Logan: Yes, sir. Mr. Bone, did you tell Greek about what you
saw and heard?

Bone: Yes.

Logan: Did Greek tell you what he thought?

Bone: He laughed and said, "Peachy will need more than
that."

Logan: Thank you, Mr. Bone. No further questions, Judge.

Judge Rice: You may be excused Mr. Bone. Because we
have put in a good day's work and the heat is troublesome,
court will be recessed until ten o'clock in the morning. I
need to conduct a short hearing in another matter.
Gentlemen, don't discuss the case until you retire to deliberate. Everyone please remain seated while the jury leaves the
courtroom.

Mr. Palmer, how are we doing on witnesses? I have a full
docket next week, so we must finish even if it means holding court on Saturday.

Palmer: The People's case will be concluded tomorrow,
Judge.

Judge Rice: Very well. Mr. Lincoln, I realize you have no obligation to call any witnesses, but…

Lincoln: We can be finished this week if we work Saturday.

Judge Rice: Thank you, gentlemen. I know this is an important case to both sides. So I want you to have the time you need. We stand in recess.

The jury's focused attention during the day was apparent to everyone in the courtroom, and it made Virginia nervous. As the jury was leaving the courtroom, Virginia quietly eased near Lincoln, Logan and Cullom to hear their muffled conversation.

"Today's testimony didn't look good," said Cullom as the last juror found the exit.

"Unfortunately, I agree," Logan added. "What do you think, Abe?"

"The testimony helped the prosecution's case, that's for certain," Lincoln lamented, "but it's to be expected. We must keep our senses and our client calm. Tomorrow will be better. Stephen, let's go back to the office and discuss tomorrow's strategy."

"I have some ideas…and I need a tall Scotch," Logan said rubbing his face with both hands.

"That might do us all some good," Cullom quipped.

"A glass of cold water will satisfy me just fine. But it's a day like this that could cause a courtroom lawyer like me to become a three-bottle man," Lincoln said, smiling. "That's for sure."

Virginia was on the verge of meltdown. What could the lawyers do to stem the tide of the prosecution's evidence? Her mind immediately recalled the worst day of her young life—the day her brother was charged and arrested.

CRICO

Although the stabbing had shaken Virginia to the bone, she was determined to find out what people in town were saying. She went to town with her brother Peyton Jr. and entered every business and gathering place. People she met sent mixed messages. Some were understanding and sympathetic—they thought Greek "got what he deserved." Others wouldn't look at her or would stop talking when they saw her. A few were angry and stated that "what Peachy had done was wrong."

When Virginia entered the general store, Ben Hart noticed her immediately. "Don't worry, Virginia," said Ben, putting his arm around his young friend. "This will all work out. We have to give people some time to think this through."

"I'm afraid," said Virginia, tearing up, her eyes still puffy from lack of sleep.

"I know, dear," said Ben.

"What have you heard?" asked Virginia.

"The sheriff came to see me yesterday. He asked me what I saw and told me he was going to Springfield as soon as he was finished taking statements from Doc and John Crafton. I think he has also talked to some of the boys who were here that day…and to Henry Frederick," Ben replied.

"What do you think will happen, Ben?" Virginia said, thinking ahead.

Ben took a breath and pressed his lips together. "I'm concerned, Virginia. The sheriff seemed troubled."

Virginia thanked Ben for being such a good friend to her and returned home to report her findings to the family. Mary Rose was worried but determined to be strong. Virginia didn't know what to say to people, but she knew that the community was divided over what had happened and that the matter was far from over.

After the stabbing, Peachy retreated to the family corncrib, where he tried to reconcile what he had been taught with what he

had done. He was terrified. Would Greek's family want revenge?
Would he be arrested and, if so, would he go to prison? His family tried to console him, and his mother assured him she would
always be by his side. But no one fully comprehended the sever-
ity of Greek's wounds—especially Peachy. So, when Greek died,
Peachy couldn't resist the impulse to run. Now it was murder and
he knew if he was found guilty, he would hang.

Fourteen days later, the sheriff and his deputy headed out to the
Harrison family farm to complete their unpleasant task. When
they arrived, Virginia was in the side yard with her mother having
lunch. Peyton and Junior were in the field.

As the sheriff and his deputy approached, the Harrison women
stood. Virginia grabbed her mother's hand and Mary Rose stiff-
ened her chin.

Stepping down from his wagon, the sheriff tipped his hat.
"Good mornin', Mary Rose…Virginia," he said, addressing them
gently. "I'm sorry, but I'm here to arrest Peachy for the murder of
Greek Crafton. Where's he at?" he asked, looking in the direction
of the field.

Mary Rose's knees weakened. "He's not here," she said, showing no emotion.

"Where can I find him?" asked the sheriff impatiently.

"I don't know," Mary Rose said as she looked at her daughter.
"He left yesterday morning, and we haven't seen him since."

The sheriff's eyes narrowed. "Well, someone needs to find him
or I will have no choice but to get some men to track him down."

"Oh! Please don't do that," Virginia said as her heart leapt to
her throat. "We'll find him."

"I'm just doin' my job, Mary Rose," the sheriff said, easing up
on the two distraught women. "We'll be back tomorrow afternoon."

"We know…we ain't mad at you," Mary Rose volunteered.

"He will be here."

The sheriff and his deputy left the way they came, leaving a trail of fine dust behind them.

As they pulled out of sight, Mary Rose turned to Virginia. "Do you know where to find him?"

"No, Ma, but I think I know where to look."

⚜

When Peachy was old enough to sit in a saddle, his father often took him and his brother to a secluded place on the North Fork of Richland Creek, where they fished and swam in the lazy waters. They went back year after year until Peachy was old enough to ride his horse there on his own.

Sometimes he would take his baby sister. Virginia would giggle incessantly when she caught a fish, but she hid her face when Peachy slid a worm or cricket on her hook.

When his sister tired of fishing, Peachy began to go by himself. It was his refuge from the pressures of life. He constructed a small platform in a mulberry tree and climbed its strong branches to sit quietly among the birds. He would be still—ever so still—until the hour was so late he would ride the entire way home at a gallop to beat the sunset.

It was in that tree—out of sight and obscured from everything but the breeze—that he did his best thinking. His childhood had not been easy. Born six weeks premature, he was always considered frail and not as manly as other young men because of his small stature. His mother, while not meaning to play favorites among her children, doted on him when he was a child and positioned him away from risk and danger as he grew older. In the mulberry tree, he felt stronger and clearer of purpose.

"Peachy," Virginia said softly. Peachy didn't hear her tender voice, so she began to climb the familiar branches of the mulberry tree. "Peachy. It's me, Virginia. Can I sit with you?"

Peachy snapped out of his trance. "I suppose. Just be careful on the third limb…it's slippery today," said Peachy without looking down.

"How are you doing, brother?" Virginia asked as she reached the weathered oak perch.

"I killed a man, Virginia. I killed him. I don't know if I can live with that," Peachy said, staring at the river.

"But…it wasn't your fault. You were only defending yourself. Greek meant to hurt you," Virginia argued.

"I guess. But I don't think he meant to kill me. I can't stop seeing his face, the look he had when I stuck the knife in his side. His mother, she…," Peachy put his face in his hands and began to sob.

"Brother…Peachy…your family cares about you. We love you and we want you to come home."

"The sheriff is looking for me, isn't he?"

"Yes…yes, he is," Virginia said, taking her brother's hand.

"You know they hang murderers, Virginia," Peachy said, looking into his sister's eyes.

"Nobody's going to hang. You ain't no murderer. But you should come back home so we can face this together," Virginia insisted.

Peachy nodded. "Do you think they'll keep me in jail until my trial?"

"I don't know, but Ma and Pa will get you a good lawyer. They will," Virginia said reassuringly.

"Well, I guess we should go then. Thanks for coming. You are always there when I need you," Peachy said, climbing down from the comfortable shelter he'd found in the tree.

The two rode together back to the Harrison farm, where they were greeted by the family, including Rev. Cartwright and Peachy's grandmother, Frances.

The following day, Sheriff Andrew returned as promised. "Let's go, Peachy," he said with authority.

"But Greek was trying to hurt him," Virginia argued.

"He'll get his chance to tell that to a jury, Virginia," the sheriff said, repeating a standard line of a law enforcement officer.

Peachy took a deep breath, looked at his mother and sister, and began walking to the wagon. Virginia broke free from Mary Rose, hugged her brother and started to cry. Brushing away her tears, she turned to the sheriff and asked, "Where you takin' him?"

"To the county jail," he said.

"Can we see him?" asked Virginia, ending her sentence in a sob.

"Of course you can, honey," the sheriff softened again.

As the three men rode off, Virginia looked at her mother. "What are we going to do, Ma?"

Mary Rose looked with a sense of determination into her daughter's green eyes, blind with tears. "As God is my witness, ain't nobody going to hang my boy," she replied.

Peachy was taken to the Sangamon County Jail, where he was held without bail. His trial was set to begin on Aug. 31.

CHAPTER 4

After checking with the court reporter for accuracy, the journalist for the *Register* detailed the events of the second day of trial for readers, who were hungry for information about the county's most talked about murder trial since the Anderson case. (George Anderson, a well-respected and admired businessman, had been murdered in the backyard of his Springfield home after someone fractured his skull with a blunt instrument. Anderson's wife and nephew, who were rumored to be having an affair, were accused of conspiring to kill him. Lincoln represented the nephew.)

TRIAL OF PEACHY QUINN HARRISON
INDICTED FOR THE MURDER OF GREEK CRAFTON

Circuit Court of Sangamon County – Hon. E.F. Rice, Judge

SECOND DAY

THURSDAY, SEPTEMBER 1, 1859

Court met pursuant to adjournment, at half past eight o'clock, and the jury being called, the trial proceeded.

The Court stated that he had learned, from the officer in charge of the jury, that one of the jurors was unwell.

Mr. Patterson, the juror alluded to, said that he was unable to serve, and, by the consent of the counsel on both sides, was discharged. After examining several alternates, Mr. Charles A. White was chosen to replace Mr. Patterson.

Mr. Palmer opened the case for the prosecution and proceeded to read the indictment and the law applicable to the case before stating the prosecution's evidence.

Mr. Lincoln stated the substance of the defense.

The examination of witnesses then commenced.

Dr. J.L. Million; CALLED, SWORN AND EXAMINED by Mr. Palmer lives in Pleasant Plains; knew the parties; knew where Crafton lived; was called to see Greek a few moments after he received the wound in Short and Hart's store. Greek was taken to my house; I dressed the wounds and supposed they were made with a sharp pointed knife; he lived until Monday evening, three days after he was hurt; I think his death was caused by the wounds received in the store. I am a practicing physician.

Henry Frederick; CALLED, SWORN AND EXAMINED by Mr. Palmer lives in Pleasant Plains; knew the parties; saw them on the Fourth of July at Clary's Grove; saw Harrison first that morning at Harrison's home; saw Greek on the road to Clary's Grove; has been friends with Harrison since they were small boys.

Palmer asked Judge Rice to declare Frederick a hostile witness. Logan vigorously objected for the defense. Judge Rice overruled the objection and declared Frederick a hostile witness.

Reluctantly, Frederick stated that while traveling to the Clary's Grove Fourth of July picnic, Harrison and he encountered Greek and John Crafton. Greek Crafton had words with Harrison. Harrison and Greek were not friends. Harrison asked Greek about his brother Peter and Greek challenged Harrison about a statement Harrison made to Peter Crafton. Greek and Harrison quarreled and Harrison called Greek a "son of a bitch." Greek came after Harrison and Frederick got them out of there. As Harrison and Frederick were leaving, Harrison yelled at Greek saying, "If you ever lay hands on me, I'll kill you."

Cross-examination by Mr. Lincoln; Greek wanted to fight Harrison that day; Harrison didn't want to fight; Greek charged Harrison and had fire in his eyes; Greek threw a dirt clod at Harrison as they rode away and it hit me in the shoulder.

Adjourned until two o'clock.

Court met pursuant to adjournment.   Two o'clock, P.M.

Sheriff Harold F. Andrew; CALLED, SWORN AND EXAMINED by Mr. Palmer is the duly elected sheriff of Sangamon County. He investigated Greek's demise and presented his findings to the Grand Jury, which returned an indictment. A warrant having been issued, he attempted to arrest Harrison who was not to be found. Failing to surrender, Harrison was later arrested. Asked where he had been, Harrison responded, "fishing."

Cross-examination by Mr. Logan; The witness only presented evidence from five witnesses to the Grand Jury.

Jon C. Bone; CALLED, SWORN AND EXAMINED by Mr. Palmer lives near Pleasant Plains; knew the parties. On seven July he was in Short and Hart's store alone. He overheard Harrison asking to buy a bowie knife with a shirt scabbard. He stated that the blade was five to six inches long.

Cross-examination by Mr. Logan; Bone told Greek about what he saw Harrison buy in the store. Greek laughed and said, "Peachy will need more than that."

It now being half past three o'clock, court was adjourned, after charging the jury and placing them in the care of the officers at the American House until ten o'clock tomorrow morning.

໑~໑౿ఌ౿ఄ

The weather on the third day of trial was a repeat of the first two. The sun was relentless in the afternoons. The residents of Sangamon County were ready for fall.

Calling Ben Hart as the prosecution's next witness created a serious dilemma for Palmer. Hart's testimony helped the prosecution's case by shoring up Bone's recollection of the timing of the bowie knife purchase. However, Hart's testimony would also create a platform for Lincoln to lay the groundwork to call into doubt the truthfulness of John Crafton's testimony. In the end, Palmer decided that the benefits of calling Ben Hart outweighed the possible harm to the People's case.

Judge Rice: Are you ready to proceed, Mr. Palmer?

Palmer: The People call Ben Hart to the stand, your Honor.

Ben Hart made a mature contrast to the down-home rabble of Peachy's friends and associates. His dark eyes were alert and serious, and he was dressed in a pressed blue shirt and dark pants. His demeanor was natural and likable. Both sides knew the jury would respect him. The only question would be, whom would he help?

Court Reporter: Please place your right hand on the Bible, Mr. Hart. Do you swear to tell the truth, the whole truth, and nothing but the truth, so help you God?

Hart: I do.

Judge Rice: Mr. Hart, having been sworn, you may be seated.

Palmer took a deep breath and approached the podium to begin his direct examination.

Palmer: Please state your name for the reporter and the jury.

Hart: Benjamin Stephen Hart.

Palmer: Where do you live, Mr. Hart?

Hart: Pleasant Plains, Sangamon County.

Palmer: I understand you run a business in Pleasant Plains.

Hart: Yes, sir. I run the general store with my partner, Nathan Short.

Palmer: What do you sell there?

Hart: Things that folks need to farm and hunt.

Palmer: Weapons?

Hart: Yes. Knives mainly. I can special-order pistols and long rifles if need be.

Palmer: Did you know Greek Crafton?

Hart: I did.

Palmer: Do you know the defendant?

Hart: Yes.

Palmer: Did you sell him a knife?

Hart: Yes.

Palmer: When?

Hart: Around the seventh or eighth of July.

Palmer: Let me show you what I have marked as State's Exhibit "A". Is that the knife you sold the defendant?

Ben took the knife in both hands, as if holding a newborn infant.

Hart: Looks like it. It was a bowie knife with a six-inch blade and German silver handle.

Palmer: Like Exhibit "A"?

Hart: Yes.

Palmer: The State would offer Exhibit "A" into evidence, your Honor.

Lincoln: No objection, your Honor.

Judge Rice: It will be received as evidence.

John Palmer questions Ben Hart

Palmer: May I pass it to the jury?

Judge Rice: You may.

Palmer carefully handed the knife, handle first, to juror Anderson, who then passed it on to his fellow jurors.

Palmer: Mr. Hart, when the defendant purchased the knife, did he say what his intentions were?

Hart: No.

Palmer: Did he look nervous when he purchased the knife?

Lincoln shot to his feet.

Lincoln: Objection, your Honor. Calls for speculation.

Judge Rice: Overruled.

Lincoln: Note our exceptions.

Judge Rice: So noted.

Palmer: Did the defendant look nervous, Mr. Hart?

Hart: He wasn't at himself.

Palmer: At himself? What do you mean?

Hart: He was out of sorts. Not his usual self.

Palmer: Thank you. Mr. Hart, let me take you back to the sixteenth of July, this year. Were you tending the store?

Hart: It was my turn to work that Saturday.

Palmer: Did anything out of the ordinary happen in your store that day?

Hart: Yes.

Palmer: To the best of your recollection, tell us what happened.

Ben looked at the jury, which was at perfect attention.

Hart: It was about 8 in the mornin', I guess. Peachy had come to the store and I showed him the paper. We were reading together when…the next thing I know Greek has Peachy in a bear hug from the back. I hollered at him to stop and I grabbed Greek to pull him off Peachy. About that time, John Crafton grabbed me and broke my grip on Greek.

Ben's calm demeanor began to fade as the events of July 16 began to flood his memory.

Palmer: Did John Crafton say anything when he pulled you away?

Hart: Yes. He said, "Leave him alone. Greek could and should whip him."

Palmer: What happened next?

Hart: The next thing I saw was Greek pulling Peachy to the door. Peachy was saying he didn't want to fight. When they were at the feed sacks, Greek pulled his arm back as if to hit Peachy. When he did, Peachy pulled his knife and stabbed him.

Palmer: How many times did he stab him?

Hart: I'm not sure.

Palmer: What happened then?

Hart: John Crafton made for Peachy. When he did, Peachy cut him, and John started throwing my goods at him.

Palmer: Is that all you saw?

Hart: No. Greek staggered out the front door and Doc held him up. Peachy ran…dropped the knife and ran.

Palmer: Was Greek bleeding?

Hart: His shirt had blood on it.

Palmer: Thank you, Mr. Hart. Pass the witness for cross-examination, your Honor.

Lincoln stood up and proceeded to the podium. He faced Ben Hart, who returned his gaze with a respectful nod, and gave Peachy a supportive glance.

Lincoln: Mr. Hart, anything like that ever happen in your store before?

Hart: Never. Never, and I hope it never happens again.

Lincoln: When John Crafton, as you say it, "made for Peachy," did he say anything?

Hart: He said, "He was not armed," referring to Greek.

Lincoln: After Peachy…after John Crafton was cut, did he say anything?

Hart: He said, "You'll pay for this" to Peachy.

Lincoln: Finally, did you hear Peachy say anything when John Crafton came after him?

Hart: Yes. He said, "Have I no friends here?" Or words like that.

Lincoln: Thank you, sir. No further questions, your Honor.

The prosecution's presentation of evidence consumed the remainder of the morning. The jury sat through the testimony of the Livingood brothers, who were at the store after Greek was stabbed. They added little to the prosecution's case. But, the dinner recess gave Palmer one more opportunity to prepare his last witness—John Crafton. He needed to end strong. John Crafton was a no-nonsense man who didn't mince words. He was the perfect witness to end the prosecution's case on a strong note.

"Call your next witness, Mr. Palmer," ordered the judge.

"The People call Jonathan Crafton to the stand," said Palmer as he nodded to the sheriff. A murmur rippled through the spectators as Crafton walked through the courtroom doors and passed the lawyers to take the oath. Crafton eased his muscular frame into the witness chair, and Palmer began his direct examination.

Palmer: Mr. Crafton, please state your full name for the gentlemen of the jury.

Crafton: My name is Jonathan Moses Crafton.

Palmer: They call you "John"?

Crafton: Yes, sir.

Palmer: Where do you live, sir?

Crafton: Just north of Pleasant Plains.

Palmer: Are you married?

Crafton: Yes, sir.

Palmer: What's your wife's name?

Crafton: Sarah.

Palmer: Do you and Mrs. Crafton have children?

The muscles in Crafton's jaw tightened with emotion as he prepared to answer the prosecutor's question.

Crafton: Up till eighteen July, we had four boys.

Palmer: What are their names?

Crafton: Greek, he was my oldest. That's what we called him. His God-given name was Jonathan. He was named after me. There's Elijah. Peter is next and then our baby boy, Moses.

Palmer: What are their ages?

Crafton: Greek was twenty-three. Elijah is twenty. Peter is eighteen and Moses is eleven.

Palmer: Where were you born and raised?

Crafton: I was born and raised in Wrightsborough, Georgia. My great-granddaddy, Moses, fought alongside Elijah Clarke against the redcoats. My granddaddy was born in the swamps of the Hornet's Nest in northeastern Georgia. After the war, they moved to Wrightsborough.

Palmer: How did you get to Illinois?

Crafton: After Greek was born, Sarah and me heard about Illinois from my uncle. We figgered it would be a good place to raise our family. We also figgered it wouldn't be as hot, but summers like this make us want to move to Minnesota.

Palmer: Amen. What's your occupation, Mr. Crafton?

Crafton: A blacksmith by trade. I also farm.

Palmer: How were your crops last year?

Crafton: Weren't worth a damn. Too much rain in the fall. They'll be better this year. I got a good stand of corn and I been told my red amber wheat is prizewinnin'.

Palmer: Very good. Do you know the defendant, Peachy Quinn Harrison?

Crafton: I do.

Palmer: Do you know his family?

Crafton: Yes, sir.

Palmer: How long have you known Mr. Harrison?

Crafton: Most his life, I reckon.

Palmer: Did he get along with your sons?

Crafton: To my way of thinkin' he did…at least till this spring.

Palmer: What happened in the spring?

Crafton crossed his powerful arms as he looked at the prisoner's dock.

Crafton: Peachy began disrespecting Greek.

Palmer: And how did he do that?

Crafton: Peachy warned Peter not to tell Greek who Peachy was courting. Then he called Greek a son of a bitch. Peter can take care of himself, but Greek took great offense to the insult to him and his mother.

Palmer: Did you hear the insult directed towards your wife and Greek?

Crafton: We were on our way to the Clary's Grove picnic when we seen Peachy and his friend Henry. I pulled alongside to say "hey." A shouting match started and Peachy said the insult.

John Crafton testifies

Palmer: How did the argument end?

Crafton: Peachy said he would kill Greek.

Palmer: Now, did you go to Short and Hart's store on July sixteenth of this year?

Crafton: Yes.

Palmer: Were you with anyone?

Crafton: My son Greek.

Palmer: In your own words, tell us what you observed that day.

Crafton: Observed?

Palmer: What did you see?

Crafton: Oh! What happened? Well, me and Greek were up early that day to go to the general store to pick up some supplies for the farm. When we got to town, Greek hitched the horse and I got down to go inside. I stopped to look at some new tools and Greek went in to find Ben. After a few seconds, I heard a ruckus. When I went to the front door, I saw Greek and Peachy locked up.

Before I could get to 'em, Ben grabbed my boy from behind. I tried to get between 'em and when I did, Peachy pulled a knife and cut my arm. When I tried to check my arm, Peachy stabbed my boy. I thought he was going to stab me, so I started heaving things at him to get away. Greek had made it out the door and Dr. Million held him. There was a lot of blood on his shirt...and...I...I didn't know what...what to do, so I...I...

Palmer: Would you like a drink of water?

Crafton: Just give me a second.

A tear slowly trickled down the blacksmith's cheek as he lifted a water glass to his lips.

Palmer: Take all the time you need, John.

Crafton: It's hard to talk about.

Palmer: We understand.

Crafton: Doc took Greek to his office and stopped the bleedin'. After, we took Greek home to his mother.

Palmer: Mr. Crafton, was your son armed?

Crafton: He's never been armed.

Palmer: Did you hear him threaten to kill or seriously injure Mr. Harrison?

Crafton: No, sir. Peachy made the threat.

Palmer: Thank you, Mr. Crafton. Pass the witness for cross-examination, your Honor.

Palmer knew the jury would remember the emotional testimony of his strong, respectable witness. What would the defense do with him?

Judge Rice: Mr. Lincoln?

To everyone's surprise, Logan stood up to question Crafton for the defense. Lincoln and Logan had carefully planned out their strategy. They both felt this move would unnerve the witness and confuse the prosecution.

Logan: We are very sorry about your loss, Mr. Crafton.

Crafton: Does that also mean your client?

Logan: Yes, sir, it does.

Crafton's lips tightened unforgivingly.

Logan: Did you see your son jump Mr. Harrison?

Crafton: No, sir.

Logan: Did you hear Peachy say he didn't want to fight?

Crafton: No, sir.

Logan: I guess it would also be true that you didn't witness Peachy grabbing the counter railing while your son tried to pull him away?

Crafton: No, sir. I didn't.

Logan knew that Crafton's testimony was at odds with the description of the events given by Ben Hart and other witnesses, so he pressed on.

Logan: When you entered Mr. Hart's store, you encouraged your son to whip Peachy, didn't you?

Crafton: That's a lie. By the time I got to them, they were toe-to-toe. I knew Greek could whip him.

Logan: So you wanted your son to whip Peachy?

Crafton: It made me no difference, sir.

Logan: Greek drew his fist back to strike Peachy, didn't he?

Crafton: I never saw nothing like that. All I remember is that I jumped between Greek and Peachy to protect my son, and Peachy cut my arm. When I checked my wound, Peachy stabbed my boy. Greek didn't have a chance.

Logan had created a significant contradiction in the prosecution's case, and Lincoln nodded for Logan to stop his examination. "Thank you, Mr. Crafton," said Logan, looking at the jury.

"No additional questions, Judge," said Palmer immediately.

Judge Rice: The hour is late, Mr. Palmer. But we must get as far as we can in the prosecution's case, notwithstanding the heat. So call your next witness.

Palmer: Judge, I'm pleased to report that the People have

concluded this portion of their case. The prosecution rests.

Judge Rice: Very well, Mr. Palmer. That makes me breathe a little easier. Gentlemen, we will be in recess until tomorrow…nine o'clock. We have concluded the People's case. Tomorrow, we will hear from the defense. If they choose to call any witnesses—they don't have to call any—but they can if they wish to do so.

Please keep in mind that the case isn't complete and you should not make up your mind until you have heard all of the evidence, arguments of counsel and my instructions on the law. Everyone remain seated while the jury leaves the courtroom.

༺∽༒∾༻

The *Register* was ready for the readers at 6 a.m. the next day. No one was disappointed in the tragic drama playing out in the courtroom.

TRIAL OF PEACHY QUINN HARRISON
INDICTED FOR THE MURDER OF GREEK CRAFTON

Circuit Court of Sangamon County – Hon. E.F. Rice, Judge

THIRD DAY

FRIDAY, SEPTEMBER 2, 1859

Court met pursuant to adjournment, at nine o'clock, and the jury being called, the trial proceeded.

Benjamin Stephen Hart; CALLED, SWORN AND EXAMINED by Mr. Palmer lives in Pleasant Plains and is one of the proprietors of the General Store there; knew the parties. On seven or eight July he sold a bowie knife to Harrison. Harrison was "out of sorts" when he bought the knife. On Saturday, sixteen July, he was tending the store. Around eight o'clock in the morning, Harrison entered the store. Greek Crafton approached Harrison from behind and grabbed him in a "bear hug." A struggle ensued and he attempted to separate the men. John Crafton pulled him away saying "Greek should whip him." As Greek was pulling Harrison to the door, Harrison stabbed Greek. John Crafton made for Harrison and Harrison cut him on the arm. Greek staggered out the front door and was assisted by Dr. Million.

Cross-examination by Mr. Lincoln; he heard John Crafton say Greek was not armed and that Harrison would "pay for this." When John Crafton came after Harrison, he said, "Have I no friends here?"

Mr. Palmer called Silas and Peter Livingood, both residents of Pleasant Plains who were witnesses at the scene, to describe Greek's condition after the stabbing. There was no cross-examination by the defense of these witnesses.

Adjourned until one o'clock.

Court met pursuant to adjournment.   One o'clock, P.M.

Jonathan Moses Crafton; CALLED, SWORN AND EXAMINED by Mr. Palmer lives north of Pleasant Plains; father to Greek and three other sons; came to Illinois from Georgia; blacksmith and farmer; knew of Harrison for many years. In the spring, Harrison began offending Greek by telling Greek's brother Peter to keep quiet about who Peachy was courting and then insulting Greek and his mother. Before the Clary's Grove picnic, Harrison insulted Greek and said he would kill him. On sixteen July he went to Hart's General Store with his son. Before he entered the General Store, he heard a "ruckus" inside. He saw Greek and Harrison "locked up." He then saw Hart grab Greek from behind. When he tried to get between Greek and Harrison, his arm was cut by Harrison with a knife and then Harrison stabbed Greek. There was a lot of blood and they took Greek to Dr. Million's office. Dr. Million stopped the bleeding and they took Greek home. Greek was not armed and Greek did not threaten to kill or injure Harrison.

Cross-examination by Mr. Logan; never saw Greek jump Harrison or hear Harrison say he didn't want to fight. He vigorously denied that he encouraged his son to "whip" Harrison.

The prosecution rested its case. It now being half past three o'clock, court was adjourned, after charging the jury and placing them in the care of the officers at the American House until nine o'clock tomorrow morning.

CHAPTER 5

Lincoln was the first lawyer to arrive at the courthouse Saturday morning. He hadn't slept very well the night before. The People had rested their case, and now it was up to the defense to call witnesses if prudent to do so. More than any decisions he had to make in a criminal trial, the calling of witnesses was the most agonizing. It was his opinion that jurors were more tolerant of witnesses called by the prosecution, because most jurors in criminal cases believed the defendant was guilty or he wouldn't be standing in the prisoner's dock. Defense witnesses, on the other hand, were more likely to be labeled liars if their testimony was called into question.

In criminal cases, due to the presumption of innocence, the defendant was not obliged to call any witnesses, and Lincoln's strategy in many cases was not to do so. He felt this strategy forced jurors to decide the case solely on the basis of the People's evidence—including who to believe.

Thinking back, Lincoln recalled several criminal cases he tried where he had made a mistake calling witnesses. He had to chuckle when he thought of the time he called a witness to the stand who, unbeknownst to him, had been drinking. The witness' sometimes erratic testimony spanned the dinner recess and when the witness failed to return to the stand, the bailiff found him sound asleep in the judge's chambers. Needless to say, the judge was not amused and ordered the bailiff to dunk the witness's head in a horse trough until he was sober enough to finish his time on the stand.

Lincoln's law career had spanned 23 years—nearly half his life. It was as much a part of him as taking a breath. It gave him access and exposure. It took him across the continent—to places he never would have seen. It allowed him to see how others practiced their profession so he could improve his. Most importantly, however, it allowed him to make a comfortable living on his terms. But the law was often a jealous mistress. On those occasions, it conflicted with his family life and his other love—politics. To be successful, he had to make troublesome sacrifices. His work required that he sometimes be away from home for weeks, sometimes months, at a time, handling, for the most part, unengaging cases of no import other than to the parties involved.

As a general practitioner, he took most anything that walked in the door, even if it only paid the most modest of fees. Until he made his reputation, he could not afford to be choosy. In this way, he built a trim, solid law practice. He discarded procrastination for diligence and preparation. He faced the "drudgery of the law," as he called it, head-on. But, he loved criminal trials because they generated high drama and got his juices flowing. A defendant's freedom was generally at the heart of the battle. Money and property could be replaced, but a man's freedom—perhaps even his life—was a commodity more precious than any material possession.

Predictably, murder cases tested him the most. He learned early that a trial lawyer, to be effective, must resist the temptation to become too attached emotionally to the client or his cause.

Otherwise, he couldn't think clearly or make sound judgments for the client's good. But how do you separate your feelings for a man or woman who may have taken the life of another and must be judged for it? You would be more than a common mortal, he felt, if you could take the same interest in an accused murderer's case whether the individual be decent or a scoundrel. If you are fond of him, you will naturally be more passionate about his case. And when you believe in him, the jury believes in you. For it is not always a choice between good and evil, right or wrong, or guilty as charged or not. The truth many times lies somewhere in the middle—to be sorted out by 12 men who are more learned in life than learned in the law.

Outright acquittals in murder cases weren't the norm, and when they happened, they were savored like a fine Plantation cigar. Surprisingly, victory for Lincoln was, on many occasions, measured by a conviction of a lesser crime and penitentiary confinement at hard labor for a shorter term of years. Of course, the prison sentences were difficult for the clients to handle, especially when they had grown to feel justified in their actions. And a criminal trial lawyer—if he cared at all—had to live with the thought of what he could have done differently to change the result. It was enough to drive many lawyers to the bottle.

Lincoln had participated in the trials of nearly 20 murder cases in his career, and he could remember all of them. His first case involved what the *Jacksonville Standard* called a "deplorable catastrophe." Two years after receiving his license to practice law, Lincoln was hired, along with his friend Stephen Logan, to represent Henry Truett.

Truett had shot and killed a popular physician, Jacob Early, over a political matter. Lincoln had represented Truett in the past and had served in the Black Hawk War under the command of Early. Honestly, of the two, Lincoln was more fond of Early. But this was an opportunity he couldn't pass by. To be counted among the lawyers already on the case would do nothing but give credibility to his fledgling law practice. Besides, Truett said he killed Early in self-defense. That made Lincoln feel better about defending the man who had killed his friend. He also had to learn that it wasn't personal. He didn't have to judge Truett. The jury would do that after the prosecution presented its evidence and Truett had his day in court to test it.

Truett's Springfield trial took five days. Two and a half of those days were devoted to picking the jury. Before a jury of 12 was seated, more than 300 men had been examined and excused for cause. This was due, in large part, to the politically charged nature of the proceedings and the familiarity of the talesmen with the defendant and the deceased.

The evidence presented showed that Truett had been in the habit of carrying pistols and was generally considered a coward. He had been appointed to the office of Registrar of the Land Office at Galena, in Jo Daviess County, a short time before the Peoria Democratic Convention in November 1837. Early was a member of the convention and served on a committee that reported a resolution disapproving of Truett's appointment and recommending his immediate removal.

About four months later, Truett came to Springfield on business and stayed at the same hotel that Early regularly patronized. Two evenings prior to the fatal encounter, the hotel proprietor discovered a pistol in the pocket of Truett's overcoat, which had been carelessly left about the hotel and used by the proprietor's son to sleep upon. On the evening of the shooting, the overcoat still had the pistol in the pocket and was hanging up in the passage adjoining the sitting room.

After supper, Early, Truett and a number of gentlemen were in the sitting room. A brief while later, all of the gentlemen left except for Truett, Early and two others. Truett presented a paper to one of the men about some private business and both left the room to discuss it. The gentleman left the hotel after the meeting and Truett returned, passing Early in the passage where the overcoat was hanging. Early returned to the sitting room, which was now occupied by the last man and Truett.

Truett confronted Early, demanding to know whether he was the author of the Peoria resolution. A heated discussion followed in which Truett called Early a damned scoundrel, rascal, hypocrite and coward. Truett brandished his pistol, according to Early's dying declarations, producing such apprehension in Early that he took a chair in his hands and raised it bottom-up in front of himself while holding out his arms in a nearly horizontal position. Truett and Early circled the room and Truett fired, dropped his pistol to the floor and ran out of the hotel. The only witness was solid on the fact that Truett brought the pistol cocked into the room, adding that he didn't hear the familiar click or see the motion of Truett's hand.

As for Early, he was stockier and taller than Truett, and it was the opinion of one of the surgeons that from the range of the missile through the body, Early must have held the chair in a striking position when he was shot. On the other hand, Early's dying declarations were that he raised the chair to keep from being shot and did not wish or intend to do any more than stop Truett from killing him.

The testimony took less than a day. The lawyers' closing arguments took two days. The prosecution argued that the killing itself implied malice. The fact of Truett getting the pistol that night after seeing Early, the expression on Truett's face before speaking to Early, the determined manner in which Truett spoke to Early, the repeated insults and provocation by a cowardly man to someone superior in size, strength and courage all went to prove that

Truett wanted to take revenge and that he had the advantage on Early by having a cocked pistol loaded for murder.

The prosecutors argued further that Early had a right to take a chair, or anything else for that matter, to protect himself from a man standing before him with a pistol, insulting and provoking him. Finally, the prosecution argued that Truett instigated the quarrel for the purpose of creating an opportunity to kill Early, and when Early lifted the chair, Truett shot him after a pretext of retreat.

The defense, on the other hand, argued that Early had a deadly weapon, to wit, a chair, within striking distance of Truett. It was the defense's position that Early could have immediately crushed Truett with the chair and that he intended to do so, or Truett believed he intended to do so. Further, the defense urged that Truett was justified in confronting Early about the authorship of the Peoria resolution and that the frailties and passions of human nature called for leniency since Truett had suffered in prison seven months awaiting trial.

Lincoln got his first taste of waiting for a jury in a high-drama case the evening after the arguments concluded. He and his fellow lawyers waited three hours before the jury returned a verdict of not guilty. It was a glorious and, to be honest, surprising victory, and word of the verdict spread like a prairie fire. He made a common mistake, however. The not guilty verdict, in what some people felt was a hopeless case before a community fond of the deceased, caused him to become overconfident in his ability to persuade a jury in self-defense cases to side with his client.

A little over a year later, he defended a boatsman named William Fraim. Fraim was working on the steamboat *Hero* docked at Frederick along the Illinois River in Schuyler County. Fraim was in a tavern with a German colleague named Neithamer when Neithamer began smoking a "segar"—as the local newspaper

described it. Fraim, who was drunk, told Neithamer not to smoke
in his face when the latter replied, "I thought the country was free
and I will smoke where I please." According to witnesses, Fraim
then lifted his hand to knock the cigar from Neithamer's mouth
when the latter raised his hand for protection. In response, Fraim,
unobserved, drew a long butcher knife from his side and drove it
to the handle in Neithamer's chest. It killed Neithamer instantly.

At trial, he argued that Fraim did not kill Neithamer out of a
malicious intent, but rather his intoxicated state negated any intent
other than acting out of a sense of self-defense. He also urged that
Fraim, at best, could only be guilty of the crime of manslaughter.
He felt good about the case when the jury retired to deliberate.
The jury took less than an hour to convict Fraim of murder, and
the judge promptly sentenced him to hang. One month later,
Fraim was hanged on a gallows one mile outside of Carthage,
Illinois.

It was the only client Lincoln ever lost to the hangman, and the
case never left his mind. After that, there was no such thing as
confidence in a jury verdict. From that point forward, he tried
every murder case as if a life hung in the balance. Because for his
client, it might very well be true.

Seventeen years would pass before his next highly public
murder trial. Sprinkled in between were more than 15 homicide
trials involving the full spectrum of clients. He defended Davy
Crockett's nephew on a charge of murder and convinced a jury
that his crime was manslaughter instead. He defended a woman,
Melissa Goings, for hitting her husband over the head with a
stick of firewood. He secured her release pending trial and she
fled, never to be heard from again. It was rumored, mainly in
jest, that he encouraged her to leave. For those who believed
such a thing, all he could think of, if anyone approached him on
the subject, was that Mrs. Goings wanted to know where she

could get a good drink of water and he told her they had mighty good water in Tennessee.

Then, in 1854, George Anderson, a well-known and highly respected citizen of Springfield, was found dead in his backyard. Anderson was a dedicated Mason and according to the newspapers "was not known to have an enemy in the world—on the contrary, he numbered as many friends as any man among us." When Anderson's body was examined, it was determined that the back part of his skull had been fractured with a blunt instrument. Later, evidence developed that Anderson might have also been poisoned with strychnine. When this fact came to light, Anderson's wife, Jane, and his nephew, Theodore, were indicted for his murder.

He and Logan represented Theodore, while four well-known lawyers represented the widow amid rumors and innuendo that Theodore and Jane were romantically involved—giving rise to the prosecution's only plausible motive. After several days of trial, the jurors were unimpressed with the People's case and found the defendants not guilty. His client always steadfastly maintained his innocence, but Lincoln was never quite sure what really happened.

Four years later, in 1858, he handled a murder case that people were still talking about. An old friend from Salem, Hannah Armstrong, asked him to represent her son, William "Duff" Armstrong. Armstrong and his friend James Norris were indicted for the murder of Preston Metzger during a fight that occurred on the outskirts of a religious camp meeting in Mason County. The local newspaper described Armstrong and Norris as "two bullies," and the allegations were that Metzger died from either a blow to the eye or a blow to the head.

The two defendants were tried separately, with Norris being tried first. The prosecution's main witness testified that from a distance of 150 feet under a bright moon, he had seen Armstrong strike Metzger with a slingshot. Norris was convicted of manslaughter and sentenced to eight years hard labor. Believing that Armstrong could not get a fair trial in Mason County after Norris' conviction, Lincoln petitioned the court for a change of venue to Cass County.

The court granted the motion, and Armstrong was tried before a Cass County jury. After establishing that the prosecution's main witness was sure that he saw Armstrong strike Metzger from the light of a bright moon "that was about the same place that the sun would be at ten o'clock in the morning," Lincoln produced an almanac for the date in question that showed that the moon had already set.

During the defense case, he presented two witnesses. The first witness testified that the alleged murder weapon was his and that he threw it away near the murder site on the day after the fight. The second witness, a physician, testified that the fatal head injury could have occurred when Metzger fell off his horse after the fight.

In his closing argument, Lincoln tried to strike a sympathetic note in an effort to supplement his evidence by telling the jury that he himself was once "a poor, friendless boy," and Armstrong's father took him into the family's house, fed and clothed him, and gave him a home. The jury promptly found Armstrong not guilty.

To this day, he mused, people believed that the jury acquitted Armstrong because of the almanac. He would always believe, however, that it was because of the testimony of his two witnesses and his closing argument. Folklore is a funny thing. It had been less than a year, but the events of that trial had taken on a life of their own. Now his career as a trial lawyer might well be defined by a murder case...for which he received no pay...that was the product of a drunken brawl at a religious meeting.

Lincoln had not always been as faithful to the practice of law as it had been to him. After he was admitted to the Illinois Bar, he was offered a position in Chicago with a well-established lawyer. It was the kind of offer that young lawyers dream of, but he turned it down to practice law in Springfield. He was a country man with country ways, and life in Springfield was more to his liking. But in those early years, his passion for politics many times exceeded his passion for the law. For 14 years he did both, but his successes in the courtroom far surpassed his successes on the stump.

When he finally decided to practice law in earnest, his partner and those close to him saw a change. He studied the law in much more depth. He believed the judges would put more trust in him if he did, and he was right.

Also, the necessity of earning a good livelihood had become essential. His financial obligations were, in fact, considerable. An old debt from a failed business venture still haunted him. He had unsuccessfully tried his hand at retail merchandising in the village of New Salem. He had sold everything from coffeepots to whiskey, but his business acumen proved lacking, so he thought he would try the practice of law.

He had a growing family. His father and stepmother, who were still living in Coles County where they had moved 18 years earlier, were financially dependent upon him. And, he was equally financially generous to his other relatives.

But his law practice quickly became "itinerant." Illinois was divided into several judicial circuits. Each circuit had at least one judge, and a select number of the best-known lawyers of the district traveled the Eighth Judicial Circuit—15 counties spread across 2,200 square miles. There were no railroads in the Eighth Judicial Circuit, so the lawyers traveled by horseback, wagons or carriages. He had no horse in the early days of his law practice and routinely borrowed one or chipped in with a half dozen or more lawyers to hire a three-seated spring wagon.

While most of the lawyers and judges found circuit riding irritating and most uncomfortable, he was amused and entertained by it. He used many of the things he saw in his stories, jokes and anecdotes and was regaled by the ramblers and settlers he met along the dusty roads. The unexpected, even if trivial, adventures and long days he experienced on the road gave him much gratification. He liked the log farmhouses, weather-beaten barns, bumpy dirt roads and lived-on back porches. He liked the farmers, laborers and nomads, and he found humor and human interest in all of them. The dirty-faced little girl with curly hair covering her eyes. The schoolboy with his front teeth missing. The small children watching with rapt amazement as birds took wing from the trees. The mother carrying her baby on her hip while hanging clothes with her free hand…or the workhorses toiling in a field as a mother sow led her squealing piglets across the road. These common sights furnished the foundation for some of his best stories. They also brought simplicity to his life. He liked that. It made him laugh and he needed that for his peace of mind.

On the circuit, the judge and lawyers usually settled in the town tavern of the county seat. For the most part, these establishments were big two-story houses with large rooms and long verandas. Nothing was exclusive about them, however. Ordinarily, the men—judge and lawyers alike—slept two to a bed with three to four beds in a room. The men ended up eating at the same table with jurors, witnesses, defendants out on bail, traveling salesmen, teamsters and ordinary laborers. The only hint of exclusiveness was the landlord's practice of seating the judge and lawyers at the head of the dining table. Most of the bar accepted this arrangement without question, but Lincoln took no interest in it.

He entered a room, on one occasion, and sat down at the foot of the table with the common folks. The landlord saw this and shouted, "Mr. Lincoln, come up here. You are in the wrong place."

To which he replied, "Have you anything better to eat up there, Joe? If not, I'll stay put."

Not surprisingly, the accommodations of the taverns were often subpar, the food was poorly cooked and the beds were insufferably hard. However, Lincoln never complained, while his colleagues grumbled incessantly. He studiously avoided criticism of what he believed were trivial matters that might hurt the feelings of others, and besides, he had things to think about other than his physical comfort. He really had little notion or desire for the "refinements of life" and almost no perception of luxury and ease.

When those sharing a room with him would be sound asleep, he would routinely rise earlier than his brothers at the bar to study. But he wouldn't just study law. At one point, he began a serious course of general education—mathematics, poetry and astronomy—and he even joined a German study club. His dedication to study at this point in his life was due to his desire to raise himself to a cultural level with the men he had met in the eastern part of the country while politicking. He often remarked that he spent his leisure time in study to make up for the "chance at an education" he didn't have when he was young. He came from a farming family, and studying was considered, even by his father, as a waste of time and an excuse for being lazy.

The circuit-riding lawyers also shared a uniform affection for him. He didn't believe himself to be superior to anyone. He treated everyone with genuine kindness. He was gentle with the young lawyers and became the much-loved senior member of the bar. For him, it was a good time—a time when lawyers did their fighting in the courtroom.

He also knew right and justice and knew how to make them applicable to the affairs of everyday life. That was an element of his character that gave him the ability to persuade a jury. He never used a word that the dullest juror could not understand. And his remarkable talent for examining witnesses did not go unnoticed. However, he was not an orator in the courtroom. He talked to the jurors in plain, sensible and candid language—almost as if in a fireside chat. The law defined him and he embraced that.

CHAPTER 6

The first time he met Peachy, Lincoln decided not to call him as a witness. Peachy became uncertain under pressure, and Palmer, a skilled cross-examiner, would rattle the young man. Moreover, Ben Hart would tell Peachy's story, and all Peachy could do by testifying was give the prosecution another issue to talk about—his truthfulness.

The decision not to call Peachy, however, was forcing Lincoln to call other witnesses to fill in important gaps that existed in his defense. Lincoln also needed to call the Rev. Peter Cartwright. After Peachy was arrested, the preacher came to see Lincoln and related a conversation he insisted he had with Greek the day Greek died. Rev. Cartwright told him he met with Greek alone after he went unannounced to the Crafton home. Ordinarily, the statements Greek made would be inadmissible as hearsay, but Cullom had researched the issue and told Lincoln he felt the law permitted the evidence to be used as a dying declaration.

Lincoln was confident in Cullom's research, but that wasn't the problem. The question was, would the jury believe the reverend? While Rev. Cartwright was a highly respected man who had an exemplary reputation as an honorable person, would the jury think a self-proclaimed, anti-death penalty minister was lying to save a good young man from the hangman?

And, there was another—more personal—reason to question the reverend's veracity. Was the preacher trying to help Greek make peace with God when he went to the Crafton home, or was he positioning himself to become a defense witness in the event of Greek's death? On Saturday morning, Lincoln was still struggling with what to do. His decision would have to be made quickly, however. It was half past eight, and spectators were beginning to drift into the courtroom.

"All rise!" announced the court crier, and everyone rose as one. "You may sit down," Judge Rice said as he took his seat on the dais. "Good morning. Will the defendant be calling any witnesses?"

"Yes, your Honor, we will," said Lincoln.

Lincoln had decided to call a few select witnesses and rest. If he could have the witnesses testify without their credibility being significantly undermined, he felt his client would be positioned as well as possible for an acquittal. But as he'd told Virginia, nothing was certain in the world of criminal jury trials.

"Mr. Lincoln, you may call your first witness."

"We call Abajiah Nottingham," said Logan, taking his place at the podium.

"Mr. Nottingham," said the judge, "please step forward and take the oath."

> *Court Reporter:* Please place your right hand on the Bible. Do you swear to tell the truth, the whole truth, and nothing but the truth, so help you God?

Abajiah Nottingham looked like his name suggested. A long brown beard filled his fair-skinned face. He lumbered to the witness chair and placed his thick hands on his knees as he took his seat.

Logan: Mr. Nottingham, where do you reside?

Nottingham: About two and a half miles northwest of Pleasant Plains.

Logan: Please speak up, sir.

Nottingham: Sorry…outside Pleasant Plains near Tallula.

Logan: Keeping some store there?

Nottingham: Yes, a grocery store.

Logan: Is the post office also kept at your house?

Nottingham: Yes, sir.

Logan: You were, I suppose, acquainted with Greek Crafton in his lifetime?

Nottingham: Slightly.

Logan: Also with Peachy Harrison?

Nottingham: More so.

Logan: Did you see the whole or any part of the scrape between Peachy Harrison and Greek Crafton on the sixteenth of July?

Nottingham: I saw some of it. I didn't see the commencement of it.

Logan: Before that day, did you hear Greek Crafton make any threats against Peachy Harrison?

Palmer: To which we object, your Honor. Testimony as to any threats by Crafton is not admissible unless evidence is shown…in connection with it…that it was brought to the knowledge of the defendant prior to the affray.

Logan: Your Honor, this goes to the heart of our case. The evidence is competent to prove Crafton's intention to inflict serious harm on our client.

Judge Rice: I believe it would be prudent for us to excuse the jury while we discuss the merits of the objection and the legal authorities on the subject. Sheriff, please escort the jury from the courtroom.

After the jury was removed from the jury box and courtroom, Judge Rice turned his attention to the objection.

Judge Rice: Mr. Logan, the prosecution believes you must establish a proper foundation for the evidence by showing the defendant knew of the threats, before the sixteenth of July, for the evidence to be admissible. My understanding of the law is that evidence of threats by the deceased, standing alone, are inadmissible…that knowledge of these threats must be proved to have been had by the prisoner before the fight. Hence, I am inclined to sustain the objection.

Logan: Sustained? But, your Honor, I believe we can lay the proper foundation and prove such knowledge.

Judge Rice: If that be the case, then I will permit the testi-

Stephen Logan argues to the court

mony. However, if you fail to establish the prisoner's knowledge, I will strike the testimony from the record and instruct the jury to disregard it. You may proceed to establish your foundation after the sheriff returns the jury to the box. We will be in recess for fifteen minutes.

Logan, relieved by the ruling, conferred with Lincoln and the confused witness to make sure everyone understood the court's ruling. When the court reconvened, Logan gripped the podium and resumed his questioning.

Logan: Mr. Nottingham, do you remember my last question?

Nottingham: Not exactly.

Logan: Before the sixteenth of July, did you hear Greek Crafton make any threats against our client?

Nottingham: Twice.

Logan: Did you tell Peachy about them before the sixteenth?

Nottingham: At the church supper.

Logan: What about the church supper?

Nottingham: Well, me and Peachy went to a church supper on the Wednesday before Saturday.

Logan: Saturday the sixteenth?

Nottingham: Yes.

Logan: Tell the jury what you heard Greek Crafton say and when and where he said it.

Palmer: Objection, Judge.

Judge Rice: Overruled. You may answer, Mr. Nottingham.

Nottingham: I can't just exactly state the day. I believe my mind is frustrated at present, but it was prior to the sixteenth. Greek remarked that he was going to whip or thrash Peachy on sight. That was at my store. That was all I believe I recollect hearing at that time.

Logan: You said there were two threats.

Nottingham: The second threat, I think, I heard on Thursday before the stabbing…at the Indian Creek picnic. I heard him say he was going to knock Peachy down and stomp him. He said he heard Peachy was carrying a pistol and a knife, a bowie knife, and he said there was about that much difference between them.

Logan: Was Greek a larger and stronger man than Peachy?

Nottingham: I think he was for sure a larger man.

Logan: Do you recollect anything else?

Nottingham: No, sir.

Logan: Pass the witness, your Honor.

Judge Rice: Any cross-examination, Mr. Palmer?

Palmer moved quickly to the podium.

Palmer: Yes, sir. Mr. Nottingham, did Greek give any reason for intending to assault Harrison?

Nottingham: Greek said he had just provocation for whipping him. That he never would suffer such impeachment as had been thrown out on him and his family—or relations and family, I think. That, I believe, is the sum and substance.

Palmer: Did Greek speak of a young lady named Rebecca?

Nottingham: No, not to my recollect.

Two more defense witnesses, John Allen and Thomas Turley, were called to testify about what they had seen in the general store, but neither had much more to offer than the prosecution's witnesses on the subject.

"Call your next witness, Mr. Lincoln," said the judge, who was getting antsy again.

"The defense calls Rev. Peter Cartwright to the stand, your Honor."

The reverend was a stout, distinguished-looking man with long, pure-white hair that was neatly brushed. He walked to the witness chair with a slight limp. There wasn't a person in Sangamon County, or Illinois for that matter, who didn't know or hadn't heard of Cartwright. Lincoln, nevertheless, took the time to detail the preacher's work.

Cartwright carefully recounted how his life had been spent in an unfailing fight against evil and his efforts to spread the Word and convert the non-believers. He told the jury he was born in Amherst County, Virginia, on the first day of September 1785 and was the presiding minister of the First Methodist Church in Pleasant Plains. He proudly related to the jury how he became a preacher when he was 16 years old and had just celebrated his 74th birthday.

Cartwright was a true "fire and brimstone" preacher who detailed his extensive travels doing the Lord's work. He explained how he had received 7,000 members into the Methodist Church, personally baptized 9,000 people, conducted over 400 funerals and preached more than 1,100 sermons. After a few more minutes getting the witness comfortable with the courtroom and eliciting the fact that Cartwright had waged an unsuccessful campaign against him for Congress, Lincoln focused his questions on the day of Greek's death.

> *Lincoln:* Reverend, how long have you labored in your calling?

> *Rev. Cartwright:* Close to fifty-eight years, sir.

> *Lincoln:* During that time, I believe, you have earned a nickname?

> *Rev. Cartwright:* Yes, some people call me "God's Plowman."

> *Lincoln:* Fitting. How long have you known the prisoner?

Cartwright's head dropped for a moment. Then, righting himself and passing his hand across his brow, he answered fondly, "I have known him since he was a babe. He has laughed and cried on my knee."

> *Lincoln:* Now, let's turn to the facts of this case. Did you

have the occasion to go to the Crafton farm place on eighteen July?

Rev. Cartwright: Yes, sir, I did.

Lincoln: While there, did you meet with Greek Crafton?

Rev. Cartwright: Yes, Mr. Lincoln.

Lincoln: Please tell the gentlemen of the jury what you saw and heard. Reflect and take it deliberately. Tell it all.

Palmer leaped to his feet. "Objection, your Honor. Mr. Lincoln is asking for hearsay."

"Judge," Lincoln snapped in response, "this is offered as Greek Crafton's dying declaration."

Judge Rice could tell this was critical testimony for the defense, but the People were also entitled to a fair trial. The judge hesitated for a few seconds. "I'm going to recess court until two o'clock. The jury can take its luncheon, but don't discuss the case. I would like the lawyers to remain while the jury leaves the courtroom."

The sheriff escorted the jury out of the courtroom and quickly returned to see what the judge was going to do.

"Mr. Lincoln," said the judge, "I'm not sure Rev. Cartwright's testimony is admissible. Nevertheless, I want to hear what he is going to say before I issue my ruling."

"I have never heard of such law," Lincoln shot back in a fiery outburst. Logan also rose to add his opinions on the subject.

The judge, however, was determined to have his way, so the defense complied with his wishes and asked Cartwright to testify out of the presence of the jury. Cartwright answered Lincoln's questions in precise detail. Then, the judge invited the two adversaries to submit their arguments orally.

Palmer attacked the preacher's testimony as unfair and inadmissible hearsay. "Your Honor, in most cases, dying declarations made by the deceased are incriminating in nature and are therefore offered into evidence by the prosecution. In this case, ironically, the defense is offering Greek Crafton's alleged dying declarations as exculpatory evidence to prove the defendant's innocence. But the same rules for admissibility apply. Since our nation was founded, the primary rule for admission of a dying declaration is that the deceased, and I quote from *The King v. Slade*, 'apprehended that he was in such a state of mortality as would inevitably oblige him soon to answer before his Maker for the truth or falsehood of his assertions'."

From memory, Palmer also cited a Georgia Supreme Court case as precedent. He had used this authority in another murder trial in Morton, Illinois, in which the defense attempted to avoid the dying declaration rule by presenting a hearsay objection. The presiding judge ruled in his favor and the citation had not left his mind. Palmer continued, "I would like to invite the court's attention to the case of *Ransom v. State of Georgia*. In *Ransom*, may it please the court, the defendant was charged with murdering his wife by beating her to death. Mrs. Ransom was found lying in a ditch with wounds about her head, face and neck and was exhausted by the loss of blood such that she was taken for dead.

"She was carried to a boardinghouse and, by medical assistance, restored to life. Over the next several hours, she recovered her senses to such a degree as to be able to give a rational account of the circumstances of her serious injuries. Mrs. Ransom's account implicated her husband as the villain, but she died a short time later. The Georgia Supreme Court found it was error to admit Mrs. Ransom's declaration because it was impossible to determine whether she apprehended her approaching dissolution. The defendant was accordingly awarded a new trial."

"Has the *Ransom* case been cited with approval by our Supreme Court?" asked Judge Rice.

"No, sir, but it's a very persuasive authority nonetheless," Palmer answered confidently.

"Point well made, Mr. Palmer," said Judge Rice.

"In summary, your Honor," Palmer said as he concluded his argument, "the testimony of Rev. Cartwright is hearsay and therefore inadmissible. Dr. Million did not testify that he told Greek his wounds were fatal. Furthermore, Greek Crafton had not given up all hope of living. Finally, Rev. Cartwright's introductory remarks about his own physical condition at the time are irrelevant. Thank you for the opportunity to address the court on this most important subject."

"Thank you, Mr. Palmer. Mr. Lincoln, what do you have to offer?"

Palmer sat down as Lincoln gathered his papers. The defense had anticipated Palmer's objection, so Lincoln was prepared to counter it. "As the court is aware, dying declarations constitute an exception to the rule rejecting hearsay evidence. And, dying declarations constitute direct evidence of the facts they are relevant to prove as distinguished from circumstantial evidence of such facts.

"Of course, the foundation that the defense must establish in this case for the admission of a dying declaration is Greek's belief that he was near death and that—in a very short time—those immortal and spiritual elements which inhabited his body would forsake it, to encounter the dread possibilities of the unknown and supernatural world beyond the grave. A dying declaration is therefore deemed to furnish a sanction equivalent to that of a solemn and positive oath administered in a court of justice."

After this lofty and passionate introduction—which was probably more suited for the audience and courtroom crowd than the judge—Lincoln got down to business. First, he summarized the history of the dying declaration exception to the hearsay rule as taken from *Blackstone's Commentaries*. Then, Lincoln cited legal precedent of his own.

"With all due respect to my learned adversary, Mr. Palmer, his precedent misses the mark. The Delaware case of *State v. Pennewill* is far more on point. In *Pennewill*, the facts revealed that the defendant was accused of murdering the deceased with a ball shot from a pistol. The deceased had apparently gone to his neighbor's after a disagreement over a rail-splitting job. The prosecution's theory, based on a dying declaration, was that when the deceased entered the door of the defendant's house, the defendant presented a pistol. As the deceased turned and ran about fifteen steps, the defendant shot him in the back. The deceased lived four days before succumbing to his wound. Before he died, however, the deceased incriminated the defendant.

"The Supreme Court of Delaware held that 'when dissolution is approaching…and the shadows of the grave are gathering in around the dying man…and his mind is impressed with the full sense of his condition, the solemnity of the scene gives to his statements a sanctity of truth more impressive and potential than the formalities of an oath and such declarations ought to be received and considered by the jury as to their effect and weight.' Of significance to this case, your Honor, is the fact that *Pennewill* turned on the overall condition of the decedent and the entirety of his statements. Greek Crafton had been mortally wounded for two days and must have known he was going to die."

Lincoln paused to let the statement sink in. "He wanted to ask for mercy and tell the truth. Since he is no longer with us, he now speaks the truth through the mouth of Rev. Cartwright, and the jury should be allowed to consider the evidence. Thank you, your

Honor."

"Thank you, Mr. Lincoln. By the way," said Judge Rice, unaffected by emotion, "has the Illinois Supreme Court approved the holding in *Pennewill*?"

"No, your Honor," said Lincoln, "but if given half the chance, I'm sure our justices would praise the wise and sound reasoning of the Delaware Supreme Court." Another spirited chorus of laughter came forth from the spectators. Palmer even managed a grin.

The judge told the packed courtroom he would make his ruling without unnecessary delay. Court was recessed while the judge retired to his chambers. The lawyers were giving the judge a real mental workout, but the dedicated jurist embraced that part of his calling.

⟡

The Harrison family had not considered that Rev. Cartwright might be barred from telling his story. The Craftons, on the other hand, were offended at the thought that Cartwright might be permitted to testify to a private meeting between their son and his minister.

Virginia timidly approached Lincoln again. She had refrained from doing so after the first day of trial out of respect for Lincoln and her expressed confidence in him. But, she couldn't help herself. "What's happening, Mr. Lincoln?" asked Virginia.

"It's just a legal matter, Virginia. It'll be all right," said Lincoln, trying to conceal his concerns. Lincoln was not sure what the judge would do, but he didn't want to upset the family unnecessarily. If the judge ruled against them, he would explain it then and tell the family he could preserve the matter for appeal if Peachy was convicted.

Virginia continued, "But it seems to me the judge should let the jury decide what to believe about Rev. Cartwright's testimony."

"Well, it's kind of complicated..." Lincoln began to say before he was interrupted by Palmer's assistant, Joseph Jamison, who was eavesdropping on the conversation.

"What would a little country girl like you know about the rules of evidence and the courtroom?" Jamison asked.

"She has a lot of common sense," Lincoln said, defending Virginia.

"She's a girl, not a lawyer. I think our colleagues in the bar would be interested to know that the great Abraham Lincoln is taking his counsel from a thirteen-year-old girl," said Jamison as he turned and walked away.

"I'm sorry, Virginia. He's a hard man to like. I think your point is well taken," said Lincoln, trying to encourage the young girl.

"It's OK. I really don't know anything about the law," said Virginia as she returned to her family.

After 30 long minutes, Judge Rice returned to the bench. Virginia thought he looked more serious than usual, and it scared her. She looked at Lincoln, who had his eyes fixed on the judge. "According to the Illinois Supreme Court in *Starkey v. the People*, in order for Rev. Cartwright's testimony to be admissible, the defense must show that Greek Crafton was *in extremis* at the time of his declaration," the judge began. "That is, there must be a demonstration that Mr. Crafton was at the point of death and in the absence of all hope of living. Also, according to *Starkey*, the court should consider all facts and circumstances—not just the declarations alone—to determine admissibility. After hearing the facts and the arguments of counsel, I'm overruling the objection. Rev. Cartwright will be permitted to testify and the jury can sort out what to believe."

Virginia breathed a sigh of relief and eyed Jamison. Jamison didn't look back. Lincoln grinned, and Palmer leaned back in his chair as if to cushion the blow. Without being told to do so, the sheriff proceeded to seat the jury, and Cartwright left the family for the witness chair. The audience knew the ruling was an important one, but only time would tell how important. Cartwright's testimony continued with Lincoln facing the jury.

Lincoln: Rev. Cartwright, do you remember my last question before the jury was excused?

Rev. Cartwright: Not really. You lawyers have got me so tangled that I don't know which end of me is up. I will try to be as collected as I can. If I understand myself, I am now to repeat what I have said once?

Lincoln: Yes, if you so recollect it…unless something else occurs to you.

Cartwright turned and studied the jury. In a voice tremulous with age and feeling, he began testifying about the day Greek died.

Rev. Cartwright: Gentlemen of the jury, I understand that this affray took place July sixteen. I was not at home nor present at the time. I knew nothing of the quarrel…pro or con…except by hearsay. I was friendly to all the parties— good friendship and fellowship as far as I knew.

I passed through the town where this affray took place on my return home from some lower counties, obtained my papers and letters from the post office and heard not one word about the affray until I got home. When I entered the room, my wife asked me if I had heard of the dreadful affair. I told her,

"No, not a word." When she repeated it, it shocked me exceedingly.

Lincoln: What happened next?

Rev. Cartwright: A day or two before this, my horse had fallen upon me and crippled me in my right hip. The day was exceedingly hot and I was exceedingly faint. I felt that I needed to comfort the Crafton family, but at first I thought I could not go. I was faint and weary, but I concluded to make the effort and I went in a wagon with my neighbor, James Zanes.

I made my way to the Crafton home and entered the living area. It was considerably crowded and all present were affected. I asked where the wounded young man was and was told by his mother that he was in the back bedroom. She escorted me to her son, who was lying on a little trundle bed that was near the floor.

I—not being able to stoop on account of the injury to my hip—knelt down by his bedside, took him by the hand and expressed my deep regret and sorrow that this fatal calamity had fallen upon him, for I looked upon it as fatal from what I had heard upon entering the home. I looked upon him as in a dying condition and felt accordingly.

Lincoln: Was the family in the room?

Rev. Cartwright: Yes, I then asked John Crafton if I could have some time alone with his son. John stood up and walked out of the room. I looked at Greek and said, "Would you pray with me?" I still had Greek's hand. After the prayer, I again expressed my deep sorrow. Greek said, I think at that moment, "The honest hour has come, and in a few moments, I expect to stand before my final judge. Do you think there will be any mercy for me?"

I then repeated my regret and sorrow at the circumstances, the fatal stab that I supposed he had received. I expressed my deep and heartfelt regret that this calamity had fallen upon him. He paused a moment, and made this reply, I think literally, "Yes," he said. "I have brought it upon myself, and I forgive Peachy."

Lincoln: What was his state of mind?

Rev. Cartwright: He then seemed as calm and composed as any man could have been in his situation, and I really wondered that he could command himself as he did. He requested religious services, and we went through them as best we could over a dying man. I have visited hundreds of dying pillows and I thought I never saw a man in a dying condition more calm and composed...more perfectly at himself. His mind seemed to be entirely fixed on his final destiny and not on the sympathetic wailing of his friends around him.

Lincoln: Then, what did you do?

Rev. Cartwright: I arose—being in extreme pain from my crippled hip—and it being extremely warm and stepped back two or three feet, not very distant. As I went into the living area, there were two doors to the room...to the north and south…and on the east and west…windows that were hoisted. I stepped back to get the air. A lady handed me a seat. I sat down to get the benefit of the air, to relieve myself, then I heard that Greek had called for me again.

When I went into his room, he said to me, "I have brought it upon myself. I forgive Peachy, and I want it said to all my friends that I have no enmity in my heart against any man. And if I die, I want it declared to all that I die in peace with God and all mankind."

Lincoln: With that, did you leave the Crafton home?

Rev. Cartwright: No, I went back to the living area and sat there in my pain I cannot tell how long. I think I got through between four and five o'clock. I am not certain as to the time. I lingered there two or three hours. The room being crowded and the doctor not able under the circumstances to keep it clear for a free circulation of the air. I requested the doctor to do so, for that was enough to kill the dying man if nothing else. I then removed outside to the shade, for the sun was getting pretty low, and soon returned home. That is the substance of what I recollect. Now, Judge, if I could be released altogether I would like it, for I have an appointment in Jacksonville tomorrow.

Judge Rice smiled. "Just a minute, Reverend. Mr. Palmer may have a few questions for you."

"Oh, I'm sorry, Judge," said Cartwright, his face flushing.

As Cartwright shared Greek's words, the courtroom was as still as a meadow at sunrise. The testimony impacted the jury. Palmer knew, if he were to call the testimony into question, he would have to cross-examine the reverend respectfully and, most importantly, delicately. Otherwise, the jury could be offended by his perceived attack on a good Christian man. The risk was great, but Palmer recognized he had no choice. Everyone was waiting. After deliberating for a few seconds, Palmer rose and slowly moved to the podium. He crossed his arms as he began to speak.

Palmer: Rev. Cartwright, it's good to see you again.

Rev. Cartwright: Likewise, Mr. Palmer.

Palmer: Let me summarize what you have testified to, if I might. If I understand your testimony, you decided on your own to go to the Crafton home?

Rev. Cartwright: Yes, sir. I thought I could comfort them.

Palmer: Now, before you went, you had heard about the stabbing, had you not?

Rev. Cartwright: Yes, sir...from my wife.

Palmer: You also didn't know the seriousness of Greek's wounds, did you?

Rev. Cartwright: Not really, sir.

Palmer: When you entered the home, you asked to see Greek?

Rev. Cartwright: Yes, I did.

Palmer: Then you told us you asked to meet with Greek alone.

Rev. Cartwright: Yes, Mr. Palmer.

Palmer: So, no one else heard what you have related to us that Greek said to you, correct?

Rev. Cartwright: That's true.

Palmer: Rev. Cartwright, Peachy Harrison is your grandson, is he not?

Rev. Cartwright: Yes, sir, he is.

Palmer: And you care for him very much.

Rev. Cartwright: Of course, sir.

Palmer: Thank you, Reverend. Oh, by the way, you have a dislike for the death penalty, do you not?

Rev. Cartwright: It's an abomination.

Palmer: Thank you for your time, Reverend.

Palmer had done the best he could cross-examining a highly respected man. He didn't know if Cartwright had manufactured Greek's dying declaration or not, but perhaps he had planted a seed of doubt.

Lincoln was impressed. Palmer had handled the cross-examination carefully and effectively. Lincoln's only decision now was whether he should ask Cartwright if he would lie under oath to save his grandson from the gallows. But, he didn't know the answer to the question. From experience, Lincoln knew you never ask a question in trial to which you don't know the answer. It was hard for him to do, but he decided to play it safe.

"I have no further questions for this witness, your Honor," said Lincoln, half rising.

"Call your next witness, Mr. Lincoln," ordered the judge.

"Judge, the defense rests," said Lincoln, looking at the jury.

"Does the prosecution have any rebuttal testimony?" asked the judge, expecting an answer in the negative.

"Yes, your Honor. The People recall Dr. Million," said Palmer, gesturing to the sheriff.

"Dr. Million, if you would please take a seat in the witness chair. Remember, you are still under oath," said Judge Rice politely.

"Yes, sir," said Dr. Million as he walked past the bar to take his seat. Palmer looked at the jury as he grabbed the podium. They were attentive and serious.

Palmer: Please state your name again for the reporter.

Dr. Million: J.L. Million, M.D.

Palmer: Dr. Million, you have previously testified in this case, have you not?

Dr. Million: Yes, in detail about my care and treatment of Greek Crafton.

Palmer: To summarize your testimony, you told us you dressed Greek's wounds at your home immediately after the affray.

Dr. Million: Yes.

Palmer: He had been stabbed with a knife, isn't that correct?

Dr. Million: Yes, twice. One wound was more of a cut. The other was a deep stab wound in his left side between the eleventh and twelfth ribs…short ribs.

Palmer: Did you tell Greek his wounds were fatal?

Dr. Million: No, I didn't.

Palmer: Did you talk to him about who inflicted his wounds?

Dr. Million: Yes, sir, several times. He said it was Peachy Harrison.

Palmer: Did you go to the Crafton home to see Greek after he left your office?

Dr. Million: I did.

Palmer: How long did you stay there?

Dr. Million: Until he passed.

Palmer: Dr. Million, during the time you were with Greek, talking to him, did he absolve Mr. Harrison's actions?

Dr. Million: No. In fact, he censured Mr. Harrison. He said Peachy provoked the incident and had no call to stab him.

Palmer: Thank you, Dr. Million. Pass the witness, your Honor.

Judge Rice: Mr. Lincoln, will there be any cross of Dr. Million?

Lincoln: Yes, your Honor. Mr. Logan will examine the doctor.

Logan took the podium. By this time, the courthouse was densely crowded. The crowd jammed the courtroom with some standing along the back wall, the hallway and the stairway leading to the balcony. The excitement was building for the final arguments and the verdict.

Logan: Dr. Million, you were not with Greek Crafton every minute of his final hours, were you?

Dr. Million: No, sir.

Logan: You were also not with Greek Crafton when he was praying with Rev. Cartwright?

Dr. Million: No, I was not.

Logan: So, you will agree that there were words spoken between Rev. Cartwright and Greek Crafton that you did not hear?

Palmer: Objection, your Honor. Mr. Logan is asking the good doctor to speculate.

Judge Rice: I'll let him answer, if he can.

Dr. Million: I'm sure they spoke, sir. I don't know what they said to each other.

Logan: Thank you, Doctor. No further questions.

Judge Rice shuffled his notes impatiently. The day was rapidly passing by and he was temporarily distracted by thoughts of the crowded docket facing him beginning early Monday morning. He knew the jurors would revolt at the suggestion of holding court after church, and rescheduling his Monday docket call was out of the question. But he had to focus on giving both sides a fair trial in the Harrison case. It was the right thing to do.

"Any further rebuttal, Mr. Palmer?" asked Judge Rice, hoping for a response by the People in the negative.

Palmer turned toward Peachy as he said, "Yes, the People call Miss Rebecca Watson to the stand."

CHAPTER 7

Peachy turned toward the rear of the courtroom as a young woman entered. The witness, Rebecca Watson, had coal-black hair and a flawless, light tawny complexion. A small nose, high cheekbones and blue eyes completed her captivating face. Her hair was parted in the middle and drawn down across her forehead to her ears. The rest of her hair was amassed above the nape of her neck in curls.

She was dressed in a pleated, muslin hoopskirt—pale purple in color—trimmed in white Chantilly lace. Her tightly fitted bodice gave a smooth round look to her bustline and shoulders that complemented her small and curvy upper body. A sash accented her waistline, and cream-colored fingerless gloves covered her small hands. A dotted and frilled cap ornamented with white lace and narrow blue ribbons of irregular length, some descending low upon her delicate shoulders, fit her appearance perfectly. She was carrying a small white parasol trimmed with white lace for protection from the blazing afternoon sun, and her grandmother's braided hairwork cross necklace hung comfortably around her slender neck.

Rebecca had a half-bashful, half-flirtatious look as she made her way through the courtroom to the witness chair. Every person in the courtroom, especially the jurors, was admiring her natural beauty.

Dead silence was followed by whispers as she approached the court reporter. Lincoln and Logan looked at each other with uncharacteristic surprise. Peachy's eyes were fixed on Rebecca until he glanced at Logan and Lincoln, who were at this point staring at him. Both were hoping for an answer to the compound question they had on their fatigued minds: *Who was this woman and what was she going to say?*

They got their answer and it wasn't good. Peachy immediately dropped his head, avoiding eye contact with his champions. Both defense lawyers, sensing trouble, rose to their feet almost simultaneously. Lincoln spoke first. "Your Honor, we are reluctant to slow the pace of the trial, but may we approach the bench?"

"Yes, Mr. Lincoln," said the judge, realizing something was up.

As Palmer, Logan and Lincoln walked briskly to the bench, Lincoln began formulating his argument. "Your Honor, we are surprised by this witness's presence. We don't know why she's here," said Lincoln in a hushed tone of voice intended to prevent the jurors from hearing his plea.

"She's a rebuttal witness, your Honor," said Palmer in a confident tone of voice, "and we are not obliged to give the defense the names of our rebuttal witnesses."

Logan responded. "That may be true...that the prosecution didn't have to reveal her name before trial...but we are still nonetheless surprised."

"They weren't surprised about the nature of their defense and this witness will reveal facts that contradict that defense," said Palmer in a louder and more tense tone of voice.

"Your Honor, I think the jurors might have heard Mr. Palmer's remark," said Logan in a whisper.

"I'm sorry, your Honor," said Palmer.

"Perhaps we should retire to my chambers to discuss this further," suggested Judge Rice.

"That procedure would probably be in order," Palmer said agreeably.

"Gentlemen of the jury," the judge began, "we must take up an issue in my chambers. So, now may be a good time for our afternoon break. I sense we are nearly finished with the testimony, so we won't be long. Please don't talk about the case amongst yourselves or with anyone else. We will be in recess for thirty minutes. Everyone please remain seated until the jury leaves the courtroom."

Judge Rice descended the dais. The sheriff escorted the judge through the door to his chambers. The lawyers followed—all six of them. Somehow their instincts told them this witness might change the outcome of the trial.

Judge Rice removed his neatly pressed robe and picked up a glass of water. "I believe the heat is much worse today," he said, sipping from his glass.

"I have a feeling things are going to get much hotter, and it reminds me of the time I was trying a case in Bellevue one July," said Lincoln, seizing the moment. "It was hotter than the devil's frying pan. Well, in any event, my opposing counsel fell ill during closing arguments. He was plainly overcome by the heat. We took a recess, but he was just not up to continuing. He had bludgeoned me in our last case against each other, so...because I didn't want to win without a fair fight...I argued his side as well as mine. I got so engrossed in arguing my opponent's cause, that I persuaded the judge to rule against me." Lincoln assumed a deadpan look as everyone in the room laughed.

Lincoln's story broke the tension and gave Logan time to think. "Judge, the defense objects to this witness's testimony. Whatever Miss Watson has to say will be irrelevant and not proper rebuttal," said Logan, attempting to flush out the prosecution.

"Well, Mr. Palmer, I suppose you should tell us why you are calling Miss Watson."

"Of course, your Honor. The defense is taking the position that the defendant is innocent because he lacked the intent to murder…that is…self-defense as a legal justification. The People must prove that the defendant killed Greek Crafton with malice aforethought. Miss Watson's testimony will provide the basis for a motive for Greek's death—jealousy and lust—other than self-defense. Also, it is proper rebuttal because the defense has claimed that Greek was out to do great bodily harm to the defendant. We believe the real motive for Greek's hostility toward Mr. Harrison was the defendant's attempt to alienate Miss Watson's affections from Greek." Palmer was never more serious.

"This is highly irregular, your Honor. May we have a moment alone with our client to discuss this dramatic turn of events?" Lincoln pleaded.

"The request seems reasonable under the circumstances," said Judge Rice. "Sheriff, please find them a private place to talk. When you are finished, please return to my chambers. Remember, gentlemen, the hour is late and we have a jury waiting."

"Thank you, your Honor," said Logan, halfway out the door.

Lincoln, Logan and Cullom followed the sheriff to a small, sparsely furnished office next to the tax collector. The deputy retrieved Peachy from his cell and brought him to the lawyers. The sheriff and deputy excused themselves but remained close to the door.

"Peachy, what the hell is going on here? What is Miss Watson going to say?" demanded Logan, obviously perturbed.

"Well, well, I…I…" Peachy stammered, "I didn't tell you about her because I was afraid you wouldn't believe me when I told you I stabbed Greek in self-defense."

"You should have told us about her. What does she have to do with all of this?" Lincoln pressed.

"She moved to Athens—it's about seventeen miles from Pleasant Plains—a couple of years ago," Peachy started to explain. "I saw her for the first time in May at Pritchard's orchard. I didn't know it then, but Greek had taken a liking to her. I had never seen a girl so beautiful, so I introduced myself to her and we began to talk. I guess we talked for about an hour. I really liked her, Mr. Lincoln," Peachy pleaded. "She was easy to talk to and her voice was like a song. I asked her if she would like to meet me at the Methodist church social in June. She said yes.

"When I got up to leave, I saw Greek's brother Peter. I walked over to speak to him and he said, 'What were you talking to Rebecca about? Greek will want to know.' Then, I asked, 'Why?' And Peter said, 'Greek's going to see her at the Clary's Grove Fourth of July picnic.' I told Peter that was Greek's right...Rebecca could see who she wanted...and that maybe he shouldn't tell Greek nothin'. I said it might be better if he— Peter—stayed away from Greek on this," Peachy concluded, his voice rising.

"What did Peter say?" asked Lincoln.

"He didn't say nothin'. He just got on his horse and left," said Peachy.

"Did you meet Rebecca at the social?" asked Logan.

"Yes, sir. We had a nice evenin'," answered Peachy.

"What did you do?" asked Logan.

"What do you mean?" replied Peachy, puzzled.

"Did you hold her hand? Did she put her arm in yours? Did you kiss her?" pressed Logan.

Peachy knew the importance of the questions, but he avoided them. "I watched her eat," said Peachy.

"What?" asked Lincoln.

"She loved her food. Her eyes would close when she took a bite. She chewed slowly and when she ate her cake, some of the chocolate stuck to her lips. We walked in the field that night...the stars..." Peachy continued.

"I've heard enough. I can hear the prosecution now, 'Passion was the leitmotiv'!" Logan interrupted.

"Was Greek there? Did anyone see you and Rebecca together?" asked Lincoln anxiously.

"Peter," said Peachy.

"Did you see Rebecca at the Fourth of July picnic?" asked Logan.

"Yes, sir," said Peachy.

"Was Greek with her?" Logan followed up.

"Yes, sir," said Peachy.

"Did Rebecca see you?" asked Lincoln.

"I think so," said Peachy.

"How do you know?" asked Logan.

"She smiled at me," said Peachy.

"Did you talk to her that day at Clary's Grove?" Logan asked.

"At the cider barrel," said Peachy.

"Did Greek see you?" asked Lincoln.

"I don't know...most likely he did. All the boys were looking at her from time to time. You couldn't help it," said Peachy defensively.

"Did you say anything to Rebecca about Greek?" said Lincoln.

"I don't recollect. I probably did," said Peachy.

"Did Rebecca ever say anything to you about Greek?" asked Logan.

Peachy became silent. He knew he needed to tell them everything, but he was afraid they wouldn't defend him like they had so far if he told them the truth.

"Did Rebecca tell you anything about Greek saying something

to her about her seeing you?" Logan repeated, looking for a straight answer.

"Well...she told me...she told me that Greek had said he didn't like me being around her," Peachy reluctantly admitted.

"Peachy, I need to talk privately with Mr. Logan and Mr. Cullom. I'll call the sheriff," said Lincoln.

"You're not mad at me, are you?" asked Peachy.

"No, Peachy. I'm not. We'll think of something," said Lincoln as he patted Peachy's shoulder.

As the sheriff took Peachy out of the room, the three lawyers looked at each other. Each knew the damning nature of Rebecca's potential testimony and they still didn't know what else she might say on the witness stand. Up to this point in the trial, Peachy's motive for killing Greek was either anger over Greek's bullying or self-preservation. Either way, Greek was the aggressor and some jurors would naturally gravitate toward Peachy as the underdog. With Rebecca's testimony, the jury could find a motive consistent with malice aforethought. That translated into murder.

"I don't know if we have a basis for excluding Rebecca's testimony," said Logan, shaking his head.

"Neither do I," lamented Lincoln.

"Hold on. Isn't Rebecca the daughter of P.K. Watson?" asked Cullom as he scrambled for his pigskin book containing the Illinois rules of evidence in trials.

"How in the world does that matter?" asked Logan, still irritated over the defense's predicament.

"Well, I know that P.K.'s mother was a Negro. He told me when I helped him with his farm purchase," Cullom replied, thumbing through the pages.

"Now I'm really confused," said Logan.

It was as if a light had gone on in Lincoln's head. He snatched the evidence book from Cullom's hand. "Well done, Mr. Cullom.

Well done," said Lincoln as he pointed to section 23 of the Illinois statutes on evidence and depositions in trials. "Here, Mr. Cullom, read this to Mr. Logan," urged Lincoln, handing the open book to Cullom.

Cullom read the law book out loud. "A Negro, mulatto or Indian shall not be a witness in any court, or any case, against a white person. A person having one-fourth part Negro blood shall be judged a mulatto."

"If P.K.'s mother is a full-blooded Negro, then Rebecca is one-fourth Negro and under Illinois law cannot testify against our client," said Lincoln soberly.

"I'll be damned," said Logan. "Let me see that."

The decision Lincoln would have to make about objecting to Rebecca's testimony using the Illinois statute was repugnant to every moral fiber of his being. As he had said many times, "Just because a law is legally right, doesn't make it morally right." But, the dilemma he faced now was a clear choice between zealously representing Peachy by objecting to testimony that could surely convict him or refusing to take advantage of a law he knew was morally wrong. He only had 10 minutes to make up his mind.

"Abe, I'm sorry I brought this up. We can't make that objection," said Cullom, realizing what he had done. "You're interested in becoming President of the United States. You have staked out your position on slavery and racism, and your opponents will make a mockery of you for using racism to defend an accused murderer."

"I'm afraid he's right," said Logan. Nonetheless, he knew what his friend would do.

Lincoln put his face in his large hands for a few seconds while he slid his long frame under a small office table. Then he looked at his friends with a fondness generally reserved for a man and his grandson. He had made his decision.

"No, my dear friend Stephen. When I passed the bar, I took an oath to do everything in my power…under the law…to represent my clients to the best of my ability. This law may be wrong and it may hurt my campaign to raise it on behalf of an accused murderer, but I must do so or be forever haunted by a decision made for me and not my client, who I am duty bound to protect. We must go to the judge with our objections."

Logan and Cullom knew in their hearts that Lincoln was right. They admired his loyalty to the profession but regretted the situation Lincoln faced. It was one of the many self-defining choices a lawyer faces along the uncertain path of his career. But they were well aware of the fact that few lawyers were strong enough to choose their client over themselves.

The three defense lawyers entered the judge's chambers precisely on time. Palmer, White and Jamison were already seated with the judge. Sheriff Andrew was standing in the corner of the room.

"Do you have an objection to this witness's testimony, gentlemen?" asked Judge Rice.

"We do, your Honor. We are relying on section twenty-three of the Illinois statutes on evidence and depositions and ask the court to exclude the testimony of Miss Watson on the ground that she is not a competent…or qualified…witness against Mr. Harrison," said Lincoln, holding his statute book for the judge to see.

"Let me see that rule, Mr. Lincoln. Does the prosecution have a rule book?" asked Judge Rice.

"Yes, your Honor," said Palmer, puzzled.

Judge Rice read the rule quietly and slowly lifted his eyes from the page. His gaze at Lincoln over his spectacles telegraphed a sense of disbelief. "What part of the rule are you relying on to support your objection?" asked Judge Rice, already confident of Lincoln's answer.

"We have good reason to believe Miss Watson is a mulatto, your Honor," said Lincoln without hesitation.

"Your Honor, this is highly irregular...to quote Mr. Logan. What Mr. Lincoln believes cannot form the basis for this objection. He must prove it," snapped Palmer, standing at the judge's desk.

Lincoln turned to Cullom. "Does Mr. Watson's mother live in Illinois?" asked Lincoln.

"No, Abe, she lives in Mississippi," said Cullom.

"In that case, your Honor, we will prove it through Miss Watson."

"I don't believe what I'm hearing. Abraham Lincoln is going to ask this lady, in full view of the public and the press, whether she's a mulatto?" Jamison blurted out, to the amazement of everyone in the room.

"No, I propose we question her in your chambers, your Honor," said Logan.

"What is your position on that, Mr. Palmer?" asked Judge Rice.

"No, objection, sir," said Palmer, fully aware that a similar procedure had been used for Rev. Cartwright and that he would appear inconsistent if he objected.

"Well, let's call her in here. Sheriff, please tell the jury to stand at ease while we conduct the examination...and bring Miss Watson to my chambers. We should also bring the prisoner in here as well," ordered Judge Rice in a voice heavy with authority.

The sheriff did as the judge directed. The jurors, hot and tired of waiting, grumbled at the news of yet another delay. Peachy was brought to the judge's chambers first. Logan asked that the court reporter also be present. The judge agreed. As Rebecca Watson was brought to the judge's chambers, it was crowded with men. The prosecution team was seated on the judge's left, the defense on the right. Peachy was seated next to Lincoln. The reporter took a seat between the attorneys, and an empty chair was placed next to him for the witness.

As Rebecca entered the door, everyone stood as the attorneys, with somber faces, watched her walk to her chair with the dignity of a highborn lady. Only Lincoln attempted to give her a reassuring look.

Peachy's courtroom demeanor vanished with Rebecca's presence. Rebecca's face was flushed and her partially covered hands had grown cold. This was hardly an unusual reaction from a witness called into a judge's chambers without warning or explanation. Sensing that, Judge Rice attempted to put Rebecca at ease by smiling and gesturing for her to be seated.

"Please have a seat, Miss Watson. And don't be intimidated by this gathering. The lawyers just want to ask you a few questions."

Rebecca stole a supportive glance at Peachy as she took her seat in the straight-backed wooden chair. Anticipating that Rebecca would be soft-spoken, the court reporter had positioned himself close to her to administer the oath and maximize his ability to hear her.

"Please place your hand on the Bible," said the reporter. "Do you swear to tell the truth, the whole truth, and nothing but the truth, so help you God?"

"I do," Rebecca said almost in a whisper.

"Mr. Lincoln, you may begin," said the judge, sliding his chair back from his desk.

> *Lincoln:* Thank you, your Honor. Miss Watson, I'm Abraham Lincoln. I believe you know my client, Peachy Quinn Harrison?

A slight smile appeared on Rebecca's face as she answered Lincoln's question in her predictably pleasant manner. "Yes, he's my friend."

Lincoln: Where do you live?

Watson: Athens.

Lincoln: That's near Pleasant Plains?

Watson: Yes, Mr. Lincoln.

Lincoln: I know it's not polite to ask a lady her age, but how old are you?

Watson: Nineteen.

Lincoln: What is your father's name, miss?

Watson: P.K. Watson.

Lincoln: And your mother?

Watson: Summer.

Lincoln: Miss Watson, it's not my desire to offend you with my next questions, but I must ask them for my client's benefit.

Watson: Yes, sir. But, I don't understand.

Lincoln: Miss Watson, did you know your grandmother—your father's mother?

Watson: Why, yes.

Lincoln: Have you met her?

Watson: Yes, in Mississippi.

Lincoln: Is she still alive?

Watson: No, she died three years ago of the fever.

Lincoln: I'm sorry. Did you ever talk to her about her life?

Watson: Yes, what is this about? Is my family on trial here?

Lincoln: I'm sorry, miss. No, they are not. But, I must...I am compelled to ask you these questions. Did you ever talk to your grandmother about her life?

Watson: Yes, once.

Lincoln: What did she tell you?

Palmer: Objection. Hearsay.

Lincoln: Judge, I'm not offering this for the truth of the matter, only to lay a foundation for her knowledge.

Judge Rice: Overruled.

Lincoln: What did she say?

Watson: Her life was very difficult. She told me her mother and father came to New Orleans on a slave boat...

Harrison: Please stop! I don't want this. Please, Mr. Lincoln.

Judge Rice: Calm down, Mr. Harrison. Mr. Lincoln, do you need another recess?

Lincoln: If that would be convenient, your Honor.

Judge Rice: Let's take fifteen minutes.

Peachy and Rebecca stood at the same time and Peachy hugged her saying, "I'm sorry. I'll make them stop."

"If it will help…" Rebecca said in tears. "I want to help you."

"Come on, Peachy," said the sheriff.

"Yes, we need to talk," said Logan. This was one time when Lincoln was without words. Two young lives immersed in such agony. He had to press on, he thought, as the defense team walked to the tiny courthouse office.

"Please, Mr. Lincoln. I don't want this. It will be in the papers…she will be the subject of gossip," pleaded Peachy.

"Maybe not," said Logan. "If the judge sustains the objection, the only way people will know is if the prosecutors make a statement to the reporters. Perhaps we could ask the judge to order the prosecution to remain silent."

"Can he do that?" said Peachy.

"I don't know, but we can try," said Logan.

Lincoln was glad someone was thinking. All of this troubled him greatly and his mind was swimming. "You realize we must do this, Peachy," said Lincoln.

"I don't want to hurt her," said Peachy.

"I know. Neither do I," said Lincoln.

"Abe has just a couple more questions, and it will be over," said Logan.

"I'm sorry about my shouting in there, but I don't want to hurt her," said Peachy.

"We are all on edge. I will tell the judge what you said," said Lincoln, gently grabbing Peachy's arm. The defense attorneys returned to the judge's chambers and apologized for Peachy's outburst. Rebecca was seated and Lincoln resumed his questioning.

Lincoln: Before we recessed, Miss Watson, you testified that your great-grandparents came to this country on a slave boat. I know this may be obvious, but were they Negro?

Watson: Yes, sir. I saw their slave papers.

Lincoln: And your grandmother was Negro?

Watson: Of course. I still don't understand why this is important.

Lincoln: Thank you, Rebecca. I'm finished, your Honor.

Judge Rice: Yes, Mr. Lincoln. Mr. Palmer, any cross-examination?

Palmer: Miss Watson, I am John Palmer.

Watson: Nice to meet you, sir.

Palmer: You and Mr. Harrison are more than friends, are you not?

Watson: We…

Lincoln: Objection, your Honor. Mr. Palmer is attempting to impeach his own witness.

Judge Rice: Mr. Palmer, Lincoln is correct. That is not permitted under our rules of evidence.

Palmer: Mr. Lincoln has stated the law correctly, but for this hearing, Miss Watson is Mr. Lincoln's witness...not mine.

Lincoln: Touché.

Judge Rice: Objection overruled.

Palmer: He's more than a friend, isn't he, Miss Watson?

Watson: Yes.

Palmer: Did you ever meet your great-grandparents?

Watson: Not that I remember.

Palmer: So, you are only assuming they were full-blooded Negro, correct?

Watson: I guess.

Palmer: Thank you, Miss Watson.

Judge Rice: Mr. Lincoln, any further questions or evidence?

Lincoln: No, your Honor.

Judge Rice: Miss Watson, you are excused. You may return to the courtroom with the sheriff.

Watson: Thank you.

Judge Rice: Gentlemen, the objection by the defense is that Miss Watson's testimony is irrelevant and that she is not a competent witness under section twenty-three. What say the prosecution?

Palmer: The defense has failed to sustain its burden of proof on the issue. Since Miss Watson is assuming her great-grandparents were Negro, there is no proof that her grandmother was a full-blooded Negro, which is required to establish that Miss Watson has one-fourth part Negro blood.

Lincoln: Mr. Palmer's argument reminds me of the witness in the assault case who was asked by the prosecutor if he actually saw the defendant bite off the victim's ear. The witness replied, "No, but I saw him spit it out." Miss Watson never saw her great-grandparents, but she was told by her Negro grandmother that they came to New Orleans on a slave ship. And she saw their slave papers…as she described them. Our burden is proof by a preponderance of the evidence and we have satisfied that burden on this issue.

Judge Rice: There is no doubt in the court's mind that Miss Watson's testimony provides a compelling motive for murder; therefore its relevance has been established by the prosecution. The jury ought to hear the evidence of motive to give it such weight as they feel it deserves. However, the court is compelled to find that Miss Watson is a mulatto, as that term is defined in section twenty-three and…as a result thereof…she cannot testify as a witness for the People in this case. Objection sustained. Let's return to the courtroom.

Logan: Judge Rice, since the court sustained the objection, would you be inclined to order the prosecution to refrain from discussing the nature of Miss Watson's testimony and the court's ruling with the press while the trial is proceeding?

Judge Rice: Mr. Palmer, I don't see that commenting to the reporters about what happened in my chambers would accomplish anything, do you?

Palmer: May I comment to the newspapers at the conclusion of the trial if they ask?

Judge Rice: After the verdict is returned, if they ask you about Miss Watson, you may answer them.

The attorneys and the judge returned to a confused courtroom crowd. The mystery woman was seated next to the sheriff on the sidewall. After the judge restored order to the courtroom, he asked the prosecution if it had any additional rebuttal witnesses. The prosecution answered in the negative.

With no further testimony, the evidence was now complete. A short recess allowed the judge to organize the instructions of law he would give to the jury. The lawyers were busy collaborating on what should be addressed during closing arguments, and the families felt a wave of uneasiness as they waited for the judge to return. When the jurors filed in and were seated, Judge Rice instructed them on their duties and the law.

"Gentlemen of the jury, now that you have heard the evidence in this case, it is time for me to instruct you on the law. To begin with, I must remind you of the indictment in this case. The grand jury has charged that on or about the sixteenth day of July, eighteen hundred fifty-nine, in this county, the defendant, Peachy Quinn Harrison, not having fear of God before his eyes, but instead having been moved and seduced by instigation of the devil, did then and there feloniously, willfully and with malice aforethought, inflict a mortal knife wound upon one Jonathan 'Greek' Crafton, which caused the death of the aforesaid Jonathan 'Greek' Crafton against the peace and dignity of the People of the State of Illinois. The indictment is signed by the Grand Jury Foreman and the Prosecuting Attorney, Mr. White.

"Keep in mind, however, that the indictment is not evidence. It is merely a way of bringing an accused to court. The prisoner is accused of committing the crime of murder willfully and with malice aforethought. The People have the burden of proving his guilt beyond a reasonable doubt. But the prisoner relies upon the defense plea of *son assault demesne*—the deceased brought on the fight. To judge the evidence in this case, you must know that willfully means on purpose with an evil design to disobey or disregard the law. To find malice, it is sufficient if a man is killed by another deliberately and intentionally without an apparently well-founded danger of great bodily harm.

"During the testimony, the People have called out the admissions of the prisoner as evidence. Having done so, they must take admissions in the prisoner's favor as well as against him. It is your duty to give any admissions such weight as you feel they deserve...whether they be damning or favorable to the accused. The defendant, on the other hand, has called out the alleged dying declarations of the deceased, Greek Crafton. Ordinarily, statements made by the deceased would not be allowed as proper evidence. But, dying declarations of the deceased may be considered by you for their truth if the proponent of the declarations—in this case the defendant—establishes that the deceased...immediately before making the statements...believed he was near death and would soon answer to his Maker for the truth or falsity of his statements. The reason for allowing the declarations is the well-known principle of a person apprehensive of immediate death and standing, as it were, in the presence of his god, binds his conscience with as high an obligation as that of an oath. Whether the declarations were made and whether the deceased made them apprehensive of immediate death are questions for you to decide.

"The defendant has also called out alleged threats by Greek Crafton to do bodily harm to him before the events which gave rise to Greek's death. To be considered by you, however, you must find that the prisoner knew of the threats before the encounter between the prisoner and the deceased in Ben Hart's store.

"Now, in an indictment for murder, the defendant may be acquitted of the charge of murder and found guilty on the same indictment for manslaughter. If, however, you should find the defendant not guilty of the charge of murder and from the evidence find him guilty of manslaughter, you will fix the length of time the accused shall be confined in the penitentiary on your verdict not to exceed eight years. Manslaughter is a homicide which, even though intentional, is committed under the influence of passion produced by an adequate or reasonable provocation, and before a reasonable time has lapsed for the blood to cool and reason to resume its habitual control, and which is not the result of wickedness of heart or cruelty of disposition. If you should find the defendant guilty of murder, his sentence will be death by hanging.

"You, as practical men, must determine beyond a reasonable doubt whether the prisoner killed Mr. Crafton and whether he did so deliberately and with malice aforethought or because of an apparently well-founded danger of great bodily harm to himself...that is in self-defense. You should not base your decision on passion or prejudice. Your verdict must be based on the facts and the law. If the accused be guilty of the crime of murder, say so. If not guilty by reason of self-defense, then that should be your verdict.

"Remember, the question before you should not be whether the People will win or lose the case. For the prosecution is always victorious when justice is done—whether the verdict be guilty or not guilty. Now it is time for the lawyers to make their final arguments. Please give them your full attention."

Looking at the prosecution table, Judge Rice said, "Mr. Palmer, you may go to the jury with your summation."

Moving to the podium, Palmer replied politely, "May it please the court, counsel and gentlemen of the jury. This has been a long and difficult trial for everyone. It has been hot and I know at times it has been difficult for you to concentrate. But I have noticed you have done a particularly good job of paying attention to the witnesses and counsel. In that spirit, I want to thank you for your service to the great state of Illinois.

"Murder trials are always stressful. The penalty, as you know, is the most severe we have in the law. However, there is a reason for that. No man should kill another without justification under the law. That is our system of justice. If a man deliberately kills another without lawful justification, then he must be held accountable. In this case, the People have the burden of proving Mr. Harrison's guilt on the charge of murder. I submit we have done that. We have done just that."

"Really," said Palmer as he left the podium for the jury rail, "this case is as clear as any you will see. For whatever reason, there was great animosity between Greek and the defendant. Both men were guilty of saying things they should not have said. At Clary's Grove, there was a verbal altercation that began with the defendant insulting Greek's mother and ended with the defendant threatening to kill Greek. A few days later, the defendant purchased a bowie knife. At that point, the defendant is armed and

Greek is not. As a matter of fact, Greek was never armed and neither was the defendant until he decided to kill Greek.

"I realize some of you may be thinking that the defendant was justified in stabbing Greek because Greek attacked him. Judge Rice has told you that the law, 'which you have been sworn to uphold,' says a man may kill another only if a well-founded danger of great bodily harm is apparent. Great bodily harm means what it says, gentlemen. There is a dispute in the testimony as to whether Greek was attempting to strike the defendant before he was stabbed. Ben Hart says yes and John Crafton says no. It matters not, however, because neither is a situation creating a well-founded danger of great—I said great—bodily harm.

"Finally, there are two pieces of evidence that the defendant deliberately intended to kill Greek. The first is that he stabbed Greek twice. Gentlemen, that was done to ensure his blows were fatal. This wasn't self-defense; it was murder—plain and simple. The second is that the defendant ran after he learned that Greek had died at his hand. The Good Book teaches us that 'the wicked flee where no man pursueth, but the righteous are bold as a lion.' Innocent men don't run, gentlemen, but the guilty generally do. It proves his state of mind. His intent to kill.

"This is a solemn occasion for all concerned. A man is dead, and we have an obligation to see that his family gets justice. The defendant is guilty of murder, and I ask you to do your duty and hand up a verdict saying as much. Thank you for your service."

Palmer returned to the prosecution's table. Jamison looked at him and said, "Well done." Palmer nodded in appreciation, even though he knew he never mentioned Rev. Cartwright's testimony. In his opinion, to do so would have required him to call Cartwright a liar. That, he thought, would be offensive to some of the jurors. His only hope was that the seed of doubt planted by him on cross-examination would grow in the privacy of the jury room. *Now, how will Lincoln and Logan handle Cartwright,* Palmer wondered.

Murder cases were the hardest on Lincoln because of the potential consequences. As an experienced courtroom lawyer, Lincoln believed it was the rare case that could be won in closing argument. It was much easier, in his opinion, to lose a case in closing argument. In dealing with juries for years, Lincoln also understood and accepted human nature. Even though the jurors promised they wouldn't make up their minds until the case was over, it was highly likely that most, if not all, of the jurors had already made up their minds—one way or the other. It was Lincoln's job to give them something to think about while at the same time avoiding a tactic that might damage the credibility of the defense.

Lincoln was at peace with his decision not to put Peachy on the stand. The biggest problem now was what to say about Rev. Cartwright. Lincoln was keenly aware that Palmer had studiously avoided mentioning Cartwright in his closing argument. That was smart strategy. It, in effect, shifted the burden to Lincoln. Cartwright was a very important witness for the defense and couldn't be ignored. But when he discussed Cartwright's testimony, he knew the jurors would be thinking about the fact that Cartwright was Peachy's grandfather and was against the death penalty. If the issue was handled poorly, it could hurt Peachy's case.

The scenarios racing through Lincoln's mind were abruptly interrupted when Judge Rice cleared his throat. "Mr. Lincoln, you may present closing arguments for the defense."

"Thank you, your Honor," Lincoln stated as he moved to stand directly behind his client. As he began to speak, Lincoln laid his hands gently on Peachy's shoulders. "May it please this honorable court. Gentlemen of the jury, distinguished counsel, this is a

Abraham Lincoln delivers closing statements

sad and tragic case. A good family has lost its eldest son. Another good family's son is looking into the face of the hangman. As a consequence, before another life is lost, we need to be sure it is the just and proper thing to do.

"I have pulled the weight of my client's fate like a plow horse for many days now. Soon that weight will be shifted to you. All I can do now is to reason with you, as the prophet Isaiah reasoned with the judges, about the evidence and the law to help you reach a fair verdict," said Lincoln as he walked from behind his client to a position about eight feet in front of the jury box. The jurors' heads were all cocked upward. "Let's carefully reflect on the testimony we heard in this courtroom."

As Lincoln spoke those words, three of the jurors crossed their arms. That posture generally meant that those particular jurors were probably not going to receive Lincoln's argument with favor. Three other jurors moved to the edge of their seats—a good sign. The other six jurors sat expressionless; there was no way to gauge what they were thinking. Lincoln was not surprised by this, however. It was the nature and beauty of the jury system that he loved so dearly. His job now was to move the six jurors to the defense position and, if he was successful, give them the tools to persuade all of the jurors to find Peachy not guilty.

Lincoln continued. "We can all agree on some of the evidence. Greek was the aggressor. My client had resisted Greek's previous attempts to fight and Greek had threatened to whip my client. Yes, my client had made threats as well. But they were made after Greek attempted to jump my client at Clary's Grove. Finally, Greek was bigger, older and stronger than my client. This point is the most significant. It provides a measure of my client's fear of great bodily harm when he was the subject of an unprovoked attack on July sixteenth in Ben Hart's store. And, even on that occasion, according to Mr. Hart, my client stated 'he didn't want to fight.' What man would not have defended himself under the circumstances?

"Now, the prosecution argues that Peachy used too much force…that he didn't have to stab Greek to stop Greek's aggression. That is a question that each one of you must answer for yourself. To do so, however, you must be sure of what was in Peachy's heart and mind. Otherwise, if you are not convinced beyond a reasonable doubt that Peachy acted with malice aforethought, you are obligated under your oath to find him not guilty.

"At this point, if you will kindly indulge me, there are two witnesses I want to discuss with you before I conclude my remarks. The first witness is John Crafton. There is no event in life more painful than the loss of a child. From personal experience, I share in the Crafton's sorrow. But, you must try to square John Crafton's testimony with that of Ben Hart. They apparently saw two different things that fateful day, and you have to decide who is telling the truth. If you believe Ben Hart, then Peachy was defending himself. If you believe John Crafton, then Peachy may be guilty of murder. If you are not sure who to believe, you have a reasonable doubt.

"So, you may be thinking, 'Abe, is there anything that was testified to that would help me decide the truth?' The answer is, 'Yes'. It comes from the mouth of Greek Crafton himself. While lying on his deathbed, the last words he uttered about this matter were, 'I brought it upon myself.'

'I brought it upon myself,' Greek said as he prepared to meet his Maker. Greek knew the truth in his heart, and he wanted to die in peace."

Lincoln had skillfully avoided any reference to Rev. Cartwright, arguing instead that the dying declaration was consistent with the events he and Logan had laid before the jury. This gave the jury a way to avoid the conclusion that Cartwright may have lied to save his grandson.

Lincoln concluded his remarks. "Gentlemen of the jury...I may venture to say...this has been a long and trying case. Your labors are now about to begin in earnest. I do not envy your sworn task but instead leave you with this belief from the depths of my bosom. There is reasonable doubt as to my client's guilt and I beg of you to practice the same forgiving spirit that Greek had shown on his deathbed and return a verdict of not guilty. Thank you for your patience."

Lincoln walked slowly to his chair. Virginia's heart soared and Mary Rose sat stoically looking at her son. The tension in the courtroom was mounting. Everyone knew a decision was near. Judge Rice looked at Lincoln and then the jury.

"Thank you, Mr. Lincoln. Gentlemen of the jury, the sheriff will now escort you to a place where you will remain until you reach a unanimous verdict. Everyone will remain seated until the jury leaves the courtroom."

After the jury filed out behind the sheriff, the judge announced: "Court will be in recess." It was 7:12 p.m. on Sept. 3.

In a simultaneous gesture of respect and civility, the lawyers met between the tables to shake hands. It is an event that most non-lawyers don't understand or appreciate. For those who love the law and the courtroom, however, it is a natural thing to do.

CHAPTER 8

While everyone was waiting for the jury to return, the *Springfield Register* reporter returned to his shared office to write his piece on the Harrison trial for the early morning edition. Pondering the much-anticipated arguments of counsel, he couldn't help but wonder what the future would hold for the able litigators. It was patently obvious that their ability to change the lives of others was limitless. But that story would have to wait for another day. It was late and his editor was waiting.

After carefully summarizing the trial testimony, the reporter focused on the closing arguments. His observations of Palmer's closing were written first. "Mr. Palmer spoke with marked ability, evincing great ingenuity in handling the testimony, interspersing remarks about the frailties of human nature and human passions, the duties of the citizens and the spirit of the law."

As for Lincoln's argument, the reporter was similarly impressed. "Mr. Lincoln's argument on behalf of the prisoner examined the evidence with great skill and earnestness, discussing the law and replying to the positions assumed by counsel for the prosecution with a subtle and relentless logic and frequent illustrations of singular fitness. The argument was delivered in an earnest, natural and energetic manner."

Summing up the trial, the reporter wrote that the "grounds, both pro and con, were strongly contested and the testimony thoroughly sifted. The jurors were now faced with, perhaps, the challenge of their lives."

At the courthouse, Virginia and the rest of the Harrison family were waiting outside the well of the courtroom for Lincoln, who had stepped over to speak to his client before the sheriff took him back to jail. Eventually, Lincoln approached them.

"How long will the jury take, Mr. Lincoln?" asked Virginia, without regard to Lincoln's previous admonitions. Lincoln replied thoughtfully, trying to calm Virginia and her family.

"There is no way to know, my dear. They could be out a few minutes or many hours. In all my years, I have never been able to predict what a jury will do with any precision. It's like trying to decide where a butterfly will alight. Every time I try, I get it wrong. All I know is we did our best."

Peyton Harrison, who hardly ever expressed himself, stuck out his hand. "We can't thank you enough, Abe. No matter what happens, we will never forget what you, Mr. Logan and Mr. Cullom have done for our family. We are deeply in your debt."

Lincoln gave Peyton a firm handshake and shook the hands of Junior and cousin Diane as well. He put his arm around Mary Rose and hugged Virginia. These moments were the most gratifying to Lincoln, even though they marked the beginning of the only part of a jury trial he hated—waiting for the jury.

During that time in every trial, Lincoln replayed every aspect of the case in his mind. He would wonder what he could have done differently to obtain a favorable outcome. One minute, fear would overtake him. The next, he would be convinced his client would be acquitted. But, he always came to the same conclusion: The outcome couldn't be appraised with any accuracy. As always, he had to settle for knowing he had put forth his best effort. That's why he was always so passionate about his criminal cases. For him, there was no other option. He couldn't shoulder the burden of knowing someone went to prison or the gallows because he failed to do all he could.

While Lincoln appeared calm on the outside, his stomach was churning and his anxiety mounting as he waited on the jury. The only way he could deal with it was to talk about something other than the case. His favorite subject was politics, of course, but there were always subjects like the weather, travels, food and his storytelling to distract him and his clients from the tormenting wait.

Nobody left the courthouse. Many stepped outside to get some air now that the hot afternoon had slipped into evening. Logan whittled on a rough piece of walnut while Cullom returned to his one-room office to work on a brief for the Illinois Supreme Court. The sheriff and his deputy zealously guarded the jury room door. No one was allowed in the jury room—not even the judge.

When the jury had a question or verdict, they were directed to knock on the door. Although the jury's deliberations were private and inviolate, the sheriff could occasionally be seen tipping his chair back, straining to hear a tidbit of information through the door.

The jury was quiet at first. After about an hour, raised voices could be heard. This went on for 10 minutes or so. Then it got quiet again for another hour. At that point, there was a knock. Everyone stopped and watched the sheriff speak to a juror as he cracked open the door. The sheriff turned and said, "The jurors want to take a recess to clear their heads."

The lawyers agreed, and the sheriff led the jurors out the back door into a small, manicured garden. There were no expressions on the jurors' faces as they walked past the lawyers and some of the spectators. About 15 minutes later, the sheriff escorted the jury back to their room. A frequently used coercive measure was sometimes employed by judges to encourage quick verdicts—the jury was denied food and drink until they reached a decision. But for this jury, food and water were the furthest things from their minds.

The Harrison family was becoming increasingly edgy, so Lincoln decided that storytelling was in order. After a while, he distracted them to the point that they were laughing. As the agonizing time passed, Lincoln's storytelling moved from oration to amateur drama and a small crowd, including some elementary-age children, gathered around him. His deliberate, animated and honest manner made them chuckle even before the punch line was delivered.

When the subject turned to food, since everyone was missing supper, someone asked Lincoln if he liked pan-fried chicken. Lincoln turned to a young boy in the crowd. The boy, about 9 years old, was wearing faded blue overalls that contrasted with his curly red hair. He was hanging on Lincoln's every word.

"Fried chicken?" Lincoln mused. "That reminds me of the time I went to my Aunt Ruby's house to visit. She was a prizewinning cook…fried pies—apple was my favorite, mashed potatoes, sweet corn, homemade soppin' biscuits…nothing better. She could fix chicken any way you could think of. She made chicken and dumplin's, chicken stew, chicken soup, barbecued chicken and yes, fried chicken. She even raised her own hand-fed birds," Lincoln said while looking directly at the young redhead.

"Now, she fed those chickens ground corn that she pulverized herself, and those chickens ended up fatter than a summer tick on a bluetick hound dog. And eggs, they would lay more eggs than a loggerhead turtle. One day my uncle, who had a great deal of trouble with his eyes—in fact he was as cross-eyed as a Siamese cat—went to the crib for what he thought was a bag of chicken feed. Instead, he got a bag full of sawdust. Well, he fed those chickens sawdust for about a week before Aunt Ruby realized what was happening. After scolding my uncle, she banned him from the chicken coop and gave it no further thought. But, a few weeks later, one of the chickens hatched six baby chicks." Lincoln then looked the little boy square in the eye and spoke with an uncommonly straight face. "You know, when Aunt Ruby examined those chicks...four of 'em had wooden legs and two were woodpeckers."

The little boy's eyes were wide with amazement when the crowd erupted into laughter. Lincoln grinned and the boy, who was initially puzzled at the laughter, slapped his brother's arm as the teasing began.

By this time, most everyone moved back into the courtroom because it had cooled down. The spectators were beginning to get tired, and the lawyers were near exhaustion. Startling everyone, a second knock was heard and the sheriff approached the door. After a brief conversation with the same juror, the sheriff yelled, "We have a verdict!"

The lawyers scrambled for their seats. The floor spectators jammed into the wooden church pew-style seats and lined up along the back and sidewalls of the dimly lit courtroom. The balcony was brimming. The hallway and stairway were crammed with people all straining to hear the proceedings. The deputy sheriff had retrieved Peachy and was staging him in the prisoner's dock. Virginia didn't know what to do with herself. Her heart was pounding so hard she could feel it in her chest. The jury door opened, and the sheriff led the jurors through the courtroom to the jury box.

Lincoln tried to make eye contact with some of the jurors without success. They were staring straight at the judge's bench.

Doubts began to enter Lincoln's mind about the outcome. *How would he explain a conviction to the Harrison family? What issues would he raise on appeal?* At this moment in all criminal trials, Lincoln wished the jury deliberations would continue forever so he would never have to hear the mind-numbing word "guilty."

After a few seconds of total silence, the sheriff called out, "All rise." When the judge took his seat, the sheriff spoke again. "Court is now in session. You may be seated."

The judge looked at the jury. He was collecting himself behind the bench, his features sinking into somber lines. Lincoln almost burst with anticipation. He couldn't look at Virginia or Mary Rose in the audience. "Gentlemen, I understand you have reached a verdict."

Foreman Anderson, seated in the first chair of the jury box, nodded and stood up. "Yes, your Honor, we have."

The final moment of the trial was at hand. The crowd collectively stopped breathing, as if its own fate was in the hands of the jury. Every sound was hushed. In a voice that seemed to stir the air, Judge Rice posed the final trial question: "What say the jury?"

The foreman looked at Peachy and then the Crafton family. Clearing his throat, he said, "We, the jury, find the defendant *not guilty* as charged in the indictment."

The announcement was received with loud and prolonged applause by the large crowd, in spite of the efforts of the judge and the officers to subdue them. Peachy put his face in his hands and began to sob. Virginia, in tears, hugged Mary Rose, who for the first time during the entire ordeal began to cry. Lincoln headed for his client as the crowd surged joyously toward the defense lawyers. The Craftons, stunned by the outcome, stormed from the courtroom.

Crack! Crack! Crack!

"Order in the court," the judge yelled. Everyone became quiet. "Mr. Harrison, having been found not guilty by a jury of your peers, you are free to go. Court is adjourned."

As Lincoln and his client left the courtroom, they were mobbed by the Harrison family, well-wishers and the press. The *Register* reporter rushed back to stop the printing press and write his front-page headline. Out of the corner of his eye, Lincoln spotted Palmer and Jamison heading to their office. He broke away from the crowd and grabbed Palmer's hand. "John, you tried a good case."

"Congratulations, Abe. You are indeed a worthy adversary."

Almost as an afterthought, Lincoln spoke again as the men separated. "Good luck in your campaign."

"Likewise, my friend," said Palmer with a smile.

Virginia, who was thanking friends for their encouragement during the trial, turned to look for Ben Hart in the lingering crowd and instead found herself face-to-face with Jamison.

"Well, little girl," Jamison started in, "your brother was lucky today. The jury must have felt sorry for him."

"But, he was innocent!" exclaimed Virginia.

"You don't know what you're talking about," Jamison replied. "He was guilty as sin and he got away with murder."

"Doesn't self-defense mean it wasn't murder?" asked Virginia, defending her brother.

"Why do you...a woman...think you know anything about the law? I'm not spending my valuable time answering your ignorant questions," said Jamison as he walked away. Unwilling to allow the encounter to spoil the moment, Virginia found Ben Hart for a heartfelt embrace.

When the celebration ended, Lincoln thanked Logan and Cullom for a job well done but declined a wagon ride home. He wanted to walk alone. The moon was in its first quarter and the flickering Argand oil streetlamps danced in the darkness. Virginia watched as Lincoln's tall silhouette, moving with his long, gangly strides, slipped out of sight. She would not see Lincoln again for 18 months.

ᏽᎦᎧᏽ

The *Register's* final article on the Harrison trial was the talk of the county.

TRIAL OF PEACHY QUINN HARRISON
INDICTED FOR THE MURDER OF GREEK CRAFTON

Circuit Court of Sangamon County – Hon. E.F. Rice, Judge

HARRISON FOUND NOT GUILTY
SATURDAY, SEPTEMBER 3, 1859

Court met pursuant to adjournment, at ten o'clock, and the jury being called, the trial proceeded.

Mr. Palmer having rested the case for the prosecution, the examination of the defense witnesses then commenced.

Abajiah Nottingham; CALLED, SWORN AND EXAMINED by Mr. Logan lives in close proximity to Pleasant Plains near Tallula; grocery store owner; knew the parties; saw some of the affray; Palmer objected to Logan's attempt to produce testimony from the witness about threats by Crafton against Harrison before the affray. The Judge permitted the questioning conditioned upon Harrison's knowledge of such threats; the witness recounted the substance of two threats, the first being Crafton was "going to whip" Harrison on sight; the second being Crafton "was going to knock Peachy down and stomp him"; both threats, according to the witness, were communicated to Harrison.

Cross-examination by Mr. Palmer; Crafton told the witness he had been provoked by Harrison when he was making the threats.

Defense witnesses John Allen and Thomas Turley of Tallula; CALLED, SWORN AND EXAMINED by Mr. Lincoln about what they witnessed after the affray. Their testimony was uneventful; there was no cross-examination by Mr. Palmer.

Reverend Peter Cartwright; CALLED, SWORN AND EXAMINED by Mr. Lincoln lives in Pleasant Plains; went to the Crafton farmplace after the affray to console the family and the victim; Palmer objected to Lincoln's attempts to produce testimony from the witness about the dying declarations of Crafton. A warm debate took place out of the presence of the jury over Lincoln's protestations; the Judge listened carefully and intently to the arguments, both pro and con, for the competency of the testimony; after retiring to consider the relative merits of each argument, the Judge returned to the courtroom to announce his decision to receive the testimony over the People's objections; the witness was then asked to repeat his testimony in front of the jury and did so with intensity and emotion; the witness, Harrison's grandfather, testified that he was friendly to all parties and after consoling the family asked to speak to young Crafton alone; the family granted his request and Cartwright, kneeling down by his bedside and taking his hand, expressed his deep regret and sorrow "for the calamity that had fallen upon him"; Crafton then asked Cartwright if he thought "there would be any mercy" for him to which Cartwright again repeated his regret and sorrow at the young man's circumstances; Crafton then said, according to the witness, "I have brought it upon myself and I forgive Peachy"; Cartwright described young Crafton as "calm" and "composed" in relating his feelings; Cartwright testified that he left young Crafton's room to get some air and was then told that young Crafton wanted to speak to him again; upon returning, young Crafton stated again, "I have brought it upon myself. I forgive Peachy, and I want it said to all my friends that I have no enmity in my heart against any man and if I die I want it declared to all that I die in peace with God and all mankind".

Cross-examination by Mr. Palmer; when he went to the Crafton home he didn't know the seriousness of young Crafton's wounds; no one else heard what he related to the jury as Crafton's dying declarations; expressed disdain for the death penalty.

Mr. Lincoln having rested the case for the defense, the examination of the prosecution rebuttal witnesses then commenced.

Dr. J.L. Million, RECALLED by the prosecution and examined by Mr. Palmer; he didn't tell young Crafton his wounds were fatal; he talked to young Crafton about who inflicted his wounds; he was at the Crafton farmplace until Greek expired; during the time he was with young Crafton, Crafton did not absolve Harrison of his actions, but in fact censured Harrison because of Harrison's provocation of the incident.

Cross-examination by Mr. Logan; the witness was not with young Crafton every minute of his final hours; and did not hear the conversation between Cartwright and Greek.

In a bizarre turn of events, Mr. Palmer called Rebecca Watson to the stand. Logan and Lincoln asked to approach the bench whereupon Palmer, Logan and Lincoln spoke under hushed breath to Judge Rice. We can only assume that they were speaking about the witness, Rebecca Watson, but later attempts to confirm that fact from Mr. Logan were rebuffed. Judge Rice then adjourned court while the lawyers followed him to his chambers. After considerable delay, the attorneys and judge returned to the crowded courtroom. Rebecca Watson had taken a seat next to Sheriff Andrew and the Judge asked if there were any addition rebuttal witnesses for the prosecution. Palmer replied that there were none. Again, no explanation was given for the peculiar courtroom proceedings related above.

After another delay, the attorneys returned to the courtroom for their arguments to the jury. It was late afternoon. Mr. Palmer spoke with marked ability, evincing great ingenuity in handling the testimony, interspersing many remarks upon human nature and human passions, the duties of the citizens and the spirit of the law.

Mr. Lincoln proceeded at the meeting of the court in the evening to the final closing argument for the defense. His speech examined the evidence with great skill and clearness, discussing the law and replying to the positions assumed by counsel for the prosecution with a subtle and relentless logic and frequent illustrations of singular fitness. The argument was delivered in an earnest, natural and energetic manner.

At the conclusion of the argument, the jury, having been charged by the Judge in the law, retired in the care of Sheriff Andrew—it then being twelve minutes after seven o'clock. The crowd, which filled the courtroom, hall, stairway and balcony densely, anxiously awaited their return. At twenty-two minutes after ten o'clock, having been out three hours and ten minutes, the jury returned, and the foreman informed the court that they had agreed upon a verdict—at the same time banding it upon a slip of paper.

His honor, Judge Rice, opened it, and while every sound in the densely packed room was hushed, and every face filled with anxiety, he handed it back to the foreman to read: "We the jury, find the defendant *Not Guilty* as charged in the indictment." The announcement was greeted with loud and prolonged applause from the Harrison supporters. The Craftons and their supporters left the courthouse in disgust.

The prisoner, Peachy Quinn Harrison, was of course immediately discharged. Whereupon he was surrounded by his friends and received their congratulations with a countenance of joy, but with a grave and dignified reserve, well-befitting the occasion.

But the Craftons were not through. Furious over the not guilty verdict, John Crafton went to Palmer's office first thing Monday morning. Drained from the intensely fought trial, Palmer was reading the *Springfield Register's* account of the closing arguments and verdict, trying not to second-guess his strategy and approach. He had received the publicity he wanted, but he had lost the biggest trial of his career, and the editorials were supportive of the jury's verdict. If only he could have called Rebecca Watson to the stand.

As Palmer finished the article, his clerk interrupted him to announce Crafton's presence. As they met, Palmer began with an apology. "I'm sorry, John. I did my best, but the jury obviously disagreed with us."

"This ain't right," Crafton pleaded. "Harrison's getting away with murder. Can't you arrest him again? Maybe manslaughter or assault?"

"John, we did the best we could. I don't know what else we could have done, but we can't charge him with anything else concerning your son's death. It would be double jeopardy."

"I told my sons we needed to let the law handle this," Crafton said, shaking his head. "I guess I should have let them…"

"John, don't try to take the law into your own hands. If you do, you may find yourself in jail," interrupted Palmer.

Jamison had entered the office unobserved during the conversation and was listening to Crafton's plea. "What else can I do?" asked Crafton.

"John, it's over," said Palmer.

"Ben Hart and the preacher did this. They lied and the jury believed them. Can't you have them arrested for lying?"

"No, John. I won't file that charge. We just need to put this behind us. I would like to stay and talk some more, but I have court in fifteen minutes," Palmer said, moving toward the door.

"Well, I'll see you," Crafton replied tersely as Palmer left the office.

"See you, John," Palmer said as the door slowly closed. "Tell your wife and sons I'm sorry."

Jamison reached for Crafton's hand. "John, come into my office. I have an idea," said Jamison.

"What is it, Mr. Jamison?" asked Crafton, still agitated.

"I think Hart and the preacher lied, too. That means they are guilty of perjury—a crime. Hart's also guilty of conspiracy, in my opinion."

John Crafton liked what he heard.

"He sold Peachy the knife and helped him get the advantage in his store, so Peachy could use it on Greek," Jamison continued. "Now, Sheriff Andrew won't arrest Hart or Cartwright without Palmer's say-so, but aren't you friends with Thomas Greene, the justice of the peace in that part of the county?"

"Why, yes," Crafton said, aroused. "We're friends. I done some metalwork for him."

"He has the legal power to arrest someone for a crime and once he does, the sheriff would be obliged to put the prisoner in the county jail to be held for trial. Then, I could prosecute him," Jamison said with a smile.

"I could see him first thing tomorrow," Crafton replied.

"I think you should. If you need me, I'll be here," Jamison said, extending his hand.

Crafton thanked Jamison and left Springfield for Ashland, where Justice of the Peace Greene lived. He made his case against Hart and Cartwright, and Greene agreed to take Hart into custody for the crimes of perjury and conspiracy to commit murder. But, Greene refused to arrest Cartwright because the reverend gave the sermon at Greene's mother's funeral. Arresting Hart pacified Crafton.

The following day, Greene went to Short & Hart's General Store and arrested Hart, who was taken to Springfield and turned over to a reluctant Sheriff Andrew. Outraged, Hart's partner, Nathan Short, went to the Harrisons about what had happened. In disbelief, they offered to go with Short to see Hart and obtain his release.

Virginia was devastated by the turn of events and wanted to do what she could to help her friend. She suggested that they go to Lincoln and seek his advice and counsel. But when they arrived at the law office, Lincoln was off campaigning, so Herndon agreed to see Hart at the jail.

Hart's initial appearance before the magistrate was scheduled for the following Monday. After Short hired Herndon to represent Hart, everyone stayed in Springfield until Hart's court date. When they arrived at the courthouse, they saw Jamison with Justice Greene and John Crafton. Virginia was incensed. *How could they treat such a good man this way?* she thought. Catching her eye in the courtroom before he presented the People's position on bail, Jamison grinned.

Magistrate William Farley opened court, calling the first case on the docket.

Magistrate Farley: Our first case this morning is the People versus Ben Hart—case number fifty-nine, eighty-nine. Mr. Jamison, are you representing the State?

Jamison: Yes, your Honor.

Magistrate Farley: Mr. Herndon, do you represent the prisoner?

Herndon: Yes, your Honor, I do.

Magistrate Farley: Very good. Mr. Hart, you are charged

with perjury and conspiracy to commit murder. How do you plead?

Herndon: The defendant pleads not guilty, your Honor.

Magistrate Farley: What's the People's position on bail?

Jamison: The People object to bail, your Honor. This matter involves the murder of Greek Crafton and these are most serious crimes.

Herndon: Your honor, Mr. Hart is an upstanding member of the village of Pleasant Plains. He is co-owner of the general store there. He has lived there for ten years. These charges are groundless, and a denial of bail would be most unfair.

Magistrate Farley: I'm familiar with this case, having read the newspaper. Mr. Hart doesn't appear to be a flight risk or risk to the public...to me...so I will set bail at one hundred dollars. This matter will be set for a probable cause hearing on September twenty-second. Any questions?

Jamison: No, sir.

Herndon: No, sir. Thank you. May I be excused?

Magistrate Farley: You may. Let's make room for the next case.

After court, Short posted Hart's bail and everyone met with Herndon outside the jail. Virginia was the first to speak. "Can they do this? This isn't right or fair."

"Legally, I'm afraid they can, Virginia," Herndon explained as he tucked a small book into his coat pocket. "The only thing we can do is hope Magistrate Farley will dismiss the case when he hears the evidence."

"That Jamison fellow did this to spite us," said Virginia.

"I'm sorry, Ben. It's all my fault," said Peachy, troubled about the situation.

"We'll be there for you like you were for us," Mary Rose said, recalling Peachy's trial.

"Damn right," said Peyton with uncharacteristic emotion.

Everyone returned to Magistrate Farley's court on Sept. 22 as instructed. Jamison and John Crafton were already seated in the courtroom when Hart and Herndon entered with the Harrisons. Magistrate Farley opened court as he had done at Hart's initial appearance and got right down to business.

Magistrate Farley: Let's see. The accused is charged with perjury and conspiracy to commit murder. A not guilty plea was entered and a probable cause hearing was set for today. Now, Mr. Hart, the People must establish to my satisfaction that there is probable cause to believe you committed the crimes of perjury and conspiracy to hold you for trial. Otherwise, the case will be dismissed. Do you understand?

Hart: Yes, sir, Judge.

Magistrate Farley: Very well. Mr. Jamison, are you ready to proceed?

Jamison: Yes, sir.

Magistrate Farley: Mr. Herndon, is the accused ready to proceed?

Herndon: Yes, your Honor.

Magistrate Farley: Let's take the perjury charge first. Summarize your proof for me, please, Mr. Jamison.

Jamison: Mr. Hart testified as a witness in the trial of Peachy Quinn Harrison, who was found not guilty of murder. At trial, Mr. Hart said that Mr. Greek Crafton was the aggressor and denied that John Crafton tried to step in front of Harrison before Harrison stabbed Greek. Mr. Hart made it appear that Harrison had no choice but to stab Greek.

Magistrate Farley: So, it was a swearing match between John Crafton and Mr. Hart?

Jamison: John…John Crafton knows what happened and Hart was in cahoots with Harrison to kill Greek.

Magistrate Farley: Is that all of the evidence you have on the perjury charge?

Jamison: I think that is enough to let a jury decide Mr. Hart's guilt on the perjury charge.

Magistrate Farley: Except for one problem, Mr. Jamison. To prove the perjury charge, you must satisfy the two-witness rule. Where is your second witness?

Jamison: Second witness?

Magistrate Farley: Yes. Where is your corroborating witness?

Jamison: I don't have one.

Magistrate Farley: In that case, I am dismissing the perjury charge.

Jamison: But…but…your Honor. The People object to a dismissal of the perjury charge.

Magistrate Farley: If you don't have another witness, your objection is overruled. Now, for the conspiracy count.

Jamison: There is a great deal of evidence on this charge, your Honor.

Magistrate Farley: Please share it with me, Mr. Jamison.

Jamison: Mr. Hart sold Peachy Harrison the murder weapon…a bowie knife…and supported Mr. Harrison's claim of self-defense by lying for him.

Magistrate Farley: I hear what you are saying, but I'm not sure that amounts to probable cause to believe Mr. Hart committed the offense of conspiracy to commit murder. Don't you have to have an agreement between them?

Jamison: That would be correct, but the agreement can be proved by circumstantial evidence, your Honor.

Magistrate Farley: What circumstantial evidence is there that Mr. Hart knew Mr. Harrison was going to stab Greek Crafton with the knife he bought from him?

Jamison: They were friends.

Magistrate Farley: I'll give you that much, but just being friends doesn't prove someone agreed to commit murder. What else?

Jamison: What else? Can I talk to Mr. Crafton?

Magistrate Farley: Yes, but be brief. I have a crowded docket today.

Jamison: Yes, sir.

Jamison leaned over and whispered to Crafton. "John, I don't think Magistrate Farley likes our case."

"He must be friends with the Harrisons or Lincoln," Crafton said tersely.

"What other evidence do we have?" Jamison asked.

"They killed my boy," Crafton said, red-faced.

"I know, John, but the judge is waiting," Jamison said nervously.

"You're the lawyer," said Crafton. Jamison turned toward an irritated Magistrate Farley.

Jamison: Judge, that would be our evidence.

Magistrate Farley: The conspiracy charge is dismissed as well. Mr. Hart, you are free to go.

Herndon: Thanks, Judge. May we be excused?

Magistrate Farley: You may.

Hart and the Harrisons watched Crafton berate Jamison as they quickly exited the courtroom. As Virginia passed Jamison, he caught her attention. "Hey, Missy, how are you doing today?"

Startled, Virginia replied, "I'm fine now."

"There will be another day," said Jamison, turning his attention again to Crafton.

⚜

After the Harrison trial, Lincoln worked hard to secure the Republican nomination for President. On Nov. 6, 1860, Lincoln was elected to be the 16th President of the United States of America. Preparing to leave his beloved hometown and law practice wasn't easy. Lincoln told his law partner to leave his name on the door of their law office. "If I live long enough, Billy, I expect to return to Springfield and practice law as if nothing had ever happened."

On Feb. 11, 1861, Lincoln made his way to the Springfield, Illinois, depot of the Great Western Railway for his long trip to Washington. In an unintended speech to a large crowd of friends and well-wishers gathered to bid him a fond good-bye, Lincoln spoke from the heart.

"My friends, no one…not in my situation…can appreciate my feeling of sadness at this parting. To this place, and to the kindness of these people, I owe everything. Here, I have lived a quarter of a century and have passed from a young to an old man. Here, my children have been born and one is buried. I now leave, not knowing when or whether I may return, with a task before me greater than that which rested upon Washington. Without the assistance of that divine being whoever attended him, I cannot succeed. With that assistance, I cannot fail. Trusting in him who can go with me and remain with you, and be everywhere for good, let us confidently hope that all will yet be well. To his care commending you—as I hope in your prayers you will commend me—I bid you an affectionate farewell."

As he turned to enter the train, Lincoln saw Virginia, who had separated from her family to find a better vantage point near the specially designed sleeping car. He motioned for her to come to the platform, where he hugged her tightly. Virginia spoke to Lincoln with a newfound reverence.

"I didn't think you would remember me, Mr. Lincoln. I know you will be a great President."

Lincoln glanced at her brilliant, sweet face and responded with heartfelt fondness and humility. "How could I forget such kind eyes, Virginia? I believe that I am up to the task. Perhaps you can write me and tell me how you think I am doing while I work to repair our divided Union."

Virginia couldn't find the words to answer him, but her eyes expressed her deep respect for him. He patted Virginia's shoulder as he kissed her on the forehead. Then he lowered his head and entered the back of the train.

Twenty-one days later, Lincoln was sworn in as President. Just over a month after his inauguration, the Civil War began.

CHAPTER 9

During his campaign for the Republican nomination, Lincoln made it clear that if elected, he would resist, with force if necessary, the promotion of slavery or the secession of the South from the Union. As he prepared for his inauguration, the passions of rebellion were being stoked into a raging fire. Sensing the nation's tension, Lincoln delivered an inaugural address of reason and pacification. But his efforts to repress the angry secessionists with words of reason had no effect on the South. From the time of his election to the day of his inauguration, there had been dissent and uncertainty, and the storm clouds of revolt grew more and more ominous.

Eventually, the South drew a line in the dirt, and the masses that made up the North dug in like a plow horse slowed by a mighty wind. Lincoln sent forth a call for volunteers and 75,000 loyal citizens, who were soon to become courageous soldiers, proudly answered his plea for help. The first to volunteer their services lived in the President's home state. They were the men who would eventually comprise the 7th Illinois Volunteer Infantry. The first company of 130 men stepped forward two days after the war began. The second company was organized four days later.

In Pleasant Plains, Peachy couldn't get over Greek's death. In spite of his acquittal, he grieved constantly over the fact that he had killed another man. His guilt was consuming him. *Did he provoke Greek? Did he need to stab him twice? Was it really about Rebecca?* These were questions he had a hard time denying.

Peachy counseled with his grandfather and shared his feelings with his mother, but their wise and tender words couldn't heal his festering wounds of the heart. His grandfather suggested that he go to the Craftons to express regret for what had happened. But they were still bitter, and their loss only made him feel worse. He felt guilty around Rebecca and began to distance himself from her. His family watched helplessly as he slipped into a life of melancholy.

In April 1861, Peachy informed his family he was joining the Union Army as a chaplain's assistant. Mary Rose and Virginia were crushed. They did all they could to convince Peachy to change his mind. The war, they believed, would be short-lived and there was no need to take the risk. But there was no reasoning with Peachy.

On the morning Peachy was to report for duty, the Harrison family piled into the wagon for the trip to Springfield. The Cartwrights had come to tell Peachy good-bye. As they started to leave the only place Peachy knew as home, his grandfather approached the overflowing wagon. "Godspeed, Peachy," he said.

"Don't worry, Grandpa," Peachy said, throwing his cloth satchel in the back of the wagon. "I'll be fine. When President Lincoln's volunteers face the rebs, they'll hightail it all the way back to Mississippi."

"Can't say that I disagree with you, son," said Rev. Cartwright. "I just want you to be careful."

"I will. I promise, Grandpa."

"Peachy, I'm very proud of your decision to volunteer for the infantry and for choosing to become a chaplain's assistant. Rev. Davis is a good man. You can learn a lot about the Good Book…and spreading the Word…from him."

"He seems like it, Grandpa."

"Peachy, I want to show you something. Your great-grandpa worked for the Great Western Railway for a time when the railroad was first forging its way west. He used this pocket watch to make sure the train was always on time. And I want you to have it…"

"No…No…I couldn't," Peachy interrupted.

"I insist, son. I insist. At seven o'clock every day, we're going to pray for you and all the soldiers in this unnecessary war, and we want you to be able to stop what you're doing and join us in prayer," Rev. Cartwright said as he rubbed the gold heirloom on his vest.

"Grandpa, I don't know what to say. I'll keep it with me always."

"Just don't let it run down," said Rev. Cartwright with a grin.

"I'll wind it first thing every morning," said Peachy as he fastened the watch chain to his suspenders and slid the timepiece into his trouser pocket.

The two men embraced. Peachy had made that a habit with his grandfather. Then he hoisted himself up next to his father, and the frisky farm horses lurched forward as the lines slapped their sturdy brown backs.

As the Harrisons arrived at Company G headquarters in Springfield, they were met by a lanky first sergeant. "You one of our new recruits?" asked the sergeant, obviously in a hurry.

"Yes, sir, I'm Peachy Quinn Harrison," said Peachy, snapping to attention.

"Well, recruit, grab your gear and follow me."

Peachy turned to face his family. He knew this wouldn't be

easy. Mary Rose, who had been fighting back tears for two weeks, couldn't check her emotions. She wrapped her arms firmly around her son as tears gently slid down her cheeks.

"I've almost lost you twice, Peachy. I can't bear the thought of what might happen to you."

"I've got to do this, Ma. I can't have any peace if I don't," Peachy confessed.

"Gettin' yourself killed won't help things, son," said Mary Rose, wiping her face.

"I don't plan on gettin' killed. I just want to help folks get through this the best I can. Maybe restoring a man's faith will save his life as well as my soul."

"Please be careful, Peachy," Virginia said as she put her arm around her mother.

"I will, Virginia. Lord willin' and the creek don't rise, I'll see you in a few months."

The sergeant was growing impatient. Peachy quickly gave his father and brother a firm handshake, kissed Virginia and his mother, and jogged off. He was led into the quartermaster's tent to take an oath of allegiance, sign his induction papers and be issued his uniform, knapsack and rifle.

"Private Harrison, you have been issued property of the United States of America and we expect you to take care of it," said the gruff quartermaster.

"Yes, sir," said Peachy again, snapping to attention.

"Each man is purchasing a sixteen-shot Henry repeating rifle for fifty dollars that will come out of your thirteen dollars-a-month pay. The volunteers offered to pay for their rifles—the sixteen-shooters—to give us an edge," said the quartermaster proudly.

"Rifle?" asked Peachy.

"Why, yes, young man. How do you expect to fight the rebs

without a rifle?" asked the quartermaster incredulously.

The sergeant held his hand over his mouth to hide his grin.

"I don't want to shoot nobody," said Peachy softly.

"Well, how do you expect to fight without a gun?" barked the quartermaster as he sat down in disbelief.

"But, I don't want to fight nobody," said Peachy, shaking his head.

"You don't want to fight nobody?"

The sergeant was now becoming concerned himself.

"Son, why did you volunteer?" asked the quartermaster.

"I'm going to be a chaplain's assistant," Peachy explained. "If you will send for Chaplain Davis, he will explain everything."

Before it was over, Peachy had the sergeant, quartermaster, Chaplain Davis and the company lieutenant engaged in a spirited argument about whether he would be required to carry a rifle. It was finally decided that Peachy would purchase and carry a rifle, but he didn't have to shoot it at anyone if he didn't want to. Everyone seemed satisfied with that arrangement.

As the process continued, Chaplain Davis told Peachy it would be good for him to go through basic training so he could understand the duties, obligations and priorities of a soldier. "Peachy, my role here is to ease human suffering, when needed. Counsel the soldiers, when requested. Administer to the injured and dying and perform all religious services for the regiment, if asked. There's no book I know of that tells you the right way to do your job. So just watch me and do what's in your heart and what you think's right."

Listening to Chaplain Davis, Peachy knew his grandfather was right about him. "I hope I'm up to this," said Peachy.

"You're from good stock, my son. This will be demanding, but I'm confident you can do it. By the way, how's that reprobate grandfather of yours?"

"Just as ornery as ever," Peachy retorted.

"Oh! One more thing," Chaplain Davis said seriously. "Don't forget to write your ma."

"Religiously," quipped Peachy.

⁂

On April 25, 1861, the regiment of the 7th Illinois, with 35 officers and 1,500 foot soldiers, was mustered into service. The men left for Alton, Illinois, where they were housed as comfortably as possible in the old state penitentiary. Peachy noted with interest how the soldiers, who were eager for battle, were instead bedded down in a home for criminals. They volunteered for a war intent on stamping out a threat to the Union and now they found themselves in the dark recesses of an old jail. But they made the best of it, marching every day and drilling tirelessly in the handling of their weapons and the strategy of warfare.

After several weeks in Alton, the 7th boarded a steamer for Cairo, where the soldiers camped at Camp Defiance. From Cairo, the regiment marched to Mound City, where the troops camped on the lush banks of the Ohio River. These were the quiet days of the 7th, although Peachy was able to study Chaplain Davis as he presided over the burial of two men who perished in unfortunate training accidents.

On the Fourth of July, the regiment marched to a scenic grove on the river to listen to a reading of the Declaration of Independence by the commanding colonel. The reading was preceded by Chaplain Davis' sermon on the virtues of loyalty to country after acknowledging a loyalty to God. Peachy listened and learned while the men's spirits were lifted, but silently he wondered if the men could ever square killing another man with loyalty to God.

Later in the month, the regiment's brief period of enlistment came to a close. An overwhelming majority of the disappointed soldiers re-enlisted for three more years. After hearing the story of the Battle of Bull Run, where the Union soldiers were soundly defeated, the men longed to carry the Union flag south.

After returning to Camp Defiance, the regiment boarded a steamer destined for the Mississippi River. Floating the muddy waters, they landed at Sulphur Springs, Missouri. They were now on rebel soil. The soldiers were loaded on a train bound for Ironton, Missouri, where they were greeted by Gen. Benjamin M. Prentiss.

"Men," the general barked, "you have been ordered here to help me drive Confederate General Jeff Thompson from Missouri."

Peachy was captivated by the beauty of the peaceful-looking countryside. It was hard for him to conceive that the tranquil valleys and rolling hills could soon erupt into a scene of Americans fighting Americans to the death.

For many days and nights, the 7th dutifully followed Gen. Prentiss in his relentless pursuit of the elusive Gen. Thompson. They marched over hills and streams, stumbling over the loose rocks, through the towns of Fredericktown and Jackson as they forged their way to Cape Girardeau. It was there the expedition ended, for Gen. Thompson had already made his well-planned exit south.

On Sept. 26, President Lincoln proclaimed a national fast. Chaplain Davis delivered a superb sermon, Peachy thought, on the high ideals of their mission and how they would soon go into battle with God on their side. Their faithful spirits, however, gave way to stark reality when one of the 7th's officers died of typhoid fever that very evening. The following day, with Peachy assisting Chaplain Davis, he was buried with full military honors.

Orders were eventually received for the regiment to march to

Fort Holt, Kentucky, to relieve the 17th Illinois Infantry. New orders to follow the river toward Columbus, Kentucky, came after a month of drilling and building houses at Fort Holt. Naval transports, which were loaded with troops and headed downriver, caught the attention of the soldiers methodically marching along the pristine shore. Something was brewing.

The 7th traveled as far as Elliot's Mill before receiving orders to remain there until further notice. After their second anxious day in camp, the soldiers heard the unmistakable thunder of cannons. A battle was raging. This marked the first time the dreadful sounds of war had fallen upon the untested regiment's ears.

An eerie silence enveloped the 7th while it patiently waited for orders to move forward into the fight. The regiment was eagerly awaiting its chance to buttress its brothers when an exhausted messenger arrived with a dispatch. Gen. Grant had fought the great Battle of Belmont and had been forced into retreat. Now, an overwhelming enemy force was bearing down on the 7th. Hurriedly, the regiment retreated to Fort Holt.

The following day, holding a flag of truce, a contingency of soldiers made its way down the river to the battlefield of Belmont to search for the dead and wounded. Sixty-four Union soldiers had been killed. Their remains were cremated on the spot where they died. As the flames leaped off the burning bodies and the wretched odor of flesh filled the air, Peachy prayed for the war's end. *Would the families of the dead ever see their final resting place? Did these men die in vain?* These questions haunted him.

The 7th remained safe at Fort Holt until Jan. 13, 1862, when it received orders to march to Landville, Kentucky, to join Gen. John McClernand's division. The plan was to move back to Columbus. As the campfires danced on the fields as far as his eye could see, Peachy wondered what the future would hold for the 7th. All indications were that Gen. Grant was planning another advance. Peachy could do nothing but survey the fields and feel sad. He knew that some of those who slept contentedly on the damp ground, with a yellow moon casting its soft light on their faces, would fall forever silent in the days to come.

The following morning, Peachy and the thousands of soldiers around him received the much-anticipated word to move forward. As they began their fateful march, it started to rain. They marched through thick mud and rain all day to arrive at their swampy campsite in the Mayfield Creek bottoms. The creek was rising and their food supplies were running low. The officers' training told them the situation looked critical. For two days, the men endured the rain and the cold, expecting orders to attack. But once again, the 7th faced disappointment. Orders were received to move back to Fort Holt.

On Feb. 3, the frustrated men boarded a new steamer for an undisclosed destination. At full speed, they traveled up the Ohio River past Paducah, Kentucky, and, as the beautiful dawn broke upon the steamer's polished decks, they found themselves on the Tennessee River with thousands of Union soldiers.

Rumor had it that Fort Henry was their final destination. With gunboats running interference for six steamers filled with men, the men finally witnessed Fort Henry's formidable walls and the flaunting Confederate Stars and Bars. Four miles from the fort, 10,000 anxious troops were staged awaiting orders. Everything felt warlike. As the hours ticked by, the campfires burned dimly while the cold rain drenched the nervous troops. Then, the gray clouds separated and the Tennessee sky became clear. The warm sun began to dry the camp and lift the men's spirits.

The 7th was assigned to the rear of the fort. From a nearby bluff, it surveyed its first rebel camp along with white smoke and a deep roar from the Union gunboat *Essex*. But the thick Tennessee mud frustrated the 7th's attempts to position its heavy artillery. It wasn't long before the ranks began to accept the fact that they were only going to be unwilling spectators at a fierce naval battle. Wanting to help, the 7th spent the day marching, with the thunder of the cannons behind it to cut off the rebel retreat. It was too late. Fort Henry had fallen and the battered rebels had quickly scattered. That night, the 7th camped in the cold woods, crushed that it had not contributed to the battle. But a rebel flag fell that day, and the soldiers were satisfied with that.

At daybreak, the troops dug 30 mangled and lifeless Confederate soldiers out of the destruction. The mutilated mass of humanity had fallen that day, Peachy mused, fighting against their old flag—against the country that nurtured them and their families in the caring arms of liberty. Rev. Cartwright was right. It was a needless and senseless war. Peachy prayed for the fallen rebel soldiers and returned to the soothing bivouac fires of Company G.

Over the next four days, another 10,000 troops landed at Fort Henry. Campfire talk was that the next assault would be on Fort Donelson. The rumor proved true. With banners flapping and flags flying, the 7th could hear the familiar report of artillery cannons as it slowly approached the Tennessee stronghold. The battle had already begun. The 7th camped two miles from the fort and remained there all night.

With the morning sunrise, after gulping down a breakfast of weak coffee and stale bread, the 7th formed a crisp battle line.

"Forward!" shouted Col. Willoughby Babcock. After a short distance, the colonel ordered the men to halt. "Unsling knapsacks and draw overcoats. Move forward double-quick time," he yelled, drawing his pistol.

Over a small hill and down a ravine, the men found the enemy. Simultaneously, a concealed rebel artillery battery met them with a savage barrage of cannon fire. The men instinctively hesitated, but Col. Babcock calmed them with a command to "stand fast."

Company G flanked the enemy battery and silenced its deadly guns. But it cost the 7th one of its faithful volunteers.

The officers considered it a miracle that more men weren't lost, but Peachy and Chaplain Davis were not consoled. The tragedy of the soldier's death was multiplied by the cold, dark February night. The regiment had been ordered to refrain from building fires because the general did not want to give away the troops' position. As the night wore on, the winter winds blew and it began to rain. Then the rain changed to sleet and snow. Some of the soldiers had no blankets; others tried to keep from freezing by pacing up and down a nearby hill. The hours seemed like days as the miserable soldiers waited for dawn.

The welcomed morning light brought warm campfires. Peachy was shivering as he stood with the men of Company G and shook his head in disbelief. To a man, even with their wet clothes and frozen blankets, heavy with ice, he heard no complaints. Looking into their suffering faces—young men of unwavering devotion to country and the cause of liberty—he felt proud to be in their midst.

It wasn't long before the rebels came into range again. Their cannonballs whizzed over the soldiers' heads, snapping off treetops and creating deadly spears in the woods around them. The Union gunboats continued to test the resolve of the fortified rebels. But only the Union sharpshooters fired back as the men of the 7th waited for the order to attack. The order was slow to come, the siege continued throughout the day and the soldiers suffered through another night of cold and snow. On the third day, the winter clouds disappeared. The calmness of the clear morning sky was short-lived, however, when the battle began to rage again. This time, the men of the 7th quickly buckled for certain conflict.

Moving swiftly through the woods behind its old, tattered flag, the regiment found itself in the middle of the fray. Peachy was horrified to see blankets of grapeshot and canister ball cutting their hellish paths through the packed ranks of the 7th as the brave men followed their standard over the walls of the fort. "Fort Donelson is ours!" shouted the Union soldiers. A white flag appeared, followed by an unconditional surrender of the rebel force and its munitions of war.

But the 7th had suffered casualties. Peachy and Chaplain Davis moved among the wounded soldiers, ministering to them and treating their injuries. The men of Company I told Peachy and Chaplain Davis that one of the dead was Capt. Noah E. Mendell. Mendell had been seriously wounded in the Battle of Fort Henry, but he'd ignored the surgeon who had forbid him from going into battle at Fort Donelson.

Mendell told his men that his first lieutenant would take command of the company and he would follow them "as long as he had strength." Because of his injuries, he was unable to buckle his sword belt around his waist. So he buckled it around his neck instead. Following close behind his company, he waved his sword above his head, cheered his men and told them to stand by their brave leader. But as the company moved forward, hissing grapeshot found its mark. A missile entered Mendell's head just beneath his right ear and exited immediately through the center of his left ear. He died instantaneously.

During Capt. Mendell's moving funeral service, Peachy listened to Chaplain Davis eulogize his death while face-to-face with the enemies of his country. "Men, a more gallant and patriotic soldier you will not find. He died as all of you would wish to die in this noble calling. You are all aware of this martyr's acts of bravery and heroism, and of his unwavering Christian beliefs, but I do not want you to leave this place without knowing something about this fine soldier's life before his time on earth was cut short by the deadly musket shot."

The men were hungry for details about their hero. "Capt. Mendell would have liked you to know that he was born in Blairsville, Pennsylvania, on November nine, eighteen thirty-seven. Consequently, he was in his twenty-fifth year at the time of his brave and glorious death. He had a lovely wife and two precious daughters. His mother died when he was just a child, but he leaves a brother—a professor at West Point—and a loving father and sister to mourn his untimely death.

"He was among the first to offer his services when the call was made for volunteers, and he was a long and respected member of Capt. John Cook's state militia company, the Springfield Zouave Grays. Upon Capt. Cook's promotion to colonel, Capt. Mendell rose to second lieutenant, in which capacity he served during three months of service. At the close of that service, he was unanimously chosen captain for three years of service." Some of the men were now moved to tears.

"Capt. Mendell is sleeping silently now. May he sleep peacefully and may the brave men of his company, should they in the coming years pass his grave, tread lightly there and shed a silent tear to his memory. His remains will be sent home to the Springfield Cemetery. We give him as a martyr to the loyal people of Springfield, and the 7th, especially his noble Company I, prays that God have mercy on his soul."

The men of Company I filed by Capt. Mendell's pine casket, touching the freshly sawed wood ever so gently as Chaplain Davis finished. Peachy took note of Chaplain Davis' words and demeanor since he was assigned the task of visiting each of the wounded soldiers. He didn't know what to say or do, but Chaplain Davis assured him if he would speak to each man as if he were that man's brother, the right words would come. Peachy accepted the instructions and set out on faith to make his visits.

On the whole, the soldiers were receptive to his contacts and appreciative of his concern, but one would trouble Peachy more than the others. The soldier received a head wound when grapeshot ricocheted off his cannon and grazed the left side of his forehead.

"Hey, soldier. How you feeling?" asked Peachy as he entered a crudely constructed lean-to.

"Not too damn good, but I'll make it. Head's a achin' and I can't stop the confounded bleedin'," said the soldier, pressing a bloodstained bandage to his wound.

"Let me take a look at that," said Peachy, reaching for the bandage.

"You a doctor?" asked the soldier as he recoiled from Peachy's reach.

"No, I'm the assistant chaplain."

"Then what the hell do you think you're doin'?" snapped the soldier.

"Well, I…I thought I might be able to help…" Peachy stammered.

"Unless you know how to stitch me up, you better stick to preachin'," interrupted the soldier.

"I'm sorry, friend." Peachy was now operating on instinct. "I didn't mean to offend you."

"No offense taken. I just don't put much stock in preachers…that's all," said the soldier, standing up slowly.

Peachy hadn't expected this. "Why not?" he asked.

"The ones I knowed do a lot of talking, but I ain't never seen much doin'," said the soldier as he sat on his cannon wheel.

Peachy was stumped. He had not known any preachers except his grandfather and Chaplain Davis. Each had set a fine example for him and others, and he had never thought of a minister not being like them. So he decided to change the subject. "Where you from?" Peachy asked, smiling.

"My family—what I have left of 'em—lives in Pennsylvania. I moved to Illinois six years ago." The soldier looked at the bloody bandage as he removed it from his forehead.

"Six years! How old are you?"

"Sixteen."

"Sixteen! Where do your mother and father live?"

"They're dead," said the soldier matter-of-factly.

"What happened?"

"They were kilt when we was crossin' the Mississippi River," the soldier recalled. "My sister drowned, too. The current caught the barge the wrong way and our wagon tumpt over. I floated ashore on my mama's kitchen table. My cousin carried me to Springfield, where I got a job in the foundry."

"At ten years old!" Peachy couldn't imagine the soldier's fear.

"Had to do something," said the soldier, giving the only response he could.

"Where did you live?"

"With the owner's brother. I worked at the foundry till I joined the infantry."

"Why did you join?"

"For the thirteen dollars a month and three square meals. They told me I could make more iffin' I got a promotion."

Struggling for the right words, Peachy told the soldier he hoped his wound got better soon and that he would find him the following day if he had no objection.

"Ain't you gonna ask me to pray with you?" asked the soldier as Peachy turned to walk away.

"I...I...I...well, I guess, if you want me to." How could he forget such a thing?

"Don't reckon I need it today. I took care of myself most of my life. Maybe you better save it for the man that's fixin' to meet his Maker." The soldier was in his element.

"As you wish," said Peachy, disappointed in his own perform-
ance. "If you change your mind, just let me know."

Breaking a slight smile, the soldier said, "I will, preacher."

As Peachy walked away, he thought to himself, *Thirteen dollars a month and three meals a day. I thought everybody joined
this army to save the Union. And, I didn't even ask him his name.*
Kicking himself for doing a poor job with the soldier, Peachy
promised himself that he would do better the next day.

The following day, Peachy headed to the soldier's campsite but
found that he had been transferred to another company. Peachy
wanted another chance to give the soldier a friend to lean on.
Perhaps he would see him again.

After four days in camp recovering from the battle at Fort
Donelson, the 7th boarded a steamer that carried the troops up the
Cumberland River. The cliffs, valleys and rolling hills adorned
with splendid cedars were awe-inspiring. Negroes, proudly waving the Union flag, flocked to the shore to watch their deliverers
steam up the river. Pleasant weather and peaceful scenes were
enough to cause the men to forget they were in the throes of war.

But the two weeks on the crowded steamer came to an end at
Pittsburg Landing. It was a beautiful Sabbath morning on April 6,
1862. "The dews have gone to Heaven and the stars have gone to
God," said Peachy as he admired the early morning sky inlaid
with crimson. The men had barely awakened when they heard the
rattle of muskets and the familiar roar from the cannon's mouth.
The 7th marched to the front line, where the soldiers were ordered
to lie down behind a well-constructed rail fence as the belching
rebel cannons began plowing deep lanes in the Union ranks.

As the fighting intensified, the Army of the Tennessee struggled desperately. The odds were decidedly against it. The Union
regiments began yielding position after position with the 7th following suit. The 7th even risked capture at one point when it was

so far in the front that it was stranded without support. Confusion reigned. Brave men were falling to the ground like raindrops. But the Army of the Tennessee fought on even as it was being methodically driven back toward the river.

Positioned only a quarter of a mile from the river, Grant formed his last line of defense. Everyone understood that if the line was broken, the battle would be lost and the Army of the Tennessee would be killed or captured. The rebel general, Albert Sidney Johnston, began making his preparations for an all-out final assault against an army that had been retreating all day. As Peachy gazed upon the gleaming bayonets along the 7th's line, he knew that every man would give all he had that day.

The armies clashed on Shiloh's plain. The sun was dulled by the heavy smoke. As sunset found its way to the battlefield, each army was holding its own. Like Napoleon at Waterloo, who prayed that nightfall or Blucher would save him, the Army of the Tennessee prayed that nightfall or Gen. Don Buell's Army of the Ohio would come to save them. Gen. Johnston made one last desperate push, but as the sun set, the battered Army of the Tennessee was still stubbornly holding its line.

With night, reinforcements came, and Peachy and Chaplain Davis led the men in prayer, thanking God for the Army of the Ohio. As darkness engulfed them, it began to rain. Members of the 7th, exhausted from the bloody battle, dropped to the ground, oblivious to the driving rain. While they slept, many wounded soldiers would die.

At daybreak, the weary soldiers were reminded that the battle was far from over. The weather had cleared, and the Army of the Ohio and the Army of the Tennessee were driving the rebels back as the battle raged furiously. For the 7th, there was destined to be yet another day of bloodshed. Thousands of Union bayonets flashed in the blazing sunlight until the rebel army was in full retreat. As night came, the great battle of Shiloh was over. Thirteen thousand soldiers had been killed or wounded over the two days of fighting.

Peachy and Chaplain Davis were particularly heartsick over the heavy losses sustained by the 7th. Fourteen men lost their lives and 43 were wounded. Large parties commissioned from each regiment began the grisly work of burying the dead of both armies. There was no way Peachy and Chaplain Davis could spend time over each soldier's grave, which troubled them greatly. Shiloh was turned into one vast graveyard, and they knew that when family members made the pilgrimage there to pay tribute to the dead, they would not be able to recognize the graves of the soldiers as fighters for or against the Stars and Stripes. For the next 20 days, the men of the 7th languished in a deplorable camp near a battlefield producing a sickening odor of rotting flesh. And with each passing day, the sick list grew longer.

Peachy became dazed by the death and suffering. He assisted Chaplain Davis at a mass service, where the dead soldiers were buried in one grave. For the next eight days, Peachy ministered to the wounded—some of whom were delirious with pain from the loss of limbs or eyes and serious head wounds.

On April 29, 1862, the 3rd Brigade, consisting of the 7th, 50th and 47th Illinois, and the 22nd Ohio marched from Pittsburg Landing in the direction of Corinth, Mississippi. Six days later, the 7th assumed a position near Corinth at the base of the Confederate Army, which was commanded by Gen. Pierre Gustave Toutant Beauregard.

While they waited, Peachy saw the men open mail and receive their hard-earned pay. Both brought pleasant smiles to the faces of the weary soldiers and a temporary reprieve from their duties. But there would be no battle. For two days earlier, the rebels blew up their magazines and ordnance stores as they evacuated their position. Peachy was more than grateful. He didn't think he could bear seeing another field like Shiloh. Instead, the soldiers moved to occupy the position the retreating rebels had held the day before.

Poking around the abandoned campsite, Peachy discovered some papers obviously overlooked in the rebels' hasty departure. While sorting through them, his eye caught a neatly folded letter, composed by a young woman and addressed to her sister. Peachy hesitated reading the private letter, not wanting to tread on the privacy of the two women, but the first few lines captivated him.

YANKEEVILLE, April 22nd, 1862

My Dear Sister:

As it may be a very long time before we again have an opportunity to write to you, Ma has made us all promise to write you a long letter; so if a thick packet comes to hand (provided it is not kidnapped), you need not be surprised.

You see by the dating of my letter that we have moved family, house servants and all into Yankeeville. We are only about one hundred miles farther from you than when we lived at Huntsville. The portion of the United States that we live in is decidedly in the most out-of-the-way place I have ever seen. Although the cars seem to run regularly, there is never a breath of news to gladden our hearts. I declare I have not seen a newspaper for two weeks and expect if I were to see one now, I should regard it as a supernatural appearance and be frightened to death.

The Rev. Mr. Wilson is here and preached for

us and was not so partial to the President of the
C.S.A. He prayed the Lord to look down upon us in
mercy as we then stood before Him, political enemies. The church was half filled with officers,
brass buttons and black feathers, strange to say,
looking as calm and collected after their exploits
as a pan of buttermilk.

I wish you could see them as they pass the
gate; sometimes on horseback, forty or fifty of
them together, with their long, murderous swords
encased in brass and dangling with terrific
clamor against the horses' sides, which produces
an effect so frightening that our faces are fear
blanched with terror, and we instinctively pull
our sunbonnets over our faces and stop our ears
with our fingers, that we may shut out as much
as possible the humiliating noise.

Do you not shudder when you think that we
are in the hands of these ruffians? We expect
every night that the town will be either shelled or
burnt, and when I wake up in the morning, I am
surprised to find myself safe and that the shells
have not yet been hurled this way; then I say to
myself in the most thankful and cheery way,
"Good morning, dear. I'm glad to see you're all
here." I miss dear little Huntsville so much, and
often think of the times we used to have swinging
together on the porch every night.

Here the streets are so guarded that one dare
not go beyond the dwelling houses, and as to
singing in concert, the town is too full of
Yankeedoodles ever to attempt it. Oh! How I long

*to see our dear soldiers again. Although I have
no near kindred in the army, each one of them is
as dear to me as a brother.*

*All our girls are proud and brave and never
lose faith. They give no quarters to the Yankees,
and as one of them remarked, "He hadn't seen a
woman smile since he had been here." But how
can we smile and be gay in their presence, when
our hearts are with Charley, over the water? If
you see any of my soldier friends up your way,
please tell them to come and escort us back. We
cannot return without protection. There is a
large party of girls here who would come with
me, and who will join us.*

*Our political canoe has run aground, and
the no-secession waves run so high that it is dangerous for a party of females to brave them
without some trusty arm to guard the vessel's bow.
I wish I could see you all. We ought not to be separated. Kiss my brother and take good care of
him, for men are so precious these war times.*

*Your loving sister,
Elizabeth*

❦

Remaining in the area for months, the 7th drilled and took turns
on the picket line. And it patrolled the area around Corinth to foil
any rebel surprise attacks. The men built houses to shield themselves from the sun's scorching rays and traded with Southern
sympathizers who brought fruit, milk, chickens and eggs. Poring
over newspapers denouncing the South and heaping praise on

President Lincoln for having the courage and wisdom to issue the great Emancipation Proclamation, the soldiers' spirits were lifted.

On Oct. 3, 1862, the 7th received orders to march in double-quick time to Corinth. A rebel force of about 25,000 men was in front of them. It joined forces with the rest of the 3rd Brigade and the four regiments formed a new line of battle. Following the quick reaction, there was a seemingly endless lull. The heat was insufferable. The men had no water and were famished. Some of the soldiers of the 7th collapsed in their tracks, fainting and exhausted under the roasting sun.

Then, without warning, the men were again ordered to advance. Reaching within themselves, they swept through the woods like a frightful wildfire. After making progress in forcing the rebels back, a fresh group of Confederate troops was hurled against their flanks, compelling them to make a hasty retreat. The battle raged furiously and the thick woods surrounding Corinth were consumed by smoke and fire. Ordered by the general to move to the rear of the division and rest, the 7th reluctantly fell back. Another regiment was ordered to take its place, and the fighting continued until dark.

By 8 a.m., the soldiers of the South gathered at the edge of the woods and charged the line of the 7th. A fierce battle followed. The charging rebel column was overwhelming, and the 7th was driven back yet again. Then the regiment rallied and seemed determined to hold its line. Reckless cannon shells were making deep furrows in the earth. The air was full of whistling miniés. Smoke from the cannons was everywhere, and everything seemed to be wrapped in flames. For a short while, the rebels reeled from the regiment's determined front and it threw them into confusion. But they reformed and made a charge across an open field in terrible array. The situation looked grim and an officer cried out, "O, noble Seventh! Stand the storm...it won't last long!" Peachy couldn't help but think that the battle was surely lost.

Then, the 7th saw the 2nd Division swing around and hurl volley after volley of grapeshot and cannonballs into the flanks of the enemy. The rebel lines began to waver. Col. Babcock ordered the 7th to move firmly forward with all of its might. The enemy buckled and began to be driven back from Corinth's field. Finally, a rebel retreat rang out and shouts of victory were heard through the Union ranks. When the 7th laid down to rest in the bloodstained field, six of its number had been killed, 43 were wounded and 21 had been taken prisoner.

As they had done many time before, Peachy and Chaplain Davis made their way through the wounded. They ministered to the men who had received severe head wounds, amputated limbs and disfiguring wounds to the face. It was a heart-wrenching sight. The following morning, the regiment passed over the battlefield, giving chase to the rebel army. Lifeless bodies were scattered everywhere. The bodies had turned black, and the soldiers turned their heads as they walked past the dreadful and sickening scene.

After marching all day, the regiment set up camp in a sweet potato patch. The men ate well that night. The next morning, the soldiers moved to the great Mississippi pineries. As they marched, they easily captured hundreds of half-starved Confederate soldiers on a dusty road lined with broken wagons, tents, cooking utensils and blown-up caissons. After raiding a nearby plantation, the soldiers, in fine fettle, circled the campfires, eating their reward and enjoying their smoking pipes. They talked of home and the tranquil days that seemed so long ago.

Marching farther south the following day, Peachy watched in disbelief as the whole country was being foraged of anything that afforded subsistence. The South was practically in a state of starvation. Unable to stand by and do nothing, Peachy and the commissary sergeant took some meat to a family of six in a nearby village. As they approached the lady of the house, who was surrounded by five hungry children, she extended both arms, denying them entry.

"Oh dear," she said, recoiling like a frightened animal. "This is Yankee meat. I don't know whether I can eat Yankee meat or not. I fear it is contaminated." Peachy could hardly believe his ears.

"What cause is worth starvation?" Peachy replied as they left the home in disgust. Undeterred, the two men found several orphan children who were crying for something to eat and gave them bread and jerky.

Having succeeded in routing the rebel army in Mississippi, the 7th marched back to Corinth, where Peachy spent his evenings perusing the journal of a captured rebel officer on the orders of a company captain.

Saturday, October 4th. — An eventful day. At four o'clock a.m., our brigade was ordered to the left, about a quarter of a mile, and halted, where we deployed forward a skirmish line which kept up a constant fire. A battery in front of the right of our regiment opened briskly and the enemy replied in the same manner. The cannonading was heavy for an hour and a half. Our regiment laid down and stood it nobly. The shells flew thick and fast, cutting off large limbs and filling the air with fragments. Many burst within twenty feet of me. It was extremely unpleasant — and I prayed for forgiveness of my sins and made up my mind to go through the tempest.

Colonel Sawyer called for volunteers to

assist the Second Texas skirmishers. I volunteered and took my company. Captain Perkins and Lieutenant Munson being taken sick directly after the severe bombardment, I led the company all the time. I went skirmishing at seven-and-a-half and returned at nine-and-a-half. Two of Captain Foster's men were killed, but none of ours. The enemy fired very fast. We got behind trees and logs, and the way bullets did fly was unpleasant to see. I think twenty must have passed within a few feet of me humming prettily. Shells tore off large limbs, and splinters struck my tree several times. We could only move from tree to tree by bending low to the ground while moving. Oh! How anxiously I watched for the bursting of the shells when the heavy roar proclaimed their coming.

At nine-and-a-half o'clock, I had my skirmishers relieved by Captain Rouser's company. Sent my men to their places and went behind a log with Major Furger. At ten o'clock, the fight opened in earnest; this was on the right. In a few moments, the left went into action in splendid style. At fifteen minutes past ten, Colonel Rogers came by us only saying, "Alabama forces!" Our regiment with the brigade rose unmindful of shell or shot and moved forward, marching about two hundred and fifty yards, and rising the crest of a hill, the whole of Corinth with its enormous fortifications burst upon our view. The United

States flag was floating over the forts and in the town.

We were now met by a perfect storm of grape, canister, cannon and minié balls. Oh! God, I never saw the like. The men fell like grass. Giving one tremendous cheer, we dashed to the bottom of the hill on which the fortifications are situated. Here we found every foot of ground covered with large trees and brush. Looking to the right or left, I saw several brigades charging at the same time—what a sight! I saw men running at full speed, stop suddenly and fall on their faces, with their brains scattered all around; others with legs or arms cut off. I gave myself to God, and got ahead of my company. The ground was literally strewed with mangled corpses. One ball passed through my pants and cut twigs close by me. It seemed that by holding out my hand I could have caught a dozen bullets.

We pushed forward, marching as it were into the mouths of the cannon. I rushed to the ditch of the fort—I jumped into it, and half way up the sloping wall; the enemy was only two or three feet from me on the other side, but could not shoot us for fear of being shot themselves. Our men were in the same predicament. Only five or six were on the wall, and thirty or forty in and around the ditch. Catesby, my companion, was on the wall beside me. A man within two feet of me put his head cautiously up to shoot into the fort, but suddenly dropped his musket, and his brains were dashed in a stream over my fine coat, which I had in my arms. Several were killed and rolled down the embankment. This was done by a regiment of Yankees. Some of our men cried "put down the flag," when it was lowered or shot into the ditch. Oh! We were butchered like dogs—for we were not supported.

Someone placed a white handkerchief on Sergeant Buck's musket, and he took it to a port hole, but the Yankees snatched it off and took him prisoner. The men were falling ten at a time. The ditch being full, and finding that we had no chance, we, the survivors, tried to save ourselves as best we could. I was so far up I could not get off quickly; I do not recollect seeing Catesby after this, but think he got off before. I trust in God he has. I and Captain Foster started together, and the air was literally filled with hissing balls. I got about twenty steps as quick as I could, about a dozen being killed in that distance. I fell down and crawled behind a large stump. Just then I saw poor Foster throw up his hands and saying "Oh! My God!" jumped about two feet off the ground and fell on his face. The top of his head seemed to cave in, and the blood spurted straight up several feet. I could see men falling as they attempted to run; some with their heads blown to pieces and others with the blood streaming from their backs. Oh! It was horrible.

One poor fellow being almost on me, told

me his name and asked me to take his
pocketbook, and if I escaped to give it to his
mother and tell her that he died like a brave
man. I asked him if he was a Christian; he
said he was. I asked him to pray, which he
did with the cannons thundering a deadly
accompaniment. Poor fellow, I forgot his
request in the excitement. His legs were literally
cut to pieces. As our men retreated, the enemy
poured into us a terrific fire. I was hardly
thirty feet from the mouths of the cannons.
Minié balls filled the stump I was behind, and
the shells burst within three or four feet from
me; one was so near it struck me and burnt my
face with powder. The grapeshot knocked large
pieces from my stump; it was gradually wearing
away. I endured the horrors of death here for
one-half hour.

Our troops formed in line and advanced a
second time to the charge with cheers, but
began firing when about half way, and I had
to endure it all. I feigned death. I was between
our own and the enemy's fire. In the first
charge, our men did not fire a gun, but
charged across the ditch and up to the very
mouths of the cannons. But our boys were shot
down like hogs; they could not stand the storms
that came from the Yankees' thundering guns.
I had no chance whatever. All around me men
were surrendering. I could do no better than
follow suit; but thank God, I am unhurt;
nothing but a merciful providence saved me.

This entry, Peachy thought, was evidence enough of the terrible war he was witnessing and the desperation of the rebels who struggled for secession.

The 7th remained in camp at Corinth until Dec. 18, 1862, when it received orders to march for West Tennessee. Fifty miles from Corinth, the general discovered the enemy had evaded him. The troops returned to Corinth by rail to find that the railroads running from Corinth to Memphis, Tennessee, were cut by the Confederacy, thereby closing off any communications with the government. But more importantly, as a result of the loss of communications, the men were only issued half rations. Isolated from the rest of the world with no mail, no news and only half rations, the soldiers seemed indifferent to their situation, which surprised Peachy.

To address the shortage of food, Companies H and I were ordered to go on a foraging expedition with the division train. They made a general sweep of every farmhouse and plantation they could find and returned with a train loaded down with corn, hogs, sheep, chickens and geese. *More Americans left to starve while the soldiers gained nourishment*, Peachy thought.

Around the campfires that night, a general discussion broke out among the men as to the fitness of Lincoln's Emancipation Proclamation, set to take effect in 1863, declaring a chained race free by the stroke of one man's pen. Peachy was surprised to learn that the proclamation had its advocates and its detractors. Some of the men were fanatical in their praise of the proclamation while others bitter in its condemnation. Peachy prayed for the time when all men would embrace the proclamation as a powerful blow against the slaveholders' rebellion.

After being cut off from communications for two weeks, the soldiers were becoming anxious over the fact that their half rations would soon be gone. For a moment, however, they were distracted by the arrival of the mail, which miraculously found its way to the camp by Pony Express. After three weeks of half rations, the men were subsisting on corn obtained by foraging and, in part, by reminding each other of the stories their grandfathers handed down of the Revolution and the seemingly hopeless struggle for independence. It fortified them.

As the 7th was nearing the brink of starvation, the trains began running again to Corinth. The time in their secluded camp, hungry and without any mail or news from the North, gave Peachy an opportunity to study human nature. If a man had faults, they would surely surface under the stress, and if he had virtues, they would shine like the blade of a newly forged saber. Pleasantly, the noble traits were seen pouring out their light throughout the camp. Peachy believed that in camp, more than any other place, a man could be convinced of the reality of human corruption and at the same time be assured of the glory of human redemption.

As January slipped by, the men, growing weary in the cold, could ignore the bad coffee and the stale crackers if they could receive mail. It made them better soldiers. However, the mail also brought the sober news that a faction in Illinois wanted to stop the prosecution of the war and capitulate to the South. Sensing an adverse effect on morale, the officers of the various regiments met and drafted resolutions for Governor Yates in Springfield. A late-night session produced a document they could all embrace.

"Whereas, Our government is now engaged in a struggle for the perpetuation of every right dear to us as American citizens, and require the united efforts of all good, true and loyal men in its behalf: and whereas, we behold with deep regret the bitter partisan spirit that is becoming dangerously vindictive and malicious in our state, the tendency of which is to frustrate the plans of the federal and state authorities in their efforts to suppress this infamous

rebellion; therefore,

"*Resolved, That having pledged ourselves with our most cherished interests in the service of our common country in this hour of national peril, we ask our friends at home to lay aside all petty jealousies and party animosities, and as one man stand by us in upholding the president in his war measures, in maintaining the authority and the dignity of the government, and in unfurling again the glorious emblem of our nationality over every city and town of rebellion.*

"*Resolved, That we tender to Governor Yates and Adjutant General Fuller our warmest thanks for their untiring zeal in organizing, arming and equipping the army Illinois has sent to the field, and for their timely attention to the wants of our sick and wounded soldiers, and we assure them of our steady and warm support in their efforts to maintain for Illinois the proud position of pre-eminent loyalty which she now occupies.*

"*Resolved, That we have watched the traitorous conduct of those members of the Illinois Legislature who misrepresent their constituents—who have been proposing a cessation of the war, avowedly to arrange terms for peace, but really to give time for the exhausted rebels to recover strength and renew their plottings to divest Governor Yates of the right and authority vested in him by our state constitution and laws, and to them we calmly and firmly say, beware of the terrible retribution that is falling upon your coadjutors at the south, and that as your crime is tenfold blacker it will swiftly smite you with tenfold more horrors, should you persist in your damnable work of treason.*

"*Resolved, That in tending our thanks to Governor Yates, and assuring him of our hearty support in his efforts to crush this inhuman rebellion, we are deeply and feelingly in 'earnest.' We have left to the protection of the laws he is to enforce, all that is dear to man—our wives, our children, our parents, our homes—and should the loathsome treason of the madmen who are trying to wrest from him a portion of his just authority render it necessary in his opinion for us to return and crush out treason there, we will promptly obey a proper order so to do, for we despise a sneaking, whining traitor in the rear much more than an open rebel in front.*

"Resolved, That we hold in contempt, and will execrate any man who in this struggle for national life, offers factious opposition to either the federal or state government in their efforts or measures for the vigorous prosecution of the war for the suppression of this godless rebellion.

"Resolved, That we are opposed to all propositions for a cessation of hostilities, or a compromise other than those propositions which the government has constantly offered; 'Return to loyalty— to the laws and common level with the other states of the Union, under the constitution as our fathers made it.'

LIEUT. COL. PHILLIPS, 9th Illinois,
President.
T.N. LETTON, Adjutant 50th Illinois,
Secretary.

The resolutions had their desired effect on the soldiers, but Peachy and Chaplain Davis were now struggling with their office. The soldiers had become reckless in their faith. "Peachy," Chaplain Davis confided, "should the angel Gabriel receive a commission as chaplain to the 7th, he would surely give it up as a bad bargain." Chaplain Davis reached for a pen and parchment. "What would you say if I ask the colonel to have a regiment church service in the hall built by the men to take their meals?"

"That's a grand idea, chaplain," said Peachy with a sense of purpose.

Everything was arranged as if the men were in a church—with the obvious absence of an organ. An adept fiddler was substituted. Chaplain Davis' sermon was about war and its applications to the Gospel. His concluding remarks hit home.

"War is atheistic, heathenish, devilish…qualify it as you may with all that civilization and Christianity can do…it is yet the mightiest reaping machine in the harvest of hell. I do not say that God has nothing to do with its running. For we believe that hidden beneath the veil of human wrath, He directs every move to His own glory. But he who drives this terrible instrument is very apt to become like it, being barred as we are from civilization and the refining and ennobling influence of female society."

The men were engrossed in his words and left the hall searching their hearts for a way to do their duty and not become blunted to the Gospel.

When February dawned its first days, the soldiers received orders to march to Davenport Mills, in north Mississippi, to get lumber. On the way, they passed a line of weary refugees winding their way to Corinth to seek protection under the Union flag.

By the middle of February, the men received orders to march to Iuka, Mississippi. From there, they headed to Tuscumbia, Alabama, passing the war's devastating bane on the stately plantations there. The men had heard that the Alabama Union Cavalry and the Kansas Jayhawkers were on the warpath—their long-awaited day of retribution had finally arrived. They torched everything that would burn.

At Tuscumbia, the 7th was ordered to South Florence on the Tennessee River. The siege was short-lived and the city surrendered shortly after the regiment's arrival. The rebels had fallen back across Town Creek, and the Union soldiers marched to intercept them. But the enemy retreated into the mountains, leaving the Union Army in undisputed possession of the dazzling Tuscumbia Valley.

CHAPTER 10

The conversation with Lincoln at the Springfield train depot moved Virginia like no other. At 15, Virginia wanted the unheard of—to become Illinois' first woman courtroom lawyer. Her parents were stunned by the news. There were no women lawyers in Illinois—much less female trial lawyers. Women couldn't sit on juries and didn't have the right to vote. It just wasn't the way things were done. Virginia pleaded with her parents to let her try. After several discussions, in which her parents pointed out how she was going to be terribly disappointed and not taken seriously, they agreed to accompany her to see Lincoln's law partner, William Herndon.

Herndon graciously received the Harrisons and listened to Virginia's bold plan. Virginia pressed her case with conviction. "Did you know that the first woman lawyer was admitted as an attorney to Lord Baltimore in sixteen forty-three?" she argued.

"No, I didn't," said Herndon, impressed with Virginia's research. To everyone's surprise, when Virginia finished, Herndon announced his idea.

"Well, this…this is something I've never thought of, Virginia. I'm not sure if the Illinois Bar and Supreme Court would accept you or not, but this is what I intend to do. I'll write President

Lincoln and seek his counsel."

Virginia shot straight up from her seat, clapping and squealing. Herndon and the Harrisons couldn't help but laugh. Everyone enjoyed the moment. When the Harrisons left the office, Herndon shook his head thinking, *Damnedest thing I ever heard. The next thing you know, a woman will want to be governor.*

In light of the serious problems facing the nation, Herndon did not expect to hear from Lincoln for a very long time. Three months passed before a letter arrived from the Executive Mansion. Herndon recognized the handwriting instantly. Since he knew the letter was in response to his query for advice regarding Virginia, he decided to summon her to Springfield so they could read the letter together. Herndon was not afraid to disappoint Virginia because he knew she would listen to Lincoln's words and take them to heart.

They opened the letter together, each expecting a different response.

Dear Billy,

It was so pleasant to receive your letter. I am pleased the office is in good order.

I must say Virginia's idea is beyond novel. What would our colleagues and the Illinois Supreme Court say? At first, I thought the idea was unworkable. However, after mature reflection, I think she deserves the opportunity. If any woman can make a success of this ambitious venture, it would be Virginia. She definitely has the mind and work ethic for the law. But most of all, she has the will.

If I might make one suggestion, however. I think Virginia needs to be told to finish her schooling. After that occurs, and if you find it convenient, perhaps you could hire her at a fair salary to be our clerk.

I must conclude now, my friend. I have a meeting shortly where some of my cabinet members are going to question my sanity.

Your Faithful Friend,

A. Lincoln

Virginia needed a moment to grasp the meaning of Lincoln's message and was momentarily speechless. But as the realization of his words hit home, her astonishment turned to pure joy. "A clerk in the law office of Lincoln and Herndon!" Virginia blurted out. "This is like a dream come true. I'll work for free!"

But Herndon wouldn't consider it. He instructed Virginia to finish her schooling and then he would put her to work—for pay.

In the spring of 1862, Virginia began working as a clerk in the law offices of Lincoln and Herndon. Virginia's first day was, without a doubt, the most exciting day of her young life. Here she was—a small-town country girl from Pleasant Plains—working in the law office of the President of the United States. Unimaginable.

Because he was required to go to an adjoining county for court early that morning, Herndon left word that he would return by mid-afternoon to give Virginia specific instructions on the duties of a law clerk. It had been explained to Virginia that the firm's last clerk had moved to Chicago to be near his ailing mother. So, the office was without a senior clerk and, more importantly, a teacher for Virginia. Herndon had accepted the fact that in the short term, at least, he would have to show Virginia the ropes.

While she waited, Virginia decided to organize the office since it was clear that it hadn't been touched for some time. Books needed to be shelved, and important papers and documents needed to be sorted and filed. The office had an odor of tobacco and musty papers. Dirty cups and dusty bottles were perched on the desks and worktable. The place needed a good cleaning.

Lincoln's desk was piled high with pleadings and letters. Virginia had heard that Lincoln routinely kept his desk messy. It seemed he was the only one who could find anything on or near it. She hoped there was nothing pressing in there. Herndon, on the other hand, appeared more orderly. *An interesting partnership*, she thought as she began to see what was involved in the operation of a law office.

Most of the documents she examined made no sense to her, but she read them anyway. Handwritten surveys, contracts, court filings, correspondence, wills and attorney's notes that appeared to be in another language bewildered her. But she continued reading them until her head was swimming. She stacked and separated the papers by name or subject, the best she could tell, until she had several large piles.

Then she proceeded to the books: *Blackstone's Commentaries on the Laws of England; Chitty's Pleadings*—two volumes containing pleading forms and precedents; *Story's Commentaries on Equity Jurisprudence; Swift's Digest of the Laws of Evidence in Civil and Criminal Cases;* and *Kent's Commentaries on American Law*. She also examined the *Revised Statutes of Illinois* and the *Illinois Supreme Court Reporter*. She became captivated by them. While she didn't comprehend all of what she was reading, she knew she was in the right place to become a properly schooled lawyer.

The *Illinois Supreme Court Reporter* quickly became her favorite. It contained a chronological compilation of cases decided by the Illinois Supreme Court on every subject—taxation, land and property disputes, breach of contract, slavery issues, will contests and her favorite, criminal law. Virginia read the books for hours as the day came to a close. Then, she was jolted out of a trance by a hand on her shoulder.

"Virginia," said Herndon after what had to be his third attempt to get her attention.

Virginia instinctively thought she had done something wrong. "Mr. Herndon, I didn't hear you come in," Virginia said. "I'm so sorry."

"Don't be," Herndon responded, placing his books on the neatly arranged table. "The ability to concentrate intensely on the law is a good trait. I honed mine like a logger's ax when Abe was in town. His boys would run through this office like a twister and he would sit by, reading a letter or the newspaper like nothing was happening. Sometimes I would go outside and sit on the bench just to read my mail." Herndon laughed fondly, but Virginia could tell that, at times, the boys had unnerved him.

"Well, it looks like you have been busy today. The place hasn't looked this good for years," said Herndon as he surveyed the bookshelves.

He proceeded to show Virginia how to place the papers she had stacked into client and important document files. He explained the difference between a deed of trust and a contract, and a court pleading and a letter brief. He told her why the books were arranged just so and the importance of keeping the *Illinois Supreme Court Reporter* up to date. Virginia loved every minute of her conversation with Herndon, and the rest of the afternoon flew by in an instant.

"Next Tuesday, I have court in Springfield. You can accompany me, and I will introduce you to the most important people in the legal process," said Herndon, smiling.

"Who would that be?" Virginia asked.

"You will see," said Herndon as he picked up his coat to leave.

At 8 a.m. Tuesday, Virginia was more than ready for her trip to the courthouse. The night before, she had stayed up late making a journal on her lessons for the past week. She didn't want to forget anything. Herndon met her at the front door of the office.

"Good morning," Herndon said cheerfully. "It's going to be a beautiful day. Are you ready to go?"

"Yes, sir," said Virginia, obviously excited. The two walked briskly to the Globe Tavern. During the morning and at lunch, a sign in the window informed patrons that the Globe Tavern was an eatery. In the evening, however, the Globe became a tavern and boardinghouse. Sarah Beck, the tavern's proprietor, started selling liquor at half past three, but most of the lawyers had cleared out by then.

Virginia was puzzled and a little stunned when she came to realize that every lawyer in town was in the Globe having coffee and breakfast. Herndon affectionately called it "holding court." The gentlemen were talking about politics, their cases and, of course, the ladies. When Virginia was spotted, the third subject was quite appropriately deferred until another time.

Virginia was introduced to everyone, and although the Globe was generally off- limits to women in the morning, most of the lawyers were pleased to make her acquaintance. Several knew her family from Peachy's trial, but it was obvious that Virginia had grown up and was, in their minds, well-connected.

As they worked the room, Virginia spotted Joseph Jamison. He had already seen her and was whispering and giggling to some of his colleagues like a schoolboy. Herndon was unaware of the tension between them, so he introduced her to Jamison and his friends enthusiastically.

"We've met," said Jamison as he gave Virginia a halfhearted handshake.

"You have?" said Herndon.

"Yes, we met at the Harrison trial. I was assisting Palmer," said Jamison.

"Of course. I forgot you were there. It was a wild night," said Herndon.

"I suppose," Jamison said tersely. "Her brother was real lucky."

"Or his lawyers were real good. Either way, the case is over," Herndon responded.

"Not for everyone, Billy. Well, Missy, I heard you were clerking at Lincoln and Herndon. Keeping the office clean and the books dusted?" said Jamison with contempt.

"I'm going to court with Mr. Herndon sometimes," said Virginia, pretending she didn't hear the snickers from Jamison's friends.

"Oh, really? I haven't seen you there," said Jamison with hauteur.

"She just started and has a great deal of work to do in the office," said Herndon in Virginia's defense.

"I'm also studying criminal law," Virginia volunteered.

With his arrogance not waning, Jamison replied, "What for? You can't practice law…you're a woman."

"Well, I'm going to try," said Virginia, elevating her voice.

"That's a waste of time. Women just don't have the temperament for practicing law. You would be too emotional," said Jamison, waving his finger in Virginia's face.

In an effort to divert attention from the unpleasant conversation, Herndon interrupted Jamison. "Did you fellas see Clyde's new buggy? When he pulls into McLean County with that rig, he'll be turning heads everywhere. Virginia, I guess we should head to the courthouse," he said, taking her arm.

"I'll see you in court, Missy…carrying Billy's saddlebag," said Jamison with a smirk. As Herndon walked Virginia out the establishment's back door, Virginia overheard Jamison say to his friends, "I wonder if she will excel in criminology or vampology?" And then laughter.

The pair headed directly to the courthouse. On the way, Herndon added, "Virginia, if you need to track down a Springfield lawyer for a signature or to serve him papers, you need to get to the Globe before nine-thirty. By following that rule, your chances of a successful mission will be greatly enhanced."

At the courthouse, Virginia met the court clerks, the county administrative employees, the sheriff's deputy and Judge Rice—who was in town for his regular term of court. Moving from office to office, Herndon gave Virginia a priceless piece of advice. "Court personnel and the sheriff's office employees love it when clerks and lawyers come in and ask for their help. If you let them believe you don't know what you are doing, they bend over backwards to help you. Also, whatever you do, don't make any courthouse or administrative office employee feel like you think you are better or smarter than them. They can make your life hell."

"Kind of like my mother taught me. You can catch more flies with honey than with vinegar," said Virginia.

"Precisely, Virginia."

Virginia was so excited and eager that Herndon occasionally was amused by her enthusiasm. And as time passed, some members of the local bar raised their eyebrows at her presence, but most gave her the encouragement and support she needed. Virginia was a quick study and became a trusted assistant to Herndon. She read law books between her clerking tasks and asked questions incessantly. She told everyone how wonderful it would be to someday clerk for President Lincoln when he returned to Springfield.

For the next two years, Virginia's work in the law of criminal offenses was confined largely to office tasks. It impressed

Herndon enough, however, that he decided it was time for Virginia to become experienced in criminal law procedure and strategy. While there were procedural rules and statutes to learn from books, the only practical way for her to absorb and learn its application was to see it firsthand in the courtroom.

So, Herndon decided to introduce Virginia to the case of *The People of the State of Illinois v. Horace Matthew Alsupp*. Now, Horace Alsupp, who had acquired the nickname "Dr. Alsupp," made most of his vacillating fortune selling healing potions and horrible-tasting elixirs. Dr. Alsupp was once described by a sitting judge as the state's most "notorious thief, forger and rapscallion"—to which he took grave offense.

Apparently, Dr. Alsupp had also tried his hand as a grifter. Grifters were generally known to practice their art of deception and subterfuge on those of substance who occasionally succumbed to lapses of greed. Horace professed that he merely cheated the cheaters. He was an honest crook, he claimed, who ultimately shared his prizes with those less fortunate. But most often, Horace explained, he was "an innocent man ensnared by ambiguous circumstances."

In Herndon's case, the state's attorney had procured a *writ of mittimus*—a judicial commitment order—to bring about the arrest of the good doctor for forgery and attempting to pass counterfeit bank mortgages to one Samuel Tyler and his brother, Robert. As Horace's court date was drawing near, Herndon asked Virginia if she would like to assist him at the preliminary hearing.

"Virginia, how would you like to accompany me to court in my next criminal case…to assist me and sit at counsel table?" he asked, looking up from a neatly arranged file.

"What's the case about? When's court? Who's the judge? The prosecutor?" Virginia replied rapid-fire.

"I guess that means yes," said Herndon, smiling.

"Oh, I'm sorry...yes...yes, that would be wonderful," said Virginia, blushing.

"Our client is the infamous Horace Alsupp...fondly known as Dr. Alsupp...a first-rate snake oil salesman, con artist and grifter," Herndon began. "He's accused of forgery and attempting to sell counterfeit mortgages to Samuel and Robert Tyler, two business-men of DeWitt County who, by reputation, have grown their net worth through shady deals and exploitation. It seems that Horace sold them five one-hundred-dollar Farmers Bank of Kentucky bank mortgages for the discounted price of three hundred fifty dollars. I'm confident the Tylers thought Horace had swindled the mortgages from some spinster... explaining the greatly discount-ed selling price, but Horace told me that he bought them for two hundred dollars from a ladies hat salesman who was down on his luck," said Herndon, raising his eyebrows.

"Well, let's get the salesman to the state's attorney," said Virginia enthusiastically.

"Wow...I wish it were that easy. Horace told me the salesman was passing through town on his way to New York and he could not remember the man's name," Herndon responded, rolling his eyes.

"Do you believe him?" asked Virginia, peering at the file.

"It's not our job to judge him, Virginia. Many people ask me, 'How can you defend someone you know is guilty?' The assump-tion they make about criminal defense lawyers is that they assume our clients have told us they committed the crime. Thankfully, we don't have to decide guilt or innocence. That's what Judge Davis or twelve unprepared jurors...pulled away from their grain fields...are asked to do. Our job is to make sure Horace's trial is fair...that the evidence is tested and true and that they—the jurors—are not tricked by the witnesses or manipulated by a pros-ecutor who would like to make their decision for them."

"Who's the prosecutor?" asked Virginia, nodding in agreement.

"Your old friend Joseph Jamison," said Herndon, grinning. "Are you ready for his insults and demeaning comments?"

"Why does he always make me feel so inferior, Billy?" Virginia sighed.

"Because you let him, Virginia."

"Well, this time will be different. I won't let him get to me," said Virginia with determination as she picked up Dr. Alsupp's file.

"Good. Let's get to work. Horace is in jail in Clinton. We need to go see him, then we need to go see the prosecutor's evidence. After that, we need to try to interview the witnesses—if they will talk to us—and plan our strategy. As you know, the preliminary hearing is to determine whether sufficient evidence exists to hold our client for the grand jury. If we can stop it there, Horace will not have to go to a jury trial.

"By the way, there's one more piece of evidence you need to know about. During one of Horace's attempts to go straight, he worked in the print shop of the *Chicago Tribune*."

"Does the prosecutor know that, Billy?" asked Virginia, bracing herself for the worst.

"I'm afraid so, Virginia. He's the one who informed me."

"Then…how do we defend Mr. Alsupp?" asked Virginia, dipping her pen into the inkwell.

"The People's circumstantial evidence is very strong…very strong," said Herndon.

"The next thing you know, they will have a witness who saw him print the mortgages," Virginia weighed in.

"I know it looks bad. But just think of it this way—if it were easy, anyone could defend him. A reputation is not built defending easy cases. Victory against the odds gets your client justice and makes you famous," said Herndon with a smile.

"If Dr. Alsupp doesn't end up spending the next five years in prison, this should be fun," said Virginia, rubbing her hands together.

Herndon and Virginia paid a visit to their client in the DeWitt County Jail and then suffered through an hour of Jamison telling them he had an open-and-shut case against their client. They studied the bank mortgages and got permission from the state's attorney to take one mortgage with them while they attempted to interview the witnesses. Robert Tyler refused to talk to them, but Samuel Tyler was amused by what he considered to be a futile effort on their part to defend an obviously guilty man. Samuel did confirm Alsupp's story about purchasing the mortgages from a salesman who was headed east. But the judge would never accept that story without some corroboration—something to back up Alsupp's claim.

In the final analysis, they needed to cast doubt on one piece of evidence—the mortgages—and corroborate another piece of evidence—the existence of the salesman.

"Virginia, the villain supposedly sold ladies headwear. Why don't you take my buggy and go to every general store in DeWitt County…if you have to…and see if anyone remembers him," said Herndon as he sat down at his desk. "I have an idea on the mortgages."

Virginia was thrilled over the prospect of actually conducting an investigation in a real criminal case. She plotted out her route by identifying every town in DeWitt County that could have a general store. Virginia was so adept at making others feel comfortable when she questioned them that before she finished, she had several volunteer "deputies" helping her out.

At last she hit pay dirt. About the time Alsupp bought the mortgages, a salesman, who said he was on his way to New York, entered a dress shop in the town of Clinton.

"I can't remember the gentleman's name, but he was peddling that new felt bonnet," said the store owner. "I passed on the purchase because I wasn't convinced the bonnet would sell to my traditional clientele," he added. "But I will gladly make the trip to DeWitt County if you need me at trial."

Virginia proudly reported her findings to Herndon. He was hoping for a little more, but what Virginia discovered would have to do. Praising Virginia for her efforts, Herndon said, "My idea on the mortgages will require a trip to Chicago to see the prosecution's key witness—the chief typesetter for the *Tribune*."

Herndon didn't know anything about printing presses, but he had one week to learn. He wanted to take Virginia with him, but Alsupp's defense fund was running low. Virginia had never been to Chicago, but there would be other cases.

While Herndon was gone, Virginia did some research and filed a few pleadings that Herndon had prepared before he left town. When he returned, he explained his findings to Virginia, who could hardly believe what she heard.

"How will you cross-examine—is it Mr. Taylor—about his work?" Virginia asked.

"There are two ways to cross-examine a prosecution witness who intends to hurt your client," Herndon instructed. "The first is to begin politely, asking a series of…sometimes unimportant… leading questions to which the answer will always be an appeasing 'yes'…all the while sedating the witness and gaining his confidence and agreement, leading him tamely down the path to a carefully planned trap. Or, you can charge in like the Union cavalry with your pistols blazing, hoping to rattle the witness and crack his testimony.

"This witness, Mr. Taylor, never liked or trusted our client and believes him to be guilty. He will try to hurt us if he can. While I would like to attack him, Virginia, I think the wiser course is to catch him off-guard, if possible."

"Do you think it will work, Billy?" asked Virginia, seeking his reassurance.

"Well, I guess we will find out soon enough. We go before Judge Davis Monday morning, like it or not."

Surprisingly, Monday came too soon for Virginia's liking. She had been preparing herself for seeing Jamison again, and her nerves were on edge over Alsupp's case and their strategy. In a preliminary hearing, the prosecution only has to establish probable cause to believe the defendant committed the crime. If so, the judge rules that there is enough evidence to hold the accused for a grand jury indictment. If not, the defendant is set free.

"Hello, Billy…Missy…good to see you," Jamison said disingenuously as the defense team entered the courtroom. "How has Missy been doing cleaning the office and arranging your files, ol' man?" Jamison couldn't contain himself. "Why don't you just plead Horace guilty? A little time in prison would probably do him some good."

Herndon was in no mood for Jamison's obnoxious remarks. "We can't plead a client guilty who's innocent," Herndon replied.

"Innocent! Did I hear you say ol' Dr. Alsupp is innocent?" asked Jamison, laughing. "His innocence was lost the day he could speak. I tell you, Alsupp's days in the sun are numbered."

Clearly irritated, Herndon replied, "If you don't mind, we'll let Judge Davis decide that."

"I think the sheriff is bringing in our client, Billy. Don't you think we should get him settled in for the hearing?" Virginia asked as she began to move Herndon toward the defense table.

"You are quite right, Virginia. Mr. Jamison, please excuse us," said Herndon as he walked to the prisoner's dock to greet his client.

Preliminary hearing days are always entertaining to watch. The lawyers are busy checking their place on the docket and trying to corner the prosecutor for one last attempt at a better deal for their client. Witnesses are nervously roaming the courthouse, wondering where they should go and what they should do next. The judge is poring over the day's case files in an effort at last-minute preparation, and the sheriff is busy corralling the defendants for their time in the prisoner's dock.

Then, apparent chaos turns to order as the crier opens court in an attention-grabbing voice: "Judge, the first case on the docket is the People of the State of Illinois versus Horace Matthew Alsupp." Everyone settled in.

"May it please the court, I represent Dr., excuse me...Mr. Alsupp, and I will be assisted—with the court's permission—by my clerk, Virginia Harrison," said Herndon respectfully.

"Good morning, Mr. Herndon. Miss Harrison, of course, is quite welcome. Is it your desire that she examine witnesses?" asked Judge Davis with a smile.

"Oh, no, your Honor. This is Miss Harrison's first time to sit at counsel table. Her responsibilities today include making sure I don't forget anything and observing a process she will one day participate in as a member of the bar," said Herndon, looking at Virginia with pride.

Jamison chuckled as he rose to address the court. "The People are ready to proceed, your Honor, if Mr. Herndon is finished fantasizing." Several members of the bar laughed while Virginia shifted in her seat.

"Very well. You may call your first witness, Mr. Jamison," said the judge.

The morning blended into the noon hour as Jamison began to build his case against the accused. He started with the Tyler brothers, who painted a picture of Alsupp as a confidence man passing fraudulent documents to unsuspecting businessmen. Next came a representative from the Farmers Bank to verify the false signature on the counterfeit mortgages and to disclaim their preparation by the bank. Then came the typesetter. Showing the witness the questioned mortgages, Jamison presented the simple fact that Alsupp had worked for a year in the print shop of the *Tribune*, where he learned the mechanics of typesetting. Of course, he was implying that Alsupp parlayed his knowledge into crafting a remarkable likeness of an official bank mortgage.

By this time, Judge Davis was shuffling his files, seemingly paying little attention, and the sheriff was inching toward Alsupp like a cat stalking an unsuspecting sparrow. As Jamison finished, Herndon felt a sense of desperation. He needed to get the judge's attention for a few minutes while he shot his only arrow at the witness.

As he quickly stood up, his chair crashed to the wooden plank floor. The crack was startling enough that the sheriff reached for his revolver.

"Please excuse my clumsiness, your Honor," Herndon apologized as he uprighted the oak chair. "I have but a few questions for the witness. Mr. Taylor, you have been a typesetter for twenty-two years, have you not?"

"I have, Mr. Herndon," said the witness proudly.

"I would daresay you probably know more about printing presses than anyone in the land, do you not?"

"Well, I do know something about them…yes, sir," said Taylor, trying to sound modest.

"The press you have at the *Tribune* is a cylinder press, is it not?"

"Built in eighteen twenty-five…yes, sir," said Taylor as he looked at the judge.

"I direct your attention to five bank mortgages…the mortgages in question in this case," said Herndon, handing the papers to the witness.

Herndon's hand was quivering as he held the papers. Virginia had never seen that before.

"Yes, sir," said Taylor as he flipped through the documents.

"Let's take the first mortgage. They all appear alike, don't they?"

"Yes, sir, except for the mortgage number," said Taylor.

"Please inspect this first mortgage for me. Inspect it with care, Mr. Taylor, for a man's liberty hangs in the balance," said Herndon as he stood beside the seated witness. "You have told us that the *Tribune* uses a cylinder printing press..."

"Yes, sir," Taylor interrupted.

"Is it not true that this mortgage looks like it was printed on a Bullock rotary press, commonly found in the East, say New York?" questioned Herndon, springing his trap.

"Well, I...I'm not exactly sure," said Taylor as he pulled on his collar.

"So you can't tell us with any degree of certainty that this mortgage...or the others for that matter...were printed on the *Tribune* printing press?" asked Herndon, looking directly into Taylor's eyes.

The judge sat upright. Jamison laid down his quill pen, and the courtroom became uncommonly quiet.

"I don't know," said Taylor, seeking out Jamison.

"When I came to see you, I asked you to print this poem for me: 'Time! What an empty vapor 'tis, And days how swift they are!' " quoted Herndon, handing the printed verse to the witness. "Do you remember that?

"Would you be so kind as to take my magnifying glass and examine the poem and one of the mortgages for me," asked Herndon as he unfolded a small magnifying glass from his vest pocket.

"Yes, Mr. Herndon," said the witness as he examined the two papers.

"Mr. Taylor, if you would look ever so closely at the mortgages, is it not true that there is a small chip in the right-hand bar of the capital 'T'?"

"Why, yes," said the witness, surprised.

"There is no such chip in the capital 'T' of the poem you printed for me on your press, is there, Mr. Taylor?" asked Herndon, slamming the door on the prosecution's theory.

"No," said the witness as he slowly removed the glass from his eye.

"Thank you, Mr. Taylor," said Herndon, returning to his seat.

Jamison was now out of witnesses and reluctantly rested his case. The defense called Horace Alsupp to the stand. Because the judge was as familiar with Dr. Alsupp's reputation as the other members of the bar, Herndon felt it wouldn't matter if Jamison made him look like a schemer. And he did. All Herndon needed was Horace's story about the hat salesman. Herndon called Virginia's witness last and rested.

The judge leaned back in his chair and looked at the ceiling as if seeking divine guidance. "Mr. Alsupp, your reputation in this county precedes you. If I were to make my decision based on your character alone, I would hold you for the grand jury's indictment. But Mr. Jamison will have to wait for your next transgression. As far-fetched as it may seem, this time I think you were the fool. Case dismissed."

Dismissals at preliminary hearings are about as common as a Platonic year. And when they happen, an air of inspiration envelops the courthouse. For a short time, members of the criminal defense bar remember why they studied criminal law and that futility can be overcome by determination. The dismissal happened so fast that Virginia thought she had missed something.

"Let's get out of here before the judge changes his mind," said Herndon, grabbing Virginia's hand. "We'll pick up Horace at the sheriff's office and get out of town."

"Yes, of course. That was really something," Virginia replied, looking over her shoulder for one last glance at the courtroom. "By the way, Billy, did you push that chair over on purpose?"

"What do you think, Virginia?"

While it was just another day in court for Herndon, Virginia had found her future. Before everyone's eyes, over the next two years, Virginia would blossom into a mature young lady with unequaled confidence.

CHAPTER 11

By the end of February, the 7th was ordered to return again to Corinth. The marching was severe. Along the way, Peachy overheard some of the men declaring that the regiment should be known as "The Footsore Seventh." Many of the men's shoes were so worn out they had wrapped their feet in rags. Just as the Continental Army could have been tracked by the blood at Valley Forge, so could this barefoot and limping army be tracked by the bloodstained rocks on the road descending the Tuscumbia Valley. But they persevered.

The 7th lodged in Corinth until the middle of May 1863. From there, the troops were ordered to Bethel, Tennessee, where they camped until June 7. While in Bethel, the regiment was told its soldiers were to be mounted on mules to begin the work of chasing down marauding bands of rebel guerillas. By July, the 7th was told, amid loud shouts and cheers, that Gen. Grant had taken Vicksburg. The regiment was proud to know its history would be forever linked to the Army of the Tennessee.

In completing their assignment, the troops were ordered to witness the execution of a deserter from the 1st Alabama Union Cavalry. At the appointed time, the regiment was carefully positioned as if it was about to drill. It was a miserably hot July day, and the trampling infantry and galloping horsemen kept a dense cloud of dust in the sultry air. Soon the procession with the prisoner appeared on the ground in front of the soldiers.

The doomed soldier, supported by Chaplain Davis, slowly walked to the front of the line. Recalling Lincoln's admonition to him in the courtroom, Peachy couldn't help but notice that the soldier possessed the appearance of a guilty man. His head was down and his shoulders slumped forward.

After the procession passed the division line, the prisoner was marched to the lonely place of execution, where his soiled, sweaty hands were bound. Then he was gently seated on his simple coffin. Chaplain Davis offered a solemn and heartfelt prayer after which a black cloth was stretched over the soldier's eyes. Six sharpshooter executioners were ordered to their position 20 feet from their human target. There was deathly silence. Even the birds seemed to recognize the moment.

The provost marshal gave the command and the Henry rifles cracked the silence. The missiles tore through the soldier's blue jacket and found his heart. He fell face forward into the dust, his disgraceful death providing a clear lesson to all who might be tempted to follow his lead.

The 7th continued its relentless search for guerillas, marching out from camp on two-day search parties until the later part of November. The search parties reached as far as Pulaski, Tennessee, and culminated in the 7th's welcomed return to Corinth. The men were exhausted, but their efforts to provide support to Corinth continued into the dead of winter.

Peachy had always done as Chaplain Davis had counseled. For that, he was universally liked by the company and the rest of the regiment. He was easy to talk to and genuine in his advice and counsel.

"Peachy, I'm going to recommend to the captain that you be

elevated to the position of chaplain," said Chaplain Davis after a hard day in camp.

"That would please me very much, Chaplain Davis. I can't thank you enough," Peachy replied.

After Chaplain Davis' recommendation, the commanding colonel wholeheartedly approved the promotion. The gesture overwhelmed Peachy, but he accepted the challenge, reminding Chaplain Davis of his aside on the day of his famous sermon on war.

On Dec. 22, some 600 miles from its home state and after two hard years of service, the 7th Illinois re-enlisted as veterans at Pulaski, Tennessee. Immediately thereafter, the soldiers headed for Illinois to enjoy a well-deserved and much-needed 30-day furlough.

On Jan. 8, with drums beating and colors flying, the men found new strength in their anticipation of home. Many thought, at times, that they would never see their beloved state and loved ones again.

They marched from Pulaski to Columbia, where they took the train to Nashville. From Nashville, they traveled to Louisville, Kentucky, where they received their pay. From Louisville, they crossed the Ohio River and headed home. After seven days of travel, the excitement was palpable as they slowly crossed the Sangamon River. Emerging from the timber, the 7th could hear the roar of cannons. The loyal citizens of Springfield had been told of the troops' arrival and were there with flags and banners to greet them.

As the train pulled into the Great Western Depot, a large crowd surged toward it. To a man, the soldiers were deeply moved by the cheering patriots. Mothers, fathers, sisters and brothers, grandparents, lovers and childhood friends were waving and applauding for the defenders of the republic. As the train came slowly to rest and the men began to leap off the rail cars, the crowd stopped lurching forward while the boys in blue formed a line to march through the city. The crowd followed the proud regiment as it moved with precision through Springfield's main streets to the statehouse yard. Along the way, the city's faithful waved their Union flags and cheered their heroes.

The 7th's old colonel, now Brig. Gen. John Cook, was standing in one of the statehouse windows. With his sonorous and familiar voice, the general said, "Colonel Rowett, by the direction of Governor Yates, you will proceed with your regiment into the Representatives Chamber."

The veterans of the 7th and its loyal supporters filled the hall. Gov. Yates stepped forward and on behalf of the loyal people of Illinois said, "Welcome! Welcome, Seventh! To your homes and friends. The heart of this great commonwealth goes out in love for you and tears for the memory of those of your number whom you have left in the sunny South."

The governor's voice began to crack. "Again, I say on behalf of the loyal people, welcome...welcome, Seventh." Overwhelmed with emotion, Gov. Yates could find no more words for the crowd, and Brig. Gen. Cook helped the governor take his seat.

Then, the general unfurled the 7th's old Fort Donelson and Shiloh flag. Remembering the past and the terrible battle flames through which the flag had been carried, the general spoke to the men for an hour, paying tribute to the regiment's dead and wounded. He then spoke to the loyal citizens of Springfield, thanking them for their support and inspiration. When he finished, there were but a few dry eyes in the huge audience.

The Harrison clan had cornered a spot in the back of the hall to greet Peachy. His sandy hair was long but tucked neatly beneath his dusty blue cap. His untrimmed beard covered his weather-beaten face. Mary Rose, who had worried about his eating habits, thought he had surprisingly gained weight. When the regiment was dismissed, Peachy walked to the Harrisons with a pride only a family member could appreciate.

"Oh, Peachy. I've been worried sick about you," Mary Rose said as she wrapped her arms around her son's neck.

"You look a little rough around the edges," joked Junior.

"It's kinda hard to shave when you're on the move all the time. But good to see that you're still as ugly as ever," Peachy retorted.

Virginia grabbed Peachy around the waist and squeezed as hard as she could.

"You're gonna break my ribs, Virginia. How did you get so strong?"

"Doin' your chores, brother," said Virginia, refusing to break her grip.

Peachy's father stood back and watched with delight. When Peachy turned his way, Peyton gave him a firm hug. "You're a sight for sore eyes, son. We're so proud of you," he said, grabbing his son's shoulders.

"Thanks, Pa. I've sure missed everyone. Did you hear about my new position?"

"We sure did, Peachy. Your Grandpa Cartwright is all swelled up. He can't wait to see you," said Peyton.

"I half expected him to be here," said Peachy, sounding disappointed.

"He would've, but he's down in his hip again," said Mary Rose.

"Let's get goin' then. I'm about starved to death," said Peachy, tugging on Virginia's arm.

"We have a surprise for you," said Virginia.

"What is it?" asked Peachy.

"I can't tell you or it won't be a surprise," said Virginia with a laugh.

"Nice rifle, Peachy," said Junior.

"Yeah, it's a Henry sixteen-shooter repeating rifle. All the men in the regiment bought their own rifles before we left Illinois. We paid fifty dollars for 'em out of our pay. Seems as though we are the only regiment in the entire Union Army to have purchased our own rifles," said Peachy, showing the weapon to his brother. "The colonel told me it has all but increased our force fivefold," he added.

"Can I shoot it when we get back to the house?" asked Junior.

"Of course. It's never been fired at anyone, but it's a great rifle," said Peachy as he handed it to his brother.

With a full wagon, the family set out for Pleasant Plains and home. Cousin Diane, Ben Hart, Sheriff Andrew, Henry Frederick, his Grandmother and Grandfather Cartwright and, of course, his dear Rebecca swarmed the wagon as it approached the barn. As they passed through the front door of the warm barn, they were greeted by the aroma of a roasting pig and an array of colorful vegetables neatly arranged on a serving table with cousin Diane's sweets. Everyone ate, drank, sang and danced into the clear winter night.

About 10 p.m., Peachy sat down next to Rev. Cartwright on the front porch under the cold, still sky. "How's that hip doin'?" asked Peachy.

"Much better since I loosened it up with that square dance."

"No offense, but you better stick to preachin'. Your do-si-do done do-sied off," laughed Peachy.

Rev. Cartwright slapped his knee and let out a whoop. Both men laughed out loud.

"Peachy, we're mighty proud of you. Chaplain Davis wrote me. He said you jumped on your work like a duck on a June bug. He told me the men had become very fond of you and listen to what you have to say."

"I guess they do, Grandpa. Some days I feel good about my

work and other days I feel so helpless. I pray for guidance every night…at seven o'clock," said Peachy, displaying his pocket watch.

"What do you say to the boys about the dead?" Rev. Cartwright asked.

"Chaplain Davis always recalls each lost soldier and has something personal to say about them. I try to do that, too, but I'm not as good at it as he is…"

"You will be in time, son," interrupted Rev. Cartwright.

"Then I recite the twenty-third Psalm. After that, I try to tell them what God says about death. I think they want to hear how God would answer their questions about life after death and not my opinions. So, under the canopy of sorrow, I share with them the eulogy Jesus prepared for himself as recorded in St. John, chapter fourteen, verses one through three…," Peachy continued.

" 'Let not your heart be troubled. Ye believe in God, believe also in me. In my Father's house are many mansions. If it were not so, I would have told you. I go to prepare a place for you. And if I go and prepare a place for you, I will come again and receive you unto myself; that where I am, there ye may be also'," said Rev. Cartwright as he finished the Scripture from memory.

"Amen, Grandpa," Peachy responded. "Is that the right thing to say?"

Rev. Cartwright paused. "It's the truth, son."

"I hope it helps them not be afraid," said Peachy.

"I hope so, too. And now it's past my bedtime, preacher," said Rev. Cartwright as he slowly got up to go inside. Peachy couldn't contain his pride. His grandfather had just called him "Preacher." Now he could devote the rest of the evening to Rebecca. They had a lot to talk about.

⧓⧓⧓

Peachy's family and friends spent practically every waking minute together during the month of his furlough. Townsfolk had them over for suppers, socials and hoedowns. Peachy told Virginia about the beautiful rivers he saw and the countryside he walked, and Junior broke in the 16-shooter on the farm fence posts.

But the departure of the soldiers from Springfield this time was more gut-wrenching than the first. The loss of life and limb brought the realities of war closer to home. This time, people separated with a frightened and forsaken look in their eyes. *Is this the last time I will ever see you? How much longer will this dreadful war last?* Their only solace was the rumor that the war was close to being over.

All of the men had been ordered to rendezvous at Camp Butler. While there, the 7th added a large number of new recruits. Peachy couldn't help but recall that when they left Springfield the first time, the same men were too young to join the army. Now they would journey to a land that might keep them for eternity. But they were so proud in their new blue uniforms.

On Feb. 23, the 7th left the safety and comforts of Illinois for Pulaski, Tennessee, where the regiment mounted mules for its next assignment. From there, the soldiers were sent to Florence, Alabama, to patrol the Tennessee River. In Florence, the regiment was divided into three detachments comprising 10 companies and was ordered to remain in the area until more troops arrived.

A week later, the soldiers' rations were gone and there was no sign of reinforcements. So they had no choice but to once again forage from the poverty-stricken Southerners. But Peachy found it too difficult to eat while he watched children crying for food. When things became too dire, the soldiers were forced to return to Pulaski, where dull monotony soon ruled the camp as they patiently waited for direction.

Finally, the command received orders to move out at once for Eastport at the Tennessee River. It marched all night. Many soldiers fell off their trusty mules while riding along the dark and unfamiliar road. Reports of the rebels crossing the river proved to have been but an idle rumor.

More orders were received for the 7th to patrol the river between Blue Water and Eastport. Peachy just couldn't get used to the devastating effects of war on the South. Confiscating all of the farmers' horses and mules, the Union Army had brought their plows to a standstill. Starvation and suffering were the only future for these people, Peachy thought, if the angel of peace did not come soon to work its merciful hand.

Days turned into weeks in the area around Florence, and Negroes by the hundreds poured into the 7th's camp for comfort and sanctuary. The regiment moved from plantation to plantation, patrolling the area while it did what it could for the refugees.

At the Taylor plantation, the soldiers were treated to the regular routine of camp and patrol duty. The men were anxious for something to break the monotony when a fair lady of the plantation seated herself at an elegantly crafted piano in the mansion's parlor. Defiantly, she played and sang "God Save the South" and "Southern Red, White and Blue" as the men admired and were amused by her spirit and impudence. As she played "Bonny South," the Union soldiers could not fault her, for she had been led to believe that the land of her birth was engaged in a righteous cause—even by some in the North.

In the plantation library, Peachy found copies of the *Cincinnati Enquirer* containing the speeches of Ohio's exiled traitor C.L. Vallandigham. The speeches predicted southern independence, and Peachy was dismayed that these words had apparently strengthened the South's cause, shutting the gates of mercy upon its suffering people.

For two more months the soldiers camped in the area. Then, flatboats were seen by the men floating down the Tennessee, signaling that hostile movements were imminent. The conventional wisdom among the commanding generals was that the rebels would attempt to cross the Tennessee there. On May 6, 1864, a supply train from Athens, Alabama, arrived at the camp on its way to regiment headquarters. After unloading, the train left the next morning, but had not been gone for an hour when an escort courier rushed into camp shouting, "The train was attacked at Shoal Creek Bridge! The train is in danger! The Seventh is requested to send one company immediately to Captain Yeager's aid."

The company rushed to the train and reported back to the captain that Confederate Gen. Phillip Dale Roddey, accompanied by about 1,500 rebels, was crossing the Tennessee. The rebels had captured a squad standing guard at Bainbridge Ferry and were now occupying the road leading to Florence. The situation was critical. A retreat was ordered to Center Star. That evening, the 7th left for Chattanooga, Tennessee. The troops camped at the foot of Lookout Mountain in the Chattanooga Valley. As Peachy looked around, uncoffined graves dotted the timeless valley and lush mountainside. There was no escape from death.

A week after their arrival, they received orders to board a train to Atlanta, Georgia. Desolation was everywhere. Trains loaded with wounded soldiers from Sherman's army passed them on their way. It was a grim reminder of what awaited them. The train stopped short of Atlanta, and the 7th was dispatched to guard the vital railroad and rout more guerillas.

On July 8, the men boarded a train for Rome, Georgia, to join their brigade. The heat was unbearable. Rome was a lovely town situated on the Etowah River. It had been transformed into an elaborate hospital for the wounded and sick soldiers of the Army of the Cumberland. Anticipating the battle at Atlanta, the 7th was chagrined to learn that it would be building barracks in Rome for the summer.

On Oct. 3, 1864, Gen. Sherman received intelligence that Confederate Gen. John Bell Hood, commanding 30,000 foot soldiers and 10,000 horse soldiers fully supplied with the munitions of war, was positioned on the north side of the Chattahoochee River moving northward. The bridge over the Chattahoochee had been washed away in a terrible storm. Gen. Nathan Bedford Forrest had severed communications between Chattanooga and Nashville, and driftwood had leveled the bridge spanning the Oostanaula River at Resaca. In addition, a large number of rebel cavalry held Big Shanty. But the men of the 7th were ignorant of the events that were about to unfold on that clear Monday morning.

Sherman had little doubt that Hood would throw his full force against the weak garrison at Allatoona Pass. Sherman had stored over two million rations there in preparation for his march to the sea. His strategy was designed to split the Confederacy, and he knew if the rations were seized, his men would be in jeopardy. Sherman sent word to Gen. John Murray Corse, Rome's commander, to take his troops to Allatoona Pass and hold it until he could arrive with reinforcements.

Gen. Corse gathered the 7th, 12th, 15th and 57th Illinois Infantries and the 39th Iowa Infantry to travel by rail toward the Allatoona hills. About 1,500 Union soldiers arrived late at night and found one division from Gen. Hood's army, commanded by Gen. French, already surrounding the garrison. Because it was dark, the rebels allowed the train to pass unmolested, believing it to be a train bound from Chattanooga loaded with additional supplies for Sherman's army. The rebels wanted to capture all they could. But the timing, although unplanned, couldn't have been better for the determined Union troops.

As soon as the train moved through the pass, the regiment quickly formed its battle lines. When all of the preparations had been made, the men were ordered to lie down on the ground to rest. But the soldiers, including Peachy, couldn't sleep. All he could think about was the coming battle and which soldiers would live to see their family and friends again.

The rebels had been working all night preparing for their assault on the fort. When the sun rose from behind the Allatoona hills, they were confident of victory. As the armies waited, a white flag was seen in the hands of a lone soldier on horseback riding slowly from the rebel lines. The rider approached and was met by one of the 7th's foot soldiers, who had been permitted to pass the fort's strong gates. A handwritten note was handed to the Union soldier, who rushed it back to his commanding officer.

Gen. Corse opened the carefully folded parchment and read aloud, "I have Allatoona surrounded by a superior force, and to stay the needless effusion of blood, I demand your surrender." General Corse looked at his courier and said, "Tell the flag bearer I am prepared for the needless effusion of blood."

When the horse soldier returned to his superior with the reply, a rebel battery opened up with a deadly round of grapeshot and canister ball upon the Union's line, killing one soldier. Then the battery became quiet. It seemed like an eternity for the soldiers in the fort before they saw an ocean of rebels—6,000 strong—sweeping down the Allatoona hills. As the rebel fire engulfed the pass in all its deadly fury, the men of the 7th opened up with their 16-shooters. The repeating rifles made them seem as though they were 10,000 strong.

The Confederate force was checked for a moment, but a second rebel regiment charged the fort's right flank. The firm line formed by the 7th and 39th Iowa in front of the fort was ordered to fall back. Now the rebel cannons were plowing deep trenches in the fertile Georgia soil, and grapeshot filled the air like locusts. Men were falling everywhere, covering the earth with the dead and dying. In the confusion, the 7th and a few companies of the 57th and the 12th Illinois, along with the 39th Iowa, took up a new position in the fort west of the railroad. At the same time, the 93rd Illinois and the 15th Illinois assumed their positions in the fort east of the railroad. Gen. Corse set up his command in the fort with the 7th where the heart of the battle was raging.

The hasty retreat into the forts seemed to embolden the rebel forces. With yells and screams, they rushed the garrisons, hell-bent on crushing the Union soldiers. Over the hills and up the ravines they charged. As the two forces clashed, the battle quickly became hand-to-hand and man-to-man. The fighting was bloody and dogged. Gen. Corse was severely wounded and fainted from blood loss. Some of the rebel soldiers reached the warehouses containing the two million rations and attempted to burn them, but they were stopped short by a company hidden in the forest to protect the warehouses. The company suffered heavy losses as it attacked and retreated into one of the forts.

Stymied, the rebels took time to regroup and gather themselves for another charge. After forming new lines, the rebels rushed the forts like madmen, determined to destroy the Union soldiers defending the forts. The Union soldiers barricaded the Allatoona walls with their bodies, and once again the rebel forces were forced back in mass confusion and frustration.

Undaunted, the Confederate soldiers rallied and prepared for a third charge. Through the awful carnage, they rushed to engage the outnumbered Union troops. Smoke from the bellowing fort cannons filled the air and red-hot missiles were returned from the scarred hills. The rebels were coming closer and closer in their third attempt to lay siege to the forts. The Union Army was exhausted. The 7th, with its Henry repeaters, had made the difference between defeat and holding the Union's position. But the soldiers were running short of ammunition and were ordered to hold their fire and let the 15th Illinois and the 39th Iowa bayonet the rebels if they made another attempt to scale the walls.

Peachy watched the wounded general, who had been placed on his mattress, rise up and cry out, "Hold Allatoona! Hold Allatoona!" Miraculously, the rebels were driven back from the fort a third time.

Please, God, let them give up, Peachy thought to himself as he surveyed the dead and wounded on both sides. But it was only wishful thinking.

Over the blood-soaked road, the rebels charged the forts for the fourth time. The 7th's garrison was now one vast slaughter pen. The Union soldiers doubted their strength to check the frenzied rebels again. Many of the 1,500 Union soldiers had been killed or wounded, and the battle raged out of control.

Managing to reload and man the artillery, the 7th, which for some time had been discordantly silent, fired its cannons directly into the faces of the desperate rebels. The charging ranks were torn in two by blasts that were repeated and repeated until the rebels gave way in despair. Putting forth a last effort with their 16-shooters, the men of the 7th drove the rebels from their fort, forcing them to flee as the awful battle came to a close.

The 7th's 16-shooters had performed a terrible work of death upon the enemy. Of the 6,000 rebels who had charged the forts on four occasions, 600 lost their lives and another 600 lay wounded upon the Allatoona fields. The Union survivors stood triumphantly, waving their tattered and blood-washed flags over the vast field of death. But they were finally brought to their senses by the reality that half their number lay dead or injured at their feet. It was practically impossible for them to move through the forts without stepping on the dead and wounded.

Soon night came and with it rain. While the men stood in the storm and rain, the glorious feeling of triumph quickly changed to sadness. Their only comfort was the knowledge that they had checked the pass from Gen. Hood's command and saved the two million rations for Sherman's army.

The beautiful dawn revealed a field of death, blood and suffering. Peachy and Chaplain Davis spent the night ministering to as many of the wounded as they could find in the rainy darkness. The 7th's losses exceeded those in the battles of Fort Donelson, Shiloh and Corinth combined. Peachy was exhausted and fighting to keep erect. The shooting had stopped, except for an occasional rebel sniper left behind to slow any chase. But the horror of the battlefield had not yet been fully appreciated. Hundreds of dead and wounded soldiers were lying in the road and clearing in front of the forts. Peachy could see some of the soldiers writhing in pain.

"I'm going out there," Peachy told one of the lieutenants.

"Why do you care if those Johnny Rebs are suffering? They tried to kill us…and you, too," snapped the lieutenant.

"I care…I care about all men," Peachy said as he stuffed bandages in a small leather bag. "My calling is to bring comfort to the suffering and the hope of salvation to the dying."

The lieutenant shook his head in disbelief. "Chaplain, they wouldn't do it for you."

"Maybe not," said Peachy as he cracked the sturdy gate. "But I'm going out there anyhow."

"Suit yourself, Chaplain. But if it were me, I would spend my time on our men," answered the lieutenant in disgust.

A guard held the gate and Peachy slipped into the opening. He could hardly move without stepping on a body. The smell of gunpowder was still in the air.

"Ain't you gonna take your Henry?" asked the guard.

"Don't need it," Peachy replied as he slowly made his way down the road.

The sight before him was overwhelming. For a moment he did not know where to begin. As he walked past several men who were obviously dead, he saw a young man on the ground in a fetal position rocking back and forth. The soldier was mumbling something Peachy couldn't understand as he reached down and touched the wounded soldier on the shoulder.

"Friend, where are you shot?"

The young man rolled over. "In the belly. Am I gonna die?" asked the soldier as dark-red blood appeared on his parched lips. Peachy knew in his heart the wound was fatal.

"Where you from?" asked Peachy.

"Alabama," said the soldier with a moan.

"You got family?" asked Peachy.

"Just my pa and sister. My ma's dead," said the soldier.

"Do they know where you are?" asked Peachy.

"I don't think so. We been movin' around lately. Ya'll got any water?" asked the soldier, coughing.

"Here. Drink slowly," said Peachy. "Would you like for me to pray with you?" he asked.

"I'd like that," said the soldier, his youthful features losing their glow.

"If you know the words, you can say them with me," said Peachy as the soldier rolled to his side.

"OK," whispered the soldier.

"The Lord is my shepherd. I shall not want. He maketh me to lie down in green pastures. He leadeth me beside the still waters. He restoreth..." A musket shot sounded from the perimeter of the field, and Peachy felt a burning sensation in his chest.

"He...He restoreth my soul. He leadeth me...me...Yea, though

I...I...I...walk through the valley of the shadow of death..." A cold feeling started in Peachy's feet and rapidly consumed his body as he became light-headed. Closing his eyes, he saw his mother standing in the front yard of their farmhouse. It was a cool fall morning.

Peachy died on the battlefield at Allatoona Pass with a Confederate soldier tightly clasping his hand.

The survivors of the battle of Allatoona Pass spent two days burying the dead and caring for the wounded, who were carefully loaded on a train bound for Rome, Georgia. At no time during the war had the men of the 7th seen so much sadness etched on the faces of their brothers. They stood around camp lonely and silent without saying a word to each other. They grieved when they saw so many of their number perish at Shiloh and on Corinth's plain, but the blood that flowed from the dead and wounded of Allatoona Pass had completely unnerved the strong-willed men. Stalwart soldiers were now weeping.

When the word of the battle of Allatoona Pass reached Gen. Sherman, he issued an order commending the gallant Union soldiers and Chaplain Harrison. "For the numbers engaged, they stood upon the bloodiest battlefield ever known upon the American continent. The general commanding avails himself of the opportunity, in the handsome defense of the Allatoona, to illustrate the most important principle of war. That fortified posts should be defended to the last, regardless of the relative numbers of the party attacking or attacked. The thanks of this army are due and are hereby accorded to Gen. Corse, Col. Tourtellotte, Col. Rowett, officers and men, for their determined and gallant defense of Allatoona, and it has made an example to illustrate the importance of preparing in time, and meeting the danger, when present, boldly, manfully and well."

Grant concluded with this postscript. "We must also remember

Chaplain Peachy Quinn Harrison, who was mortally wounded ministering to the enemy. His death was not in vain. He was providing comfort to an American."

Still reeling from the battle at Allatoona Pass, the 7th marched to Rome, where it joined Sherman's army. Sherman was staged to march to Atlanta and the 7th was going to be part of that force. Seventy thousand strong, the soldiers marched to Atlanta. But before the 7th had arrived, Atlanta was burning and the end of the war was at hand.

⁓◦⌇◦⌇⌇◦

The news of her brother's death hit Virginia especially hard. The whole town of Pleasant Plains mourned the shocking loss and grieved with the Harrison family. Her brother's trial had started Virginia's journey and now she became more determined than ever. But the law would have to wait while she went home to console her heartbroken mother.

A soldier who had taken possession of Peachy's personal effects was given directions to the Harrison farm by a local Springfield resident. As he came into view of the neatly kept farmhouse, he saw a small woman working in a flower garden. She stood as the soldier dismounted his military-issued mule—a gift from his government for his faithful service.

"Morning, ma'am," said the soldier as he approached the woman. "Is this the Harrison place?"

"It is, young man," said Mary Rose. "Can I help you?"

"Yes, ma'am," said the soldier, removing his blue cap. "They call me Scout. I'm not really a scout—my daddy started calling me Scout after he sent me to find his prizewinning mule and I got lost."

"Well, Scout, it's nice to meet you. I'm Mary Rose Harrison and this here is my daughter, Virginia," she said as she pointed toward the front door.

"My pleasure, ma'am. I'm with or…I was with the 7th Illinois, Company A. I have something for you that belonged to Chaplain Harrison."

The soldier handed Mary Rose a carefully wrapped bundle. As Mary Rose unwrapped the items of clothing, sadness consumed her. Chaplain Davis had sent word of Peachy's death, but no details had been given other than he died bravely helping an enemy soldier.

Virginia grabbed her mother's arm. "Junior!" Virginia shouted. "Junior, please come quickly," she shouted again impatiently.

From habit, the soldier stood motionless while the women tried to regain their composure.

"Thank you so much," Mary Rose said as she unfolded a dress uniform jacket.

"Chaplain Harrison was a good man. He was nice to me when I once got hurt. After that, I heard about other men he was good to. He changed my mind about preachers—at least some of 'em—and I never got to tell him. I figured I should tell you," said the soldier.

In the breast pocket of the jacket, Mary Rose found a gold pocket watch and a small Bible. She had given the Bible to Peachy when he was home on furlough.

"Oh! I almost forgot. I also got his Henry. He never shot it much—it's like new," said the soldier as he retrieved the weapon from his saddle holster.

Mary Rose took the rifle and handed it to Junior. "He would have wanted you to have this. He remarked to me about how much you admired it when he was here," she said.

"Thanks, Ma," said Junior, turning the rifle in his hands.

"I want you to have the pocket watch, Virginia. It will keep you on time for court and all those lawyer things."

"Mother, I couldn't. I really couldn't," said Virginia, shaking her head.

"He would have wanted it that way and I am sure Grandpa Cartwright would agree," said Mary Rose, folding her daughter's hands around the timepiece.

"Where's he buried, Scout?" asked Mary Rose, turning her attention to the soldier.

"Allatoona Pass, Georgia, ma'am. The grave is marked with a nice stone marker so y'all can visit him sometime."

Mary Rose put the jacket gently to her face.

"We had a memorial service here. Rev. Cartwright presided, but it wasn't right without him," said Virginia.

"Well, ma'am, I better be gettin' along," said the soldier, turning toward his mule. "I got to be headed back to Springfield where I'm from."

"You got family there?" asked Virginia.

"Naw, just a job," said Scout.

"Why don't you stay for dinner then?" asked Virginia. "Mother's going to make fried chicken, and my cousin sent over a cherry pie."

"Yes, of course. Please stay," said Mary Rose, reaching for the soldier's hand.

"You twisted my arm. I've been off work four years, so I guess another day ain't gonna make no difference," said the soldier as he climbed the stairs with the family to the front door.

CHAPTER 12

After a month, Virginia returned to Springfield and resumed her law office duties. Lincoln was re-elected to a second term as President in the fall of 1864, but privately, Virginia was hoping he would lose. She wanted him to come home to practice law, and the recent pictures she had seen of him troubled her greatly. Lincoln's face was gaunt and haggard and showed signs of a man under tremendous stress.

On Saturday, April 15, 1865, the morning sun had barely crested the horizon when Virginia opened her eyes from a restless night of sleep. She always slept soundly, but last night was different. Virginia thought her tossing and turning had been unusual, but Friday had been an extraordinarily busy day, and there were many duties awaiting her attention on Monday. That, she felt, was probably the reason.

After slipping on her favorite yellow dress and grabbing a slice of Diane's bread, Virginia walked to her neighbor's house for her weekly cup of South American coffee and a dose of local legal gossip. Entering the back door, she saw her friend staring out the kitchen window.

"Hey, Mr. Patterson," said Virginia cheerfully. Mr. Patterson didn't turn around for a few seconds, but when he did, he was wiping his eyes. "What's wrong?" Virginia asked, walking toward him.

"Virginia, I'm afraid I must tell you about a tragic…a truly tragic event."

Virginia couldn't speak. Mr. Patterson's eyes set the stage for what followed. "President Lincoln has been mortally wounded by an assassin."

"This can't be true," said Virginia, her voice cracking. "Who would do such a thing?"

Mr. Patterson just stared at her.

Virginia turned and ran to the law office, hoping to find Herndon. As she entered the office, she found him slumped over his chair, crying. There was a half-empty glass and a whiskey bottle on his desk.

"It's true…isn't it?" Virginia asked softly.

Hardly able to collect enough breath to speak, Herndon replied, "Yes, Virginia, it's true. Abe is gone. What are we to do?"

Springfield was rocked by the news. Its favorite son murdered. The citizens devoured every newspaper, bulletin or telegram they could find to learn more about the murder and the efforts to find the culprits. Virginia couldn't make any sense out of the assassination. The war was over. President Lincoln was trying to bring people together and smother the flames of hatred. She was now adrift in a sea of uncertainty. Herndon's drinking had escalated and Virginia didn't know what to do about the office.

On Saturday morning, April 29, 1865, Virginia visited Ben Hart in Pleasant Plains. Seeing him always made her feel better. And calm. As the two friends exchanged greetings, she noticed a copy of *Harper's Weekly* on the counter with a sketch of John Wilkes Booth on the front cover. Booth had been cornered and subsequently killed during his attempted capture. Reading the articles about Booth aloud, Hart came to an editorial about Lincoln.

"Virginia, listen to this," said Hart as he drew the paper closer to his face. "So wise and good, so loved and trusted, his death is a personal blow to every faithful American household; nor will any life be a more cherished tradition, nor any name be longer and more tenderly beloved by this nation, than that of Abraham Lincoln. The genial gentleness of his manner, his homely simplicity, the cheerful humor that never failed are now seen to have been but the tender light that played around the rugged heights of his strong and noble nature. In his second inaugural address, he counseled us to begin rebuilding our nation 'with malice toward none, with charity for all.' So, when his fatal blow was struck and those *kind eyes* that never looked sternly upon a human being closed forever, the assassins lost their best friend."

Hart placed the paper on the counter.

"That is what he said about me," Virginia said.

"Said what?" asked Hart.

"Kind eyes…at the train depot before he left for Washington, he said I had kind eyes."

"He knew you," said Hart. "He knew you by your eyes."

"I'm so angry, Ben. It solved nothing and Billy just can't accept that Abe is gone…his partner is gone and he will never practice law with him again. What should I do? How can I help him? First my brother and now my friend…and for nothing. It isn't fair. I think I'll just go back home."

Ben Hart had never seen Virginia so distraught. "That is where you are wrong, Virginia. Both men were doing what they loved…and what they needed to do…when they were killed. They both were content knowing they were doing what they were called to do," Hart said, putting his arm around his friend. "I know you are bitter, Virginia. But you have work to do. Herndon needs you now more than ever. You must become his mission…his purpose in the law. He has become your teacher. Let him know you need his help to fulfill your dream."

"It's hard, Ben," said Virginia as tears filled her weary eyes.

"Life's hard, Virginia. But don't ever give up," Hart said as he pulled her to his chest.

"This is why men say women are too emotional and don't have the temperament for the law," said Virginia, wiping the warm tears from her face.

"Crying is not a sign of being incapable, Virginia. It just reveals your tenderness."

Hearing Hart's words, Virginia remembered the look in Lincoln's eyes when he told her mother he would take her brother's case. Instead of being bitter, Lincoln would want her to wrap the people she touched in kindness. And that is exactly what she set out to do.

Virginia's work in the law office preparing briefs, doing legal research and interviewing clients became more intense over the next four years. Her trips to court became more frequent and her participation in the cases became more involved. In October 1869, she took and passed the Illinois Bar Examination. In June 1870, to the surprise of no one, Virginia was certified to the Illinois Supreme Court for admission to the bar.

With unequaled anticipation, Virginia and her supporters waited for word from the Illinois Supreme Court. But many months passed before a letter from the Supreme Court arrived at the law office. The letter was from the Supreme Court reporter:

"The Court instructs me to inform you that it is compelled to deny your application for a license to practice as an attorney-at-law in the courts of this state upon the grounds that you would not be bound by the obligations necessary to be assumed where

*the relation of attorney and client shall
exist by reason of the disability imposed by
your gender."*

Virginia's disappointment pierced her spirit. Herndon felt naive for believing Virginia could get her license to practice law without a fight. He had not prepared her well enough for disappointment and it bothered him greatly. It had nothing to do with what was fair or right. Instead, they were battling a deep-seated mind-set and an irrational fear of change that often hamstrung the legal profession establishment. Even Lincoln had fallen prey, from time to time, to an uncomfortable feeling when a woman entered the male legal arena. But Herndon felt Lincoln would have divorced his emotion from the injustice. So how would Herndon convince his colleagues of their error?

Herndon had to give Virginia at least a scintilla of hope, so he immersed himself in the law books for an answer. In researching the law and applicable rules of the Illinois Supreme Court, Herndon learned that the Supreme Court's own rules provided that Virginia's application should have been considered by seven members of the full court—not summarily denied in a letter from the reporter. If Virginia could get in front of the justices, perhaps they would recognize her worth.

"We need to prepare a petition…that will be filed with the Illinois Supreme Court…asking for a hearing. If the justices deny the request, it would have to be in a public document that could find its way to the press. Women may not have the right to vote, but they have the right to demonstrate, and the Supreme Court shuns publicity—particularly bad publicity—since its members are all elected to their positions," Herndon explained.

"I like that idea," said Virginia, "and I will help draft the petition."

They decided to call it an application for a hearing "In the Matter of Virginia Faye Harrison, for a License to Practice Law." It took them four days to prepare the pleading. When it was finished, Virginia asked Herndon a procedural question. "Who's going to represent me, Billy? Will you?"

"There's nothing that would please me more," answered Herndon, "but I can't."

"Why not?" asked Virginia.

"Ordinarily, a lawyer who represents himself…or herself in your case…has a fool for a client. But the judges need to see and hear from you as an advocate. The only way that can happen is for you to face them head-on," said Herndon, clenching his fist.

"I can't do it," Virginia responded, her voice filled with emotion. "I've never argued to a judge in court before…much less seven."

"We will practice before you go to court," said Herndon, trying to calm his friend. "You can be schooled on the procedures and what you need to say. I have a friend who used to be the attorney general of Illinois. The attorney general represents the state before the Supreme Court. He's argued many cases before them."

"What if I can't talk?" asked Virginia.

"That would be hard to believe," said Herndon, smiling. "As long as I have known you, you've never been short on words."

"Are you accusing me of talking too much?" Virginia asked as the tension left her body.

"Well, let's put it this way. I think talking is the least of your worries."

"You're going to court with me though, aren't you, Billy?" asked Virginia.

"You must be joking, Virginia. I wouldn't miss this for the crown jewels of the English throne. Harrison versus the legal establishment. It's like David versus Goliath."

"All right, what do we do next?" asked Virginia, eager to go to work.

"Our petition needs to be prepared and filed first thing Monday with the Supreme Court clerk. Then we need to get you ready," said Herndon.

"Are you certain I can do this?" asked Virginia.

"I'm not certain of anything anymore. All I know is you're going to try," said Herndon, closing his law books.

The petition was signed and filed with the clerk on Monday as planned. Virginia's case was set for Feb. 29, 1871. There was no turning back now.

"We need to hold a mock court hearing. My friend... 'General' James A. McDonald...and I will coach you on what to say. But first we need to meet with the General to get his advice on the best approach to take with the justices," said Herndon enthusiastically.

The General practiced law in Ottawa, La Salle County, and Herndon planned to meet with him the next term of court in Decatur, Macon County. That gave Herndon and Virginia a week to research their legal arguments and outline the issues before the meeting. Herndon's task was to persuade his old friend that their cause was worth the fight.

❧

When Herndon returned from Decatur, he had good news for Virginia. The General agreed to meet with them in three days to discuss how they would approach this sensitive issue—both legally and strategically. The General asked that Virginia wear the clothes she intended to wear to the Supreme Court when she came to the meeting. It seemed like an odd request, but at this point, Virginia was more than agreeable.

As promised, the General arrived at the Herndon law office precisely on time. He was a tall man—solidly built—with neatly trimmed black hair. He wore black-rimmed spectacles, and a gold watch chain curved from his watch pocket to his vest. His dress was impeccable—the very picture of respectability. Even his boots stood out—not a scuff in sight.

Herndon greeted his old friend with utmost sincerity. "General, good to see you. This is Virginia," said Herndon with pride.

"Where are the clothes you intend to wear to court, Miss Harrison?" asked the General without so much as a hello.

"Why, I…I have them on," said Virginia, caught off-guard.

"You can't wear that, it's yellow…"

"And blue," Virginia interrupted.

"And you look like a pretty young woman," said the General as he removed his hat.

"Well, my mother…" said Virginia defending herself.

"Your mother isn't a male Supreme Court justice," barked the General.

"What would you like for me to wear…bib overalls and a corn-cob pipe?" replied Virginia sarcastically.

"At least she has a sharp tongue, Billy," the General eased up. "But this is no joking matter. The justices can't look at her and think 'young lady.' They've got to see her as a mature woman who can command their respect…not a young girl in a courtroom full of men."

"Do you have any suggestions?" Herndon asked, appreciating his wise friend's astute perception of the justices.

"She needs to wear a straight black dress with a high white collar and jabot…black lace-up shoes and her hair pulled back," said the General matter-of-factly.

"Like a schoolmarm," interrupted Herndon.

"…And don't powder your nose," added the General.

Virginia was speechless. As the two men finished their plans for her appearance, she made an attempt to voice her opinion. "I look awful in black. I think dark green would be fine, wouldn't it? And my hair…it's much prettier loose than it is pulled back. I'll look like I'm forty," pleaded Virginia.

"Exactly!" shouted the General.

"We don't want you looking young or pretty. You can dress that way after you get your license," Herndon interjected in a consoling tone.

"Fine," Virginia replied through tight lips, "just as long as no one I know comes to court with us."

"On the contrary," replied the General in a voice worthy of his title. "We need every one of your family and friends there. Some of them can vote."

The General picked up his walking stick and top hat and turned to the red-faced young woman. "The first lesson is over. I will see you Tuesday morning at nine o'clock sharp," ordered the General.

"We'll be here," Herndon answered quickly.

"Yes, we'll be there. And thank you," Virginia added, her head held high.

"Don't thank me yet. Your application hasn't been granted," snapped the General as he quickly left the office.

Virginia could hold back her temper no longer. "Billy, does he always look like he just smelled cow manure?"

"He cares or he wouldn't be here," Herndon answered.

"But he didn't say one kind thing," said Virginia, shaking her head. "Does he ever smile?"

"If he does, he's never done it around me," Herndon responded with a chuckle.

"Was he a good attorney general, Billy?"

"The best. The Supreme Court adored him. All business and tough as nails," Herndon replied.

"Then I'll be here Tuesday dressed like I am going to a funeral," said Virginia.

"Let's just hope it's not your own," Herndon joked.

For the next two weeks, Herndon and Virginia practiced Virginia's planned presentation and refined their legal arguments. Herndon would pretend he was a justice and would pepper Virginia with probing questions concerning her knowledge of the law and why women should be licensed to practice law. Herndon and the General had agreed the General would return to Springfield for a mock court hearing two days before Virginia's appearance before the Illinois Supreme Court.

When that day arrived, Herndon, Virginia and the General obtained permission to use the courtroom of the United States District Judge located on the second floor of the Tinsley Building for their practice hearing. To prepare Virginia for her appearance, Herndon also suggested that they take her to the Illinois Supreme Court to see where she would present her arguments.

The courtroom was located in the statehouse building in Springfield. As they entered, Virginia could feel the tension in her body mounting as she surveyed the impressive room. She walked up to the hand-rubbed oak podium and took a deep breath while she gazed at the setting in awe. Pictures of previous Supreme Court justices adorned the pale green walls. The woodwork, which had been installed with great care and affection, was trimmed with gold leaf.

A magnificent brass chandelier of candles hung from the ceiling. The room was further illuminated by candled sconces and desk candleholders that added a measure of warmth and elegance to the courtroom. The lighting flickered off the massive bench that hid all but the crimson backs of seven classical chairs.

A long counsel table was placed behind the podium and was covered with a dark-green velvet cloth. There was an American flag to the left of the bench and a magnificent pedestaled wooden eagle to the right. A red velvet curtain with gold trim encircled the

Chief Justice's chair.

The General and Herndon took their places at the table as a show of support. Since this was an application hearing for a license, and within the total discretion of the court, there would be no opposing counsel.

"The clerk of the Northern Grand Division is William Turney. He will sit to your right as you are standing at the podium. He will enter the courtroom through that side door and open court promptly at nine o'clock," said the General.

"Seven justices will be hearing the petition," added Herndon.

"Do you know them?" queried Virginia.

"Yes, this is the January term. We are in the North Central Grand Division. The judges will be Chief Justice Stephen Murphy, Justice Lawrence, Justice Walker, Justice Scott, Justice Thornton, Justice McAllister and Justice Sheldon," said the General as he called the roll from memory.

"Murphy is a very stern fellow who is a stickler on the rules," the General continued. "Lawrence and Scott are very conservative. Walker, McAllister and Sheldon are more moderate...and quiet...while Thornton is probably the most liberal of the bunch, if there is such a thing on the Supreme Court."

"But Murphy has been known to take an occasional nip before the arguments, which smoothes out his prickly personality," said Herndon with a grin.

"Let's hope he drinks a pint or so before the hearing," quipped Virginia.

"There's no hope for Lawrence and Scott. In my opinion, you can count on them being against you, Virginia," said Herndon.

"I agree. I suggest you try to get Thornton on your side and hope he swings Walker, McAllister and Sheldon," said the General.

"Perfect strategy. But be respectful and direct with Lawrence and Scott," said Herndon.

"My knees are beginning to get weak just talking about this," said Virginia.

"Just don't faint. You can hang onto the podium for support if you need to," said Herndon, patting Virginia's hand.

"That's comforting, Billy," Virginia added wryly.

The three returned to the United States District Court, and the General played the part of Justice Murphy. Virginia fielded his questions while Herndon observed and took notes. The General had several good suggestions, including an admonition to speak up when addressing the court. Virginia handled the criticism and suggestions like a true veteran.

It was a long two days for Virginia, but Wednesday morning finally came. They got to the statehouse early so Virginia could begin feeling at ease with the process. At precisely 9 a.m., the clerk entered the courtroom.

Clerk: All rise. Oyez! Oyez! Oyez! The North Central Grand Division of the Supreme Court of Illinois…Stephen Murphy presiding…is hereby in session. All ye who have business before this court draw near and ye shall be heard. God save this court and the State of Illinois. You may be seated.

Chief Justice: Good morning, everyone. Are there any motions? Hearing none…our first case this morning is the Matter of Virginia Faye Harrison. A petition for a license to practice law. Are you Virginia Harrison?

Virginia: Yes, your Honor.

Chief Justice: Miss Harrison, you will have thirty minutes to argue your case. We have several cases today and we must keep a tight schedule. So I expect you to be mindful of your time limit.

Virginia: Yes, your Honor. May it please this honorable court. My name is Virginia Faye Harrison and I am the petitioner in this matter. As my application states, at the June term of court last year, I applied for a license as an attorney at law…presenting the required certificates of character and qualifications.

Justice Lawrence: We have no doubt as to your fitness and qualifications, Miss Harrison. You have been very fortunate to have learned the profession in such a prestigious law firm.

Virginia: I couldn't agree more, Justice Lawrence. But…my application for a license was refused because I am a woman. As a result, I filed a printed argument requesting this hearing to address…

Justice Walker: In which your right to a license was most earnestly and ably maintained…I might add.

Virginia: Thank you, Justice Walker. I now challenge the decision to deny my request for a license on the basis of my sex…arguing instead that the Illinois statute authorizing licensing by this court does not exclude women.

Justice Lawrence: Miss Harrison, would you agree that an attorney is an officer of the court holding his commission at the pleasure of this court, according to our statute?

Virginia: Yes, Justice Lawrence. But your discretion in

granting or denying a license, subject to the requirements of qualifications and good moral character, should not be an arbitrary one.

Justice Lawrence: Yes, but wouldn't you agree that we should always keep in mind that our charge should be governed by the intent of the legislature and the proper administration of justice?

Virginia: To a degree. I agree that this court should always be concerned with the proper administration of justice. However, the intent of the legislature should only be considered in interpreting a statute when that statute is unclear.

Justice Walker: The statement you make is true with respect to most interpretations of a statute, but wouldn't legislative intent be important in determining a statute's scope?

Virginia: In this case, I don't believe so, sir.

Chief Justice: So, the issue for us is whether…in the existing social relations between men and women…it would promote the proper administration of justice and the general well-being of society to permit women to engage in the trial of cases in court. Would you agree?

Virginia: Yes, your Honor. I would agree…to a point…that is one issue. But the legal issue is whether the statute excludes women.

Chief Justice: I realize that you do not believe legislative intent is important for determining our statutes' scope…in your case…but is there anything in the statutes passed by our legislature that would suggest that the legislature contemplated…that the legislature intended for women to be licensed to practice law?

Virginia: The twenty-eighth section of chapter ninety of the revised statutes of eighteen forty-five provides that "whenever any person is referred to in the statute by words importing the masculine gender, females, as well as males shall be deemed to be included."

Justice Lawrence: But doesn't the thirty-sixth section of chapter ninety provide that this rule of construction shall not apply if the interpretation would be repugnant to the provision of the statute?

Virginia: Yes, your Honor. But treating women the same as men should never be repugnant to the law.

Justice Lawrence: I think the real issue in this matter is whether the admission of a woman to the office of attorney-at-law was contemplated by the legislature.

Justice Thornton: But the statute doesn't exclude any person, does it Miss Harrison?

Virginia: No, Justice Thornton.

Justice Lawrence: When our statute was enacted, Miss Harrison, did we adopt the common law of England?

Virginia: Yes, your Honor.

Justice Lawrence: And with a few exceptions, the statutes of that country passed prior to the fourth year of James the First?

Virginia: Yes, your Honor.

Justice Lawrence: Wasn't it true that female attorneys-at-law were unknown in England?

Virginia: Yes, your Honor.

Justice Lawrence: I'm convinced that the proposition that a woman should enter the courts of Westminster Hall as a barrister would have astonished the English...

Virginia: I don't...

Chief Justice: No less, perhaps, than she should be elected to a seat in the House of Commons.

Justice Walker: But this wouldn't be the first time we twisted the tail of the British lion.

The chuckles distracted Virginia for an instant.

Virginia: And I...I would also submit that the Fourteenth Amendment of the United States Constitution supersedes a construction of our statute that excludes women.

Chief Justice: Miss Harrison, I see your time is about to expire. You may have one final argument in conclusion.

Virginia collected her thoughts and then addressed the court with the poise of an experienced courtroom lawyer.

Virginia: Thank you for the opportunity to address this court. Chief Justice Murphy, I submit that the profession of the law, like the clerical profession and that of medicine, is a vocation open to every citizen of this state...and the United States for that matter. And while the legislature may proscribe qualifications for entering upon this noble pursuit, they cannot exclude a class of citizens from admission to the bar. A qualification to which a whole class of citizens never can attain is not a regulation of admission, it is...as to such class...a prohibition.

For example, the legislature could not...in specifying the qualifications...require the candidate to be a white citizen. This would be the exclusion of all colored citizens, without regard to age, character or learning. Yet no reasonable mind can draw a distinction between such an act and the custom, usage or law of a state which denies this privilege to all female citizens...without regard to age, character or learning.

If the legislature may declare that no female citizen shall be permitted to practice law, it may as well declare that no colored citizen shall practice law. For the only provision in the Constitution of the United States which secures to colored male citizens the privilege of admission to the bar is the provision that "No state shall make or enforce any law which shall abridge the privileges or immunities of a citizen." And if this provision protects the colored citizen, then it protects every citizen...colored or white...male or female.

I have been denied admission to my chosen profession not

on the basis of my intelligence, integrity or honor, but on the basis of my sex. There may be cases in which a client's right can only be rescued by the exercise of the rough qualities possessed by men. However, there may also be causes in which the calm voice of a woman would accomplish more. In the final analysis, it should be left to the taste or judgment of the clients to determine whether to retain a man or a woman. But the broad shield of the Constitution should protect us all.

Thank you for your time and studied attention.

Chief Justice: Thank you, Miss Harrison. We will be in recess for one hour, at which time we will return to announce our ruling.

The recess reminded Virginia of the time they waited for the verdict in her brother's case. Both Herndon and the General complimented Virginia on her argument and told her they thought the hearing went as well as could be expected. And her family and friends were so proud of her. Everything seemed, however, to move in slow motion. The minutes seemed like hours. Precisely one hour later, Mr. Turney's voice boomed again.

Clerk: All rise. Court is in session. You may be seated.

Chief Justice: When our statute was passed, it was regarded as an almost axiomatic truth that God designed the sexes to occupy different spheres of action, and that it belonged to men to make, apply and execute the laws. A direct participation in the affairs of government...in even the most elementary form—namely the right to vote—was not then claimed and has not yet been conceded. In view of these facts, we are certainly justified in saying that when the legislature gave...to this court...the power of granting licenses to practice law, it was not with the slightest expectation that this privilege be extended equally to men and to women.

Neither has there been any legislation since that period which would justify us in presuming a change in the legislative intent. Our laws today in regard to women are substantially what they have always been. Whatever may be our individual opinions as to the admission of women to the bar, we do not deem ourselves at liberty to exercise our power in a mode never contemplated by the legislature...and inconsistent with the usages of courts at common law...from the origin to the present day. But it is not merely an immense innovation in our own usages...as a court...that we are asked to make. This step, if taken by us, would mean that...in the opinion of this tribunal...every civil office in this state may be fulfilled by women. Governors, judges and sheriffs. This we are not yet prepared to hold.

In our opinion, it is not the province of this court to attempt...by giving a new interpretation to an ancient statute...to introduce so important a change in the legal position of one-half the people. Courts of justice were not intended to be made the instruments of pushing forward measures of popular reform. If it be desirable that those offices which we have borrowed from the English law...and which from their origin some centuries ago down to the present time have been filled exclusively by men...should also be made accessible to women, then let the change be made, but let it be made by that department of the government to which the Constitution has entrusted the power of changing the laws.

There are some departments of the legal profession in which you can appropriately labor, Miss Harrison. Whether...on the other hand...to engage in the hot strifes of the bar, in the presence of the public, and with momentous verdicts the prizes of the struggle, would tend to destroy the deference and delicacy with which it is the pride of our ruder sex to treat you, is another matter certainly worthy of your consideration. If one day the legislature chooses to remove the existing barriers and authorizes us to issue licenses equally to men and women, we shall cheerfully obey, trusting to the good sense and sound judgment of women themselves, to seek those departments of the practice in which they can labor without reasonable objection. The application is, therefore, denied.

Justice Thornton: I must respectfully dissent. It is true that at common law only males were admitted to the bar. But, this country was founded on a higher principle...one of equality under the laws. The legislature accepted persons from the bar only on the basis of character and learning. Miss Harrison's character and learning is not disputed by this court. If the legislature wanted to exclude women from our profession, it could have said so. I would grant the application.

Chief Justice: We will be in recess.

Clerk: All rise.

As the judges left the courtroom, Virginia turned to Herndon and the General and dropped her head in despair. "Why did I do this? My parents told me it wasn't possible."

Herndon tried to comfort Virginia. "You did it because it was your dream. If you hadn't tried, you would have always wondered how things might have been."

"I don't know if it's worth it," said Virginia, teary eyed.

"Virginia, there are some things that are just worth doing, no matter what," said the General.

"What do I do now?" asked Virginia.

"We're going to take this issue to the Illinois legislature. Abe made many friends there and I'm certain they will help us," said Herndon, as he stuffed his papers into his satchel.

"If the Supreme Court wants a law, we'll get them one," said the General, grabbing his walking stick. Virginia's family and friends consoled her as the two friends left the statehouse.

While contacting members of the legislature, Herndon discovered that three other women living near Chicago were going through the same painful process as Virginia. One of them, Alta Hulett, had even begun drafting the nation's first law prohibiting sex discrimination in employment. Virginia and Herndon pitched in to help her bring about passage of the law. It was a slow process, however, and Virginia was becoming impatient. In frustration, she decided to visit Judge Rice to see if he could help.

"I'm sorry, Virginia," Judge Rice explained. "There is no lawyer I would rather help than you, but I can't involve myself in politics because of my position as a judge."

However, he had an idea. He was confident Virginia knew more about the law and trial work than most of the lawyers in town. She had nine years of experience. She was a quick study and, above all, she loved the law.

❦

CHAPTER 13

I t was Christmas Eve when Judge Rice summoned Virginia to his office. With Virginia seated next to his old walnut desk, the judge reflected aloud. "Virginia, I've been giving this woman lawyer issue a great deal of thought. With all due respect to my brethren on the Illinois Supreme Court, I respectfully disagree with them."

Virginia remained uncharacteristically silent as Judge Rice handed her a written and signed order.

IN THE CIRCUIT COURT
OF SANGAMON COUNTY, ILLINOIS

In the Matter of
Virginia Faye Harrison

ORDER

Although the Illinois Supreme Court has refused to license a woman, the court believes, and therefore orders, that Virginia Faye Harrison is properly educated and qualified to practice law.

With the spirit of the age, and by virtue of my authority as a Circuit Judge, IT IS HEREBY ORDERED AND DECREED that said Virginia Faye Harrison be and is hereby authorized to practice law in the Circuit Court of Sangamon County from this day forward.

Dated: This twenty-fourth day of December, 1871.

Edward Y. Rice Jr.
Circuit Judge

When Virginia looked up, a crowd of courthouse employees and lawyers was standing in the door. To cheering and applause, Virginia jumped up and threw her arms around Judge Rice. "Oh! Pardon me...please, your Honor. That was most unprofessional," said Virginia over the prolonged applause.

"That was the first time I was ever embraced by a lawyer over a ruling. But I might say...I liked it," said Judge Rice to uproarious laughter.

A few months later, to the delight of the town, Virginia opened the first law office in Pleasant Plains and began the general practice of law. She spent her first two years trying to raise the confidence level of the locals in her abilities. Some people found it hard to take her seriously since they remembered her as the talkative, slender little girl who flitted happily from project to project. Others gave her a chance to prove herself by hiring her to collect small debts, draft sales contracts, close real estate transactions or handle simple probate matters. And, on occasion, she would be asked to represent someone charged with a crime.

The women were most fond of her, but for the most part, it was customary for the men to hire the lawyers. Men were predictably skeptical of her at first. But they eventually grew to respect her intelligence, diligence and attention to detail. If a matter went to court, she was well prepared and articulate. She knew she had to be if she wanted to be heard and not patronized. Every case took double the effort on her part, for the male establishment was not easily convinced of the merits of women in the law. And she never wore yellow—at least not to court.

Life as a solo practitioner was also a challenge financially. Herndon and others taught her the law and legal procedures well. But the everyday business of the law was another matter. No one taught her how to set and collect fees and expenses. The concept of making a living practicing law is simple enough, but what to charge for a case and when to collect it is a never-ending struggle for a practitioner. She learned from Lincoln's speeches that "a lawyer's stock-in-trade" was his, or in this case her, time. Lincoln preached the gospel of fairness and ethics in setting fees. Fair enough, she believed.

However, she came to disagree with his philosophy of not collecting a legal fee in advance. Lincoln didn't believe a lawyer would handle a case with the same level of enthusiasm if he were paid in advance. Of course, his philosophy was true of many lawyers. But those lawyers were generally unreliable sorts who worked harder getting out of work than they did addressing it. Their work ethic had its foundation in procrastination and short-cuts.

The truly good lawyers could be counted on to work diligently and with zeal—no matter how they were paid. However, the truly good lawyers counted on being paid as promised and that wasn't always the case. Most clients meant well, but their enthusiasm for payment diminished when the pressure of the legal matter was lifted. This was particularly so in criminal cases. Clients would sometimes bolt, never to be seen again after an attorney spent hours securing their release. Those clients for whom the lawyer obtained a dismissal or an acquittal were loath to pay their fees and expenses because of the belief that they were wrongly

accused from the beginning. And those clients who were convicted or pleaded guilty had more on their minds than paying a
lawyer.

No, Virginia found the opposite of Lincoln's teachings on setting and collecting fees and expenses to be true for her. The
clients needed an investment in their cases, and she needed to pay
her bills so she could represent more clients. No one would be
helped, she learned, if she went out of business representing people for little or nothing.

Virginia's first office was a small room attached to Short &
Hart's General Store. It was used for storage until Virginia asked
to use it as a law office. Virginia made it more than presentable.
It was clean and comfortable. People would drop by for a visit,
and her mother brought her lunch most days, if Virginia was in
town.

With the support of many people, Virginia managed to make a
respectable living in the law and her practice grew steadily.
Eventually, she came to need more space for her library, a worktable and chairs and perhaps even a clerk of her own. So when the
proprietor of Patty's Seamstress Shop decided to merge into the
general store, Virginia seized the opportunity to rent the two-
room space.

Her first day in the new, larger office, after spending the week-
end with her family moving and decorating, started out rather
uneventful. She had two visitors: Mr. Hart's wife, who brought
her a bouquet of wildflowers, and her mother, who brought
lunch—cold fried chicken, boiled potatoes, a slice of watermelon
and lemonade. But in the afternoon, she was surprised by her
mentor and old friend Billy Herndon, who was accompanied by
an attractive young woman and her bewildered father.

"Hey, Billy. How's the ol' circuit rider?" asked Virginia as she
met the trio at her front door.

"I would be much better if you moved to town and became my partner," said Herndon, hugging her shoulder.

"Hi, I'm Virginia Harrison," said Virginia, extending her hand to the young woman and the man in that order.

"Virginia, this is Samantha Carnall and her father, Kenneth," said Herndon, taking the lead.

"Pleased to meet you," said the Carnalls in unison.

"I heard you were moving to a new office and I thought you might need a new client to help pay the bills," said Herndon with a smile.

"Your office is very attractive," said Samantha, examining the interior walls.

"It still needs a little more furniture and some paint, but I like it," said Virginia with pride.

"Virginia, Samantha's case is rather troublesome and somewhat delicate. She has been slandered in the most cruel of ways," Herndon explained seriously.

"I've never handled a slander case before, Billy. Why do you think I would be the best lawyer to represent Samantha?" asked Virginia, looking at the Carnalls.

"Well, first of all, you are as smart as a whip and most capable of handling this case. *Chitty* will get you started. Secondly, I thought Samantha needed a woman lawyer and, finally, you have had some experience with the defendant."

"Who's the defendant?" Virginia asked.

"Your old friend Joseph Jamison," said Herndon.

"You're not joking with me, are you, Billy?" asked Virginia seriously.

"Not this time, Virginia," Herndon replied just as seriously.

"Samantha…may I call you…" Virginia began.

"Yes, Miss Harrison. Most of my friends call me Sammie, but you can call me anything that makes you comfortable," Samantha interrupted.

"All right, Sammie. Why don't you tell me what happened?" asked Virginia, reaching for some paper and her quill pen.

"Virginia, I think I should excuse myself now. I've got a court appearance this afternoon and I need to prepare," said Herndon, standing up.

"Sure you can't stay for supper?" asked Virginia, escorting Herndon to the door.

"Not today, Virginia. But I'll be back next week to see Mr. Hart and I'll be happy to eat with you. Say hey to your family for me," said Herndon, mounting his horse.

"Thanks, Billy. I will take good care of Miss Carnall," Virginia said as she waved good-bye.

"I know. That's why I brought her here," said Herndon, tipping his hat.

Virginia returned to her worktable and the Carnalls, who were now spreading out some papers for her to examine.

"I'm sorry, where were we?" Virginia asked.

"I wanted to show you some accounts I keep for the school. You see, I'm a teacher…a teacher of common schools…and as such I am charged with keeping the attendance…schedules of my students and—on oath—reporting those to the school administrators for my pay. My rate of pay is based on the number of students I have had in my classes during the month," Samantha carefully explained.

"I see. But what does that have to do with Mr. Jamison?" Virginia asked as she read over the schedules.

"Mr. Jamison was representing the school board in his capacity as the county attorney for Sangamon County," Samantha began.

"I thought he moved back to Chicago," said Virginia.

"He did, but he didn't like working for his father. So he moved back to Springfield," Samantha replied.

"Too bad. So what happened?" Virginia asked again.

"I met him at a school board meeting and we talked…just casually…about the weather and those sorts of things. He…well…he began to flirt with me after a few meetings…and…well I didn't care for it much," Samantha related.

"Yes, he thinks a great deal of himself, doesn't he?" Virginia remarked.

"And…at last month's meeting, he said some things that were…well… inappropriate," Samantha continued.

"Like what?" Virginia asked.

Virginia could see that Samantha was becoming uncomfortable talking in front of her father.

"Mr. Carnall…Kenneth…my neighbor Ben Hart just got in a shipment of hunting knives. I'll bet he would be happy to show them to you," said Virginia politely.

"Oh, yes…of course. I'll be right back, sweet pea," Kenneth said to Samantha as he gathered himself for a quick exit.

"Take your time, Daddy," said Samantha, looking at Virginia with appreciation.

"Go ahead, Samantha," said Virginia as Mr. Carnall left the office.

"He told me I had nicely shaped bosoms and that he hoped to see more of them one day. Why…why would he say such a thing to me?" asked Samantha, her ocean-blue eyes filling with tears.

"Go on," said Virginia, disgusted.

"I tried to ignore him, but he wouldn't leave me alone. So I told him if he didn't leave me alone, I would report him to the superintendent."

"Did you tell your father?" Virginia asked.

"No. I was ashamed. I didn't want him to know that someone of Mr. Jamison's position would have such little respect for me."

"How long have you lived and taught in Sangamon County?" asked Virginia, changing the subject.

"I moved here three years ago when I turned nineteen. Daddy moved here from Wisconsin last spring after my mother died. I was hired as a teacher…after living in Illinois a month…because I had been trained in teaching," Samantha said as she regained her composure.

"I'm sure you are very good at what you do, and your students adore you," said Virginia, grinning.

Samantha's smile lit up her delicate facial features. For a second, she forgot about her problems and remembered why she became a teacher.

"What did Jamison say to you after you threatened to report him?" inquired Virginia as she probed for more facts.

"Nothing. He said nothing, but he never talked to me again. I thought it was over until my best friend, Margaret, told me her gentleman friend told her that Mr. Jamison said…in front of several members of the school board…that I had lied on my schedules to get more pay…lied to the board about the number of students attending my classes," said Samantha, barely holding back her emotions. "But it's not true, Virginia. I did no such thing."

"I'm confident that is so," said Virginia reassuringly.

"But, there is more, Virginia. He told these men that I had run away from Wisconsin with a married man, a man named Branston Phillips, who lives in Macon County, and that we lived together…lived as man and wife. Then he told them my father had better take me back to Wisconsin…to the bad house where he found me and then the sores on my neck would vanish," Samantha blurted out as she burst into tears.

"That son of a bitch! Oh! I'm sorry, Sammie. Forgive me for my foul mouth. I've spent too much time in the Globe with the men lately."

"What am I to do, Virginia? Everyone's talking about me. The looks...whispers...some of the people I thought were my friends will not even stop to talk to me. Should I move away from Illinois? I don't want to leave my students. They're counting on me," Samantha sobbed.

Virginia moved around the table to console her new client. Her stomach felt like it was in her throat. How does a lawyer keep her distance in cases like this? If she became too emotionally involved in Samantha's case, she would lose her objectivity. That would be harmful to her client. On the other hand, this young woman did nothing to deserve this and she might not be able to do anything about it.

"That's what he wants, Samantha," said Virginia, breaking a long silence.

"What can we do then?" Samantha asked.

"We can file a suit in Circuit Court. It will be an action of trespass on the case for words...I'm sorry...a lawsuit for slander. We will ask for money damages, probably at least three thousand dollars. We will get an accountant to review the schedules you have and to testify they are in good order...and we will call every person that heard Jamison publish the slanderous words. Then we will call Branston Phillips to dispute what Jamison said about both of you and call your father to prove he didn't find you at a bad house. Finally, we will call your physician to prove that you have no sores on your neck and you will testify to the injury this has caused to your good name," Virginia carefully explained.

"What's a bad house, Virginia?" Samantha asked.

"Well," Virginia hesitated, "it means a brothel...a house for the practice of fornication and prostitution."

"Oh, my! Why would he say such a thing?" asked Samantha, dejected.

"He was attacking you to diminish your standing…and to cause you to leave the county before you exposed him for the scoundrel he is," said Virginia calmly.

"But all of this will take a lot of your time and cost a lot of money, won't it, Virginia?" Samantha asked. "My teacher's pay is very small."

"This is how we can do this, Samantha, if you agree. You will provide me thirty-five dollars for court fees and other expenses, sheriff's fees for serving subpoenas and my office expenses. If we are successful and collect a judgment against Mr. Jamison, you will pay me twenty-five percent of the award. If we are unsuccessful, you will not be obligated to pay me any fees," Virginia explained.

"But, I can't do that. I must pay you for your services…something. It just wouldn't be right for you to work and not get paid," Samantha insisted.

"All right…let's compromise. In addition to the expense money, you pay me fifty dollars…at ten dollars per month…plus fifteen percent of any money collected from your suit," Virginia suggested.

"I don't know how to thank you, Virginia. I didn't know where to turn."

"There is one more thing you need to know, Samantha. Your case will be a spectacle. The newspapers will print what goes on, and the courthouse will be full of busybodies and sightseers. Your personal life will be on trial, and truth is a defense for Jamison. There is no doubt he spoke the words, so his only defense is that his words were true. You will be vindicated if we win the case, but if we lose…it will be much, much worse for you," Virginia warned.

"I understand," Samantha replied.

"You should talk to your father first and seek his advice.

Sooner or later, he will find out what happened," Virginia counseled.

"I will. But Jamison should be held accountable for his maliciousness."

"I certainly agree, Samantha. You can return tomorrow and tell me of your decision. When you return, if you want to proceed, I have some homework for my client the teacher. I'll need a list of the names of all persons who overheard Jamison's statements and, if you have them, every school schedule you prepared and swore to since you were hired. I also need to know where Mr. Phillips lives and the name of your physician," said Virginia as she meticulously wrote out a list of things she needed.

"Hi, Daddy," said Samantha as her father approached the office door.

"We were just finishing up. Did you enjoy visiting with Ben?" asked Virginia as she handed the list to Samantha.

"He's quite the storyteller, Virginia. He even had some good ones on you," Kenneth said as Samantha stood with him to leave the office.

"Thank you…thank you so much, Virginia," said Samantha, grabbing Virginia's hands.

"You are quite welcome, Sammie. I will do my very best for you…I promise," Virginia replied.

Virginia shook Kenneth's hand and gave her new client a hug. As they left her office, Virginia walked to the window and watched them lock arms while they crossed the dusty street to their wagon.

But now, her thoughts weren't on Samantha's case. They were on Lincoln. Why did she remember him at times like this? It wasn't his stature as President or reputation as an accomplished politician, his recognized status as a stellar courtroom lawyer or even his commanding presence. It was the way he touched people. The gentle way he patted a shoulder or greeted a stranger. The way he held a child or caressed a stray pet. The way he caught your eye as he spoke and took time to listen to your troubles—no matter how trivial they might have seemed. It was his steadfast kindness.

In the final analysis, Virginia thought, everyone has the capacity for kindness and many have the will. But through the ages, only a few are truly remembered for it.

Author's Note

Several years ago, I read an article in my local newspaper about the discovery of a handwritten transcript of one of Abraham Lincoln's jury trials. It fascinated me so much that I made an effort to obtain a copy. After becoming discouraged with the inability to talk to the person in possession of the transcript, I forgot about it.

Then in 2005, my wife, Pat, and I made a trip to Springfield, Illinois, to see the recently opened Abraham Lincoln Presidential Library and Museum. Purely by chance, a copy of the original transcript of *People of the State of Illinois v. Peachy Quinn Harrison* came into my hands. I read it in its entirety, thinking it was the closest anyone today could ever get to hearing Lincoln speak in the courtroom. For me, it was a thrill to read his words. That transcript and an article I read in the April 29, 1865, issue of *Harper's Weekly* inspired me to write *Kind Eyes*.

Although there are hundreds of books in existence about Lincoln, including very well-written books about his law practice[1], I could not find one book—historical or otherwise—that dealt with Lincoln's life as a criminal defense trial lawyer. So I set out to explore some of the trial strategies and issues that Lincoln in all likelihood employed and faced as a criminal defense lawyer.

In addition, since I grew up in Illinois (my mother, Virginia, was born in Bloomington), I thought that weaving a story about a fictional character into the history of Lincoln as a trial lawyer might capture a reader's imagination.

Where possible, I used people, events and testimony from the actual trial. However, I created characters and events to enhance the trial's drama, and I tailored some of the trial testimony to fit the story line.

Peachy Quinn Harrison was the defendant in the actual case. While I am not sure how Peachy got his name, I think he was actually known as "Quinn." In addition, based on a trip my wife and I made to Pleasant Plains, including a visit to its cemetery, I believe Peachy had a father and brother named Peyton. Mary Rose, however, is a fictional name for his mother.

In the actual trial, Abraham Lincoln, Stephen T. Logan and Shelby M. Cullom represented Harrison, and District Attorney James B. White and John M. Palmer appeared for the State.

Judge Edward Young Rice Jr. presided and Dr. J.L. Million, Jon Bone, Abajiah Nottingham and Rev. Peter Cartwright were witnesses. Their dialogue in this book is very similar to their trial testimony. But Benjamin Hart wasn't a witness in the trial. His partner, Nathan Short, actually testified to most of the facts attributed to Hart. Of course, Hart's many conversations with Virginia are fictional.

John Crafton testified at trial, but he was Greek's brother—not his father. Crafton's testimony was rewritten to fit the story line. And Henry Frederick was not a witness in the actual case, but the prosecution did call Harrison's friend Frederick Henry.

While researching the Harrison trial in the superb work of the Lincoln Legal Papers entitled *The Law Practice of Abraham Lincoln*, I found one short newspaper article containing a reference that suggested a woman may have created the tension between Peachy and Greek. The article was written before Peachy was arrested, and the subject was never mentioned again in the newspaper or at trial. But that's how I came up with the fictional Rebecca Watson.

"General" James A. McDonald, Sheriff H.F. Andrew, Joseph R. Jamison and Samantha Carnall are fictional characters. But, Carnall's slander case against Jamison was based on a case Lincoln handled involving a schoolteacher named Emily Fancher.

Of course, Virginia is fictional, as is her Illinois Supreme Court hearing. But her hearing is based on some of the actual struggles of Alta M. Hulett and Myra Bradwell, pioneers in the fight for women in the law in Illinois. In 1873, at age 19, Hulett was the first woman admitted to the Illinois Bar. The struggles of Bradwell are detailed in *Myra Bradwell: Crusader at Law*[2] and the reported cases of *In Re Bradwell*[3] and *Bradwell v. People of State of Illinois*[4], which provided a great deal of the dialogue in Virginia's hearing.

I included the substance of some of the actual newspaper articles about the Harrison trial, including editorials, to give the reader a sense of history, the newspaper reporters' attention to factual detail and the mood of the community. Unfortunately, the trial transcript did not contain the trial hearings, opening statements or closing arguments of counsel. I created those based on my experience, although I don't profess to possess the ability to think or speak like Abraham Lincoln or John Palmer. I do, however, understand what must have been factually and legally important to the lawyers trying the Harrison case.

As for the 7th Illinois' valiant efforts in the Civil War, many of the historic details came from the memoirs of D. Leib Ambrose[5], one of its number.

Finally, all of Virginia's legal experiences with William Herndon are fictional. While I have often thought about how

Herndon must have felt losing his friend and law partner to an assassin's bullet, I wanted Lincoln's enthusiasm for the law to live on through Herndon. I am also confident Lincoln would have returned to the private practice of law with Herndon in Springfield after serving as President. Anyone who tried criminal cases the way Lincoln did loved the courtroom and the feeling one gets when speaking to 12 citizens about the fate of another.

For those readers who may be interested in the lives of some of the people involved in the Harrison trial, my research revealed the following:

• Peachy Quinn Harrison was not killed in the Civil War. All indications are that he married, had a family and lived a normal life until his death at age 83.

• Judge Edward Young Rice was born in Kentucky and was admitted to the Kentucky Bar in 1844. He moved to Montgomery County, Illinois, and was subsequently elected to the state legislature. He served as Montgomery County judge and as a Master in Chancery. In 1857, he was elected judge of the 18th Circuit of Illinois. After the Harrison trial, Rice was elected to Congress, where he served one two-year term.

• Stephen T. Logan was a celebrated lawyer and jurist who long stood at the head of the Illinois Bar. He was born in Kentucky and began studying law under the guidance of his uncle Judge Christopher Tompkins. At the age of 20, he was admitted to the Kentucky Bar. In 1832, Logan moved to Illinois and settled in Springfield, where he resided for the rest of his life. In 1835, he was elected to the office of circuit judge and served for two years, after which he resigned and resumed his legal practice, including a three-year partnership with Lincoln. Logan was elected to the state legislature in 1842 and served in that capacity until 1861. In 1860, he was a delegate to the Chicago Republican Convention, which nominated Abraham Lincoln for the presidency. Until the time of his death at age 80, Logan remained a highly regarded member of the Illinois Bar.

• Shelby M. Cullom was born in Kentucky. He came with his family to Illinois and was admitted to the Illinois Bar in 1855. He served as Springfield's city attorney and was elected to the state legislature in 1856. In 1864, Cullom was elected to Congress. He served as governor of Illinois from 1877 to 1883 and was subsequently elected to the U.S. Senate, where he served for 31 years. Notably, Cullom and another U.S. senator were responsible for passage of the Lincoln Memorial Bill, which was signed by President William Howard Taft in 1911.

• John M. Palmer was born in Kentucky. His grandfather was a soldier of the Revolution. He came to Illinois with his family in 1831 and was admitted to the Illinois Bar in 1839. Palmer was elected state senator in 1852, and in 1859—the year of the Harrison trial—he was a candidate for Congress. Palmer also served as a Civil War officer for the 14th Illinois Infantry and rose through the ranks to become a brigadier general. In 1868, Palmer was elected governor of Illinois and was subsequently elected to the U.S. Senate.

• Rev. Peter Cartwright was probably the United States' most colorful and effective frontier circuit-riding preacher. Raised in Logan County, Kentucky, commonly referred to as "Rogue's Hollow" because its population included so many vile sorts, Cartwright was a wild young man before being converted at a camp meeting of the Cane Ridge Revival. Described as "raw-boned," Cartwright, a Methodist, rode the circuit in Kentucky, Illinois and Tennessee for 65 years. He moved to Sangamon County, Illinois, in 1823. His fervent work against slavery caused him to briefly enter politics. He defeated Abe Lincoln in a race for the state legislature and lost to Lincoln in a bid for Congress. Cartwright and his wife, Frances, are buried in Pleasant Plains,

Illinois.

One of the truly remarkable things about the Harrison case was the preparation of an official transcript (or record) of the proceedings. At the time, the use of court reporters was not customary. In fact, it was rare—particularly in criminal cases—because of the lack of court reporters and the expense. Generally, if a criminal case was appealed, the parties and the judge would construct the "record" and the defendant would appeal pursuant to a "Bill of Exceptions." In the Harrison case, Robert Roberts Hitt traveled to Springfield from Chicago to report the case. Based on my research, it appears that Hitt may have been hired by one of the newspapers in order to ensure the accuracy of the reporting and, perhaps, to preserve what apparently turned out to be Lincoln's last high-profile criminal trial.

Hitt reported several interesting cases in addition to the Harrison case. For example, he reported the trial of John Hossack, indicted for rescuing a fugitive slave from the U.S. Marshal at Ottawa, Illinois. Apparently not totally satisfied with court reporting, Hitt entered politics, serving as assistant secretary of state and later as a congressman.

As I read the Harrison transcript, I couldn't help but note that many things that occurred in the trial are still handled the same way in criminal trials every day. The extensive voir dire of prospective jurors, the sequestration of witnesses, the court's admonition to jurors at recesses and at the conclusion of a day's testimony, the use of humor during the examination of witnesses, objections to evidence and hearings held out of the presence of the jurors, and a defendant who does not testify in his own defense are all common occurrences in modern-day criminal trials.

As a lawyer, I'd be remiss if I didn't conclude this note by saying that *Kind Eyes* is a work of fiction, taking license with historical and geographical facts and making no claim to textbook reliability. References to real people, events, businesses, establishments, organizations or locales are intended only to provide a sense of authenticity and may be used fictitiously. As for fictional characters, any resemblance to actual persons, living or dead, is entirely coincidental. All character incidents and dialogue are drawn from the author's imagination and are not to be construed as real.

1   Dirck, Brian. *Lincoln the Lawyer.* University of Illinois Press, 2007; Steiner, Mark E. *An Honest Calling.* Northern Illinois University Press, 2006; Herndon, William H. and Weik, Jesse W. *Herndon's Lincoln,* 1889, Knox College Lincoln Studies Center and the University of Illinois Press Urbana and Chicago reprint.

2   3 Chicago History 3 (Fall 1974)

3   55 Ill. 535 (1869)

4   83 U.S. 130, 21 L.Ed. 442, 16 Wall. 130 (1872)

5   Ambrose, D. Leib. *History of the Seventh Regiment, Illinois Volunteer Infantry,* 1868.

ABOUT THE AUTHOR

Sam Perroni, the celebrated former Arkansas criminal defense attorney and federal prosecutor, lives in Little Rock with his wife, Pat. He is currently an Adjunct Professor of White Collar Crime at the William H. Bowen School of Law and Of Counsel with the law firm of Perroni & Koehler.